LEARN FRENCH (FRANÇAIS) THE FAST AND FUN WAY

by Elisabeth Bourquin Leete
Academy at Charlemont

Heywood Wald, Coordinating Editor
Chairman, Department of Foreign Languages
Martin Van Buren High School, New York

To help you pace your learning, we've included stopwatches *like the one above* throughout the book to mark each 15-minute interval. You can read one of these units each day or pace yourself according to your needs.

CONTENTS

All inquiries should be addressed to:
Barron's Educational Series, Inc.
250 Wireless Boulevard
Hauppauge, New York 11788

Library of Congress Catalog Card No. 83-26577

International Standard Book No. 0-8120-2852-X

Library of Congress Cataloging-in-Publication Data
Leete, Elisabeth Bourquin.
Learn French the fast and fun way.

1. French language—Conversation and phrase-books—English. 2. French language—Text-books for foreign speakers—English. I. Title.
PC2121.L455 1985 448.3'421 83-26577
ISBN 0-8120-2852-X

Cover and Book Design Milton Glaser, Inc.
Illustrations Juan Suarez

PRINTED IN THE UNITED STATES OF AMERICA
3456 880 16 15 14 13

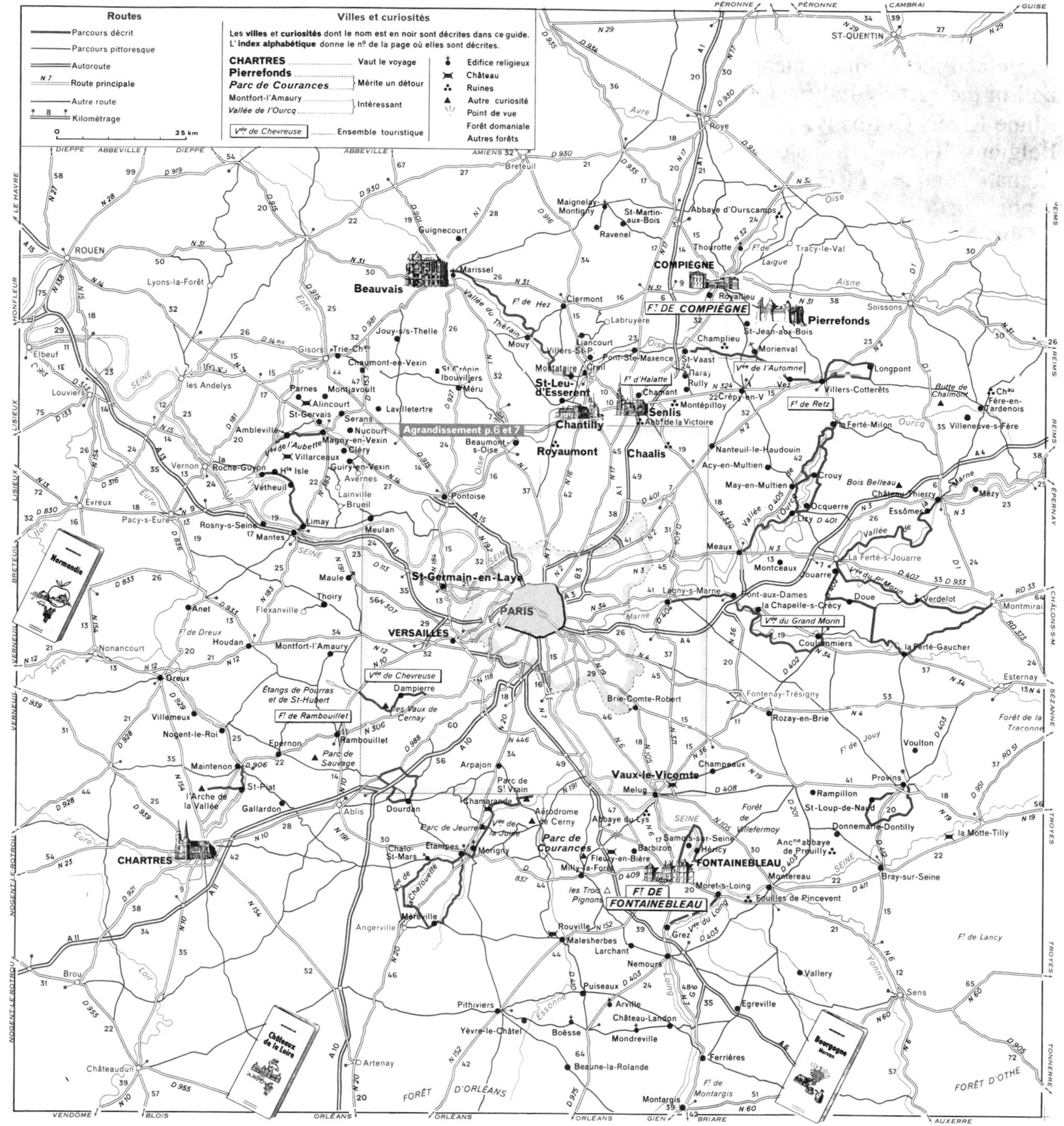

(From Michelin Guide, Environs de Paris, *20th edition. Reprinted with permission.)*

French is a language and culture shared not only by the 52 million people of European France but by many millions more in adjoining Belgium, Luxembourg and Switzerland and in the Canadian Province of Quebec, the Caribbean islands of Martinique, Guadeloupe and Haiti, French possessions in the Atlantic and Pacific, and former French colonies in South America, Asia and, especially, Africa. French is also employed extensively as an international language of diplomatic exchange.

Shaped somewhat like a hexagon, France comprises nearly 213,000 square miles. It is bounded by the English Channel in the north, the Atlantic Ocean in the west, the Pyrénées, Spain and the Mediterranean in the south, and in the east by Italy, Switzerland, the Rhine River, Germany, Luxembourg and Belgium. Its modern history dates to the Roman Conquest of Gaul in the first century B.C.

From Paris, the nation's political and cultural capital, the visitor may strike out in any direction assured that the trip will be rewarding in every sense—historically, culturally, scenically, with the happy bonus of fine wines and cuisine distinctive to every region of France. Paris itself has a concentration of magnificent sightseeing and entertainment opportunities—art museums such as the Louvre and Jeu de Paume, echoes of France's days of glory and the Napoleonic era at the Hôtel des Invalides, the Île de la Cité and Notre Dame Cathedral, lovely parks such as the Tuileries and Bois de Boulogne. And, of course, there is the Eiffel Tower.

Public transportation by rail, air and bus is excellent, and France is also blessed with a network of autoroutes together with well-mapped secondary roads, favored by many motorists wishing to gain a more intimate sense of French village and country life. Much of what the traveler may wish to see lies within a day's journey from Paris—Normandy and Brittany to the north and northwest; Marseilles, the Côte d'Azur, the Provence and the Mediterranean beaches to the south; Bordeaux, the Bay of Biscay and the Pyrénées to the southwest; to the southeast, the Alps and Mont Blanc, the Rhône Alps, and the Jura and Vosges mountains; and, to the east, the Rhine River, Champagne, Lorraine and Alsace.

Learning the language adds much interest, pleasure and satisfaction to a trip to France. Of equal importance to many is the access gained to some of the important bases of Western civilization. French philosophers, political theorists, statesmen, artists, writers and scientists have substantially influenced the cultural and political aspects of our world.

Last but not least, you will find in French-speaking countries—as you would in any other part of the world—that your efforts to communicate in the language are rewarded by kindness and offers of friendship.

FRENCH PRONUNCIATION—A FEW SIMPLE RULES

Is French difficult to pronounce? Not at all. French follows a few simple rules, and once you know these, you'll have no problem saying what you want and understanding those who speak to you. There are two basic principles of French pronunciation:

1. Not all letters are pronounced, as they most often are in English. Remember, however, that even in English, we have some silent letters—the *p* in *pneumonia*, for example.
2. The French like to link words. Sometimes a whole sentence may sound to you like one long word, especially in the beginning. For instance, you will find in the dialogue in the first unit, the sentence:

   J'habite aux États-Unis. I live in the United States.

   The sentence should sound like:

   zha-bee-toh-zay-ta-zew-nee

Linking is compulsory in many situations, especially between words that logically belong together, but is optional in other situations. In a few cases, it may seem appropriate to link the words, but it is not permitted (for example, after the conjunction et, which means "and"). You'll learn the rules for linking up words as you work your way through this book.

The pronunciation tables which follow will help you get started on the road to France and its language. Practice pronouncing the words a few times while you also learn some basic vocabulary. You'll become familiar with how French people pronounce their vowels and consonants, so you'll know how to pronounce a new word when you see it on a road sign or included in an informational brochure. But, to make it all even easier, every time we introduce a new word in this book, we show you how to pronounce it.

VOWELS

French Letters	Symbol	Pronunciation/Example
a, à	a	This is a short *A*, as in *cat*. Example: *ma* (ma) my.
a, â	ah	A long *AH*, as in *father*. Example: *pas* (pah) step.
é, final er, ez, et	ay	*A* as in *day*. Example *musée* (mew-zay) museum.
e + 2 consonants, e, ê, è	eh	This is a short *E*, as in *ever*. Example: *appelle* (a-pehl) call.
e	uh	*E*, as in English word *the*. Example: *le* (luh) the.
eu	ūh	This sound does not exist in English. The sound is between *UH* and *EW*. Example: *peu* (pūh) little.
i, y	ee	The sound of *EE*, as in *meet*. Example: *valise* (va-leez) suitcase.
o	o	A short *U*, as in *up*. Example: *homme* (om) man.
o, ô	oh	A long *O*, as in *open*. Example: *tôt* (toh) soon.
oi, oi	wa	Pronounced *WA*, as in *watch*. Example: *toi* (twa) you (familiar).
ou	oo	Pronounced *OO*, as in *tooth*. Example: *ouvrir* (oo-vreer) to open.
u	ew	This sound does not exist in English. Say EE; round your lips. Example: *tu* (tew) you (familiar).
u + vowel	wee	Pronounced *WEE*, as in *whee*. Example: *huit* (weet) eight.

CONSONANTS

French Letter(s)	Symbol	Pronunciation/Example
b, d, f, k, l, m, n, p, s, t, v, z	—	The corresponding English sound for these French consonants is the same.
c (before e, i, y)	s	This consonant is pronounced *SS*. Example: *merci* (mehr-see) thank you.
ç (before a, o, u)	s	This consonant is pronounced *SS*. Example: *garçon* (gar-sohn) boy.
c (before a, o, u)	k	The *c* without the accent mark is a hard *K*, as in *kind*. Example: *comment* (ko-mahn) how.
g (before e, i, y)	zh	Pronounced like the soft *S* in *pleasure*. Example: *rouge* (roozh) red.
ge (before a, o, u)	zh	Pronounced like the soft *S* in pleasure.
g (before a, o, u)	g	Pronounced like the hard *G* in *go*. Example: *Chicago* (Shee-kah-goh).
gn	ny	Like the sound *NI* in *onion*. Example: *oignon* (o-nyohn) onion.
h	—	The *h* is always silent. Example: *hôtel* (oh-tehl) hotel.
j	zh	Pronounced like the soft *S* in *pleasure*. Example: *je* (zhuh) I.
qu, final q	k	Pronounced like the hard *K* in *kind*. Example: *cinq* (sank) five.
r	r	This sound does not exist in English; roll the *R* at the top of back of mouth, as for gargling. Example *rouge* (roozh) red.
ss	s	The double *s* sound is pronounced *SS*. Example: *poisson* (pwa-sohn) fish.
s (at the beginning of word)	s	Pronounced *SS*. Example: *son* (sohn) his (or hers).
s (next to consonant between vowels)	z	Pronounced *Z*. Example: *poison* (pwah-zohn) poison.
t (before i + vowel)	s	Pronounced *SS*. Example: *nation* (na-syon) nation.
th	t	Pronounced like the short *T* in *top*. Example: *thé* (tay) tea.
x	ks	Pronounced *EKS*, as in *excellent*. Example: *excellent* (eck-se-lahn).
x	s	Pronounced *SS* in these words only: *dix* (dees) ten, *six* (sees) six.

NASAL SOUNDS

These are very common in French and occur when a *single* N or M follows a vowel. The N and the M are not vocalized. The tip of the tongue does not touch the roof of the mouth.

French Letters	Symbol	Pronunciation/Example
an, am, en, em	ahn	This nasal sound is similar to *ON,* as in the English word *on*. Example: *France* (frahns).
in, im, ain, aim, ien, ym	an	This sound is similar to *AN,* as in *can*. Example: *bien* (byan) well, good.
on, om	ohn	Similar to *ON,* as in *long*. Example: *bon* (bohn) good.
un, um	uhn	Similar to *UN,* as in *under*. Example: *un* (uhn) one.

When words LE, LA ("the"), and some pronouns, adverbs and conjunctions which end with an E precede a word that begins with a vowel sound, the final vowel is dropped and replaced by an apostrophe.

EXAMPLE: la + auto = l'auto
le + homme = l'homme

When words merge like this, it is called **elision**.

French syllables all have the same length and approximately the same amount of stress. The last syllable of a word group is slightly emphasized, not by saying it louder, but by making it a little longer.

HOW ENGLISH AND FRENCH ARE SIMILAR

In many ways, French is very much like English. For example, simple French sentences generally follow the same arrangement as English ones:

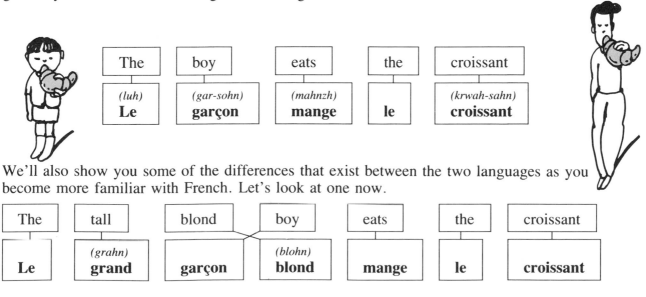

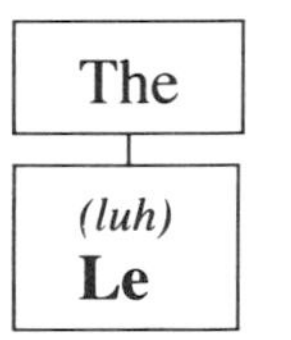

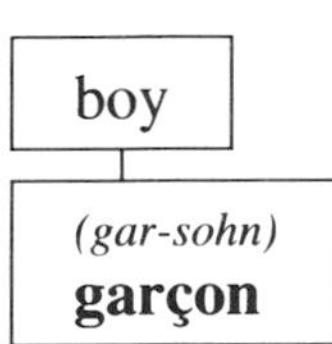

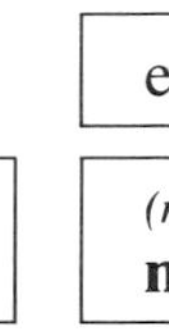

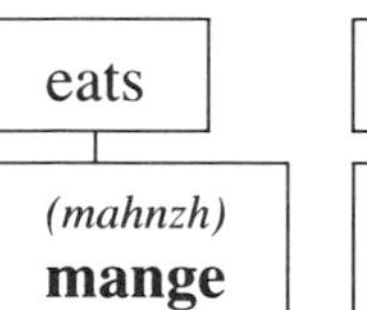

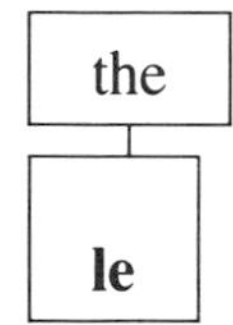

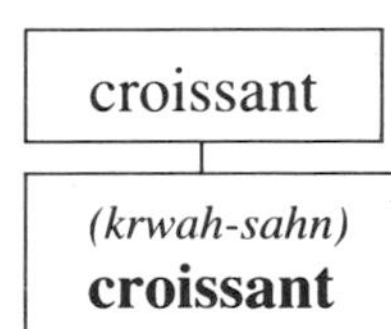

We'll also show you some of the differences that exist between the two languages as you become more familiar with French. Let's look at one now.

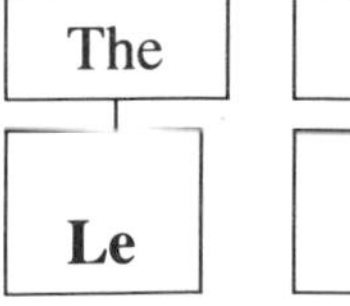

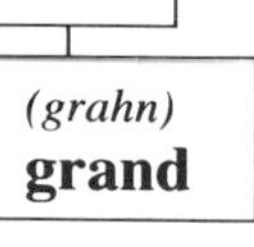

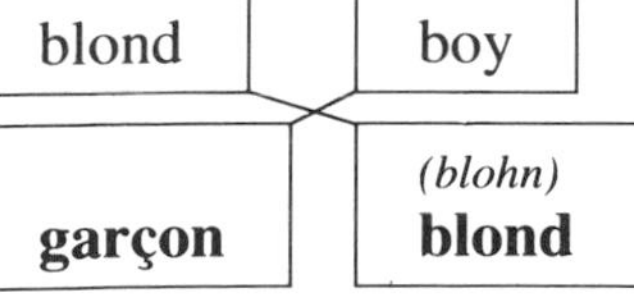

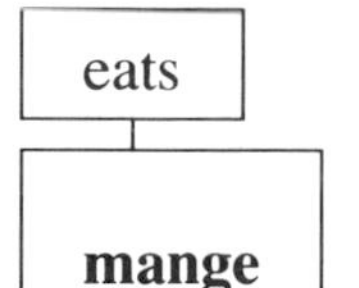

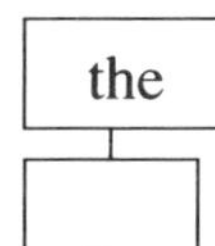

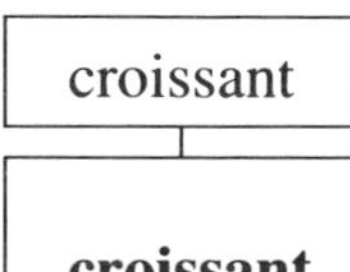

For now, think about the ways French and English words are alike. You can learn many French words simply by recognizing a few patterns in word endings.

ENGLISH WORDS ENDING IN	FRENCH WORDS ENDING IN
-ION	-ION
correction	*(ko-rek-syohn)* **correction**
occasion	*(o-ka-zyohn)* **occasion**
nation	*(na-syohn)* **nation**
station	*(sta-syohn)* **station**
education	*(ay-dew-ka-syohn)* **éducation**
function	*(fohnk-syohn)* **fonction**
-TY	-TÉ
city	*(see-tay)* **cité**
sincerity	*(san-say-ree-tay)* **sincérité**
unity	*(ew-nee-tay)* **unité**
possibility	*(po-see-bee-lee-tay)* **possibilité**
-IST	-ISTE
dentist	*(dahn-teest)* **dentiste**
violinist	*(vyo-lo-neest)* **violoniste**
pianist	*(pya-neest)* **pianiste**
-OR	-EUR
actor	*(ak-tūhr)* **acteur**
sculptor	*(skewl-tūhr)* **sculpteur**
vigor	*(vee-gūhr)* **vigueur**
color	*(koo-lūhr)* **couleur**

Did you realize how much French you already know? In many cases, the only difference is the PRONUNCIATION. In fact, you may not have realized that you've been speaking French for years! Here are just a few expressions which are part of everyday American language.

(foh) (pah)
faux pas

(rahn-day-voo)
rendez-vous

(gaf)
gaffe

(day-zha) (vew)
déjà vu

(bohn-bohn)
bonbon

(ba-geht)
baguette

(ehs-kar-goh)
escargot

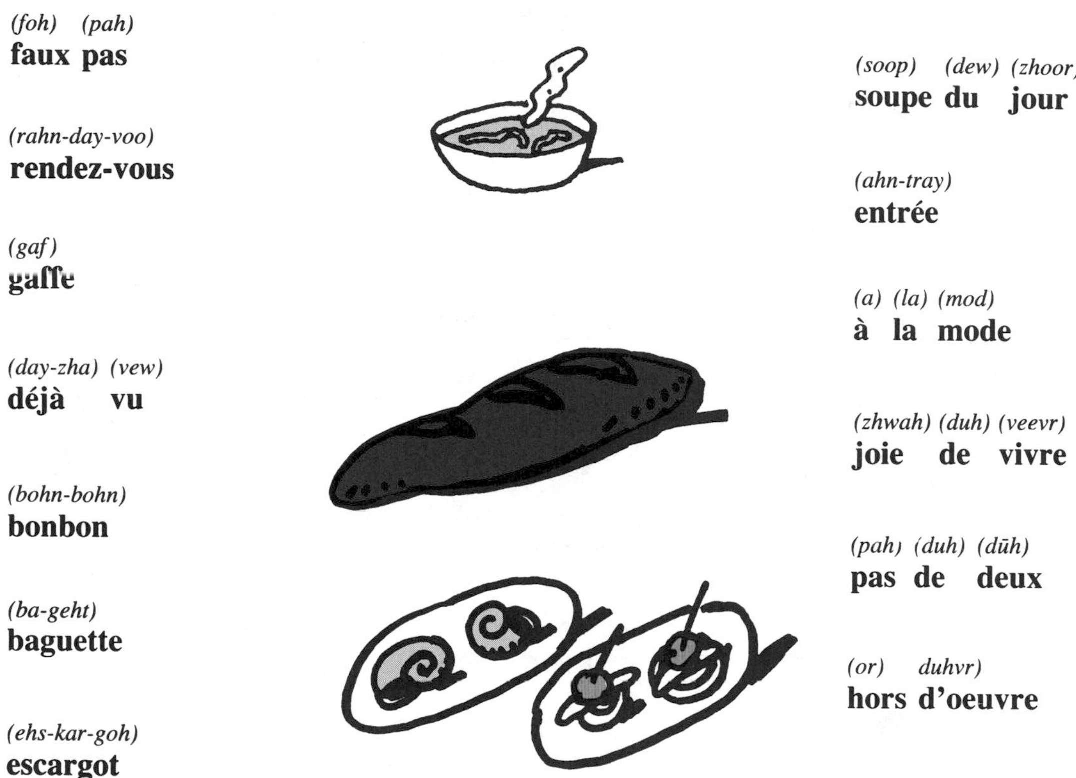

(soop) (dew) (zhoor)
soupe du jour

(ahn-tray)
entrée

(a) (la) (mod)
à la mode

(zhwah) (duh) (veevr)
joie de vivre

(pah) (duh) (dūh)
pas de deux

(or) duhvr)
hors d'oeuvre

Now you can start building upon what you already know. We don't promise it will be a cinch, but we can guarantee it will be fun, especially when you begin trying to communicate with fluent French speakers. Just put in 15 minutes a day at a pace comfortable for you.

GETTING TO KNOW PEOPLE

(fuh-sohn) (ko-ne-sahns)
Faisons Connaissance

1 *(kohn-vehr-sohn)* Conversons
Let's Talk

Knowing how to greet people and how to start a conversation is important, and you should learn those skills first. Read the following dialogue several times, pronouncing each line carefully out loud. The dialogue contains some basic words and expressions that will be useful to you.

Mark Smith, his wife Mary, their daughter Anne, and their son Paul have just arrived at Charles de Gaulle Airport in Paris, and they can't find their luggage. Mark approaches an airline employee:

(bohn-zhoor) (muh-syuh) MARC **Bonjour, Monsieur.**	Hello/Good day, Sir.
(ahn-plwa-yay) (voo) (day-zee-ray) EMPLOYÉ **Bonjour. Vous désirez** *(kehl-kuh) (shohz)* **quelque chose?**	Hello/Good day. May I help you? (*lit.* Do you want anything?)
(wee) (zhuh) (shehrsh) (may) MARC **Oui. Je cherche mes** *(va-leez)* **valises.**	Yes. I am looking for my suitcases.
(byan) (ko-mahn) (voo) EMPLOYÉ **Bien. Comment vous** *(za-play) (voo)* **appelez-vous?**	Well/O.K. What is your name? (*lit.* How do you call yourself?)
(zhuh) (ma-pehl) MARC **Je m'appelle Marc Smith.**	My name is Mark Smith.
(luh) (new-may-roh) (duh) (votr) (vol) EMPLOYÉ **Le numéro de votre vol et** *(o-ree-zheen)* **l'origine?**	Your flight number and origin?
(trwah)(sahn) (trahnt) MARC **Le vol Air France trois cent trente-** *(trwah) (duh)* **trois de New York.**	Air France flight 333 from New York.

(uhn) (mo-mahn) (seel) (voo) (pleh)
EMPLOYÉ **Un moment, s'il vous plaît.** — One moment, please.

(zhahn)
As the clerk looks through some papers on this desk, Jean, a French business friend, sees Mark.

(sa-lew) (ko-mahn) (va-tew)
JEAN **Salut, Marc! Comment vas-tu?** — Hi, Mark. How are you?

(zhuh) (vay) (byan) (ay) (twa)
MARC **Jean! Je vais bien, et toi?** — John! I am well. And you?

(treh) (tew) (eh) (ee-see) (ahn)
JEAN **Très bien. Tu es ici en**

(va-kahns)
vacances? — Very well. Are you here on a holiday?

(zhuh) (tuh) (pray-zahnt) (ma) (fa-mee-y)
MARC **Oui. Je te présente ma famille.** — Yes. Let me introduce my family.

(fam) (fee-y)
Ma femme Marie, ma fille Anne, et

(mohn) (fees)
mon fils Paul. — My wife Mary, my daughter Anne, and my son Paul.

(ahn-shahn-tay)
JEAN **Enchanté!** — Delighted!

(ehks-kew-zay-mwa) (voh)
EMPLOYÉ **Excusez-moi, Monsieur. Vos**

(a-reev) (a-vehk) (luh) (pro-shan)
valises arrivent avec le prochain

(na-vyohn)
avion. — Excuse me, Sir. Your suitcases are arriving on the next plane.

MARC	*(zewt)* **Zut!**	Darn it!
JEAN	*(pa-syahns) (neh) (pah) (zahn)* **Patience Marc. Tu n'es pas en** *(na-may-reek)* **Amérique!**	Be patient, Mark. You are not in America!
MARC *(à l'employé)*	**Merci, Monsieur.**	Thank you, Sir.
	(oh) (ruh-vwar) **Au revoir!**	Good-bye.
EMPLOYÉ	*(voo) (zahn) (pree)* **Je vous en prie.**	You are welcome.
JEAN	*(tool) (mohnd)* **Au revoir, tout le monde!**	Good-bye, everybody.
TOUT LE MONDE	*(a byan-toh)* **À bientôt!**	See you soon!

Match the French expressions from the dialogue with their English equivalents:

1. Comment vous appelez-vous?	a. May I help you?
2. Je te présente ma famille.	b. My name is . . .
3. Zut!	c. What's your name?
4. Vous désirez quelque chose?	d. Hi, how are you?
5. Je vous en prie.	e. I am well.
6. Je vais bien.	f. Let me introduce my family.
7. À bientôt.	g. Delighted!
8. Je m'appelle . . .	h. Darn it!
9. Enchanté!	i. You are welcome
10. Salut. Comment vas-tu?	j. See you soon.

ANSWERS

Matching **1.** c **2.** f **3.** h **4.** a **5.** i **6.** e **7.** j **8.** b **9.** g **10.** d

(lay) LES *(zhahn)* GENS ET LES *(shohz)* CHOSES

People and Things

One of the first things you need to know is what to call certain things or people—words we call nouns. You will need to know what a French noun looks like, and how to make it plural. Unlike English nouns, all French nouns have a gender (masculine or feminine); like English nouns, they can be either singular or plural. Look carefully at the following examples of nouns given in their singular and plural forms, and write them on the blank line in the space provided.

Singular and Plural

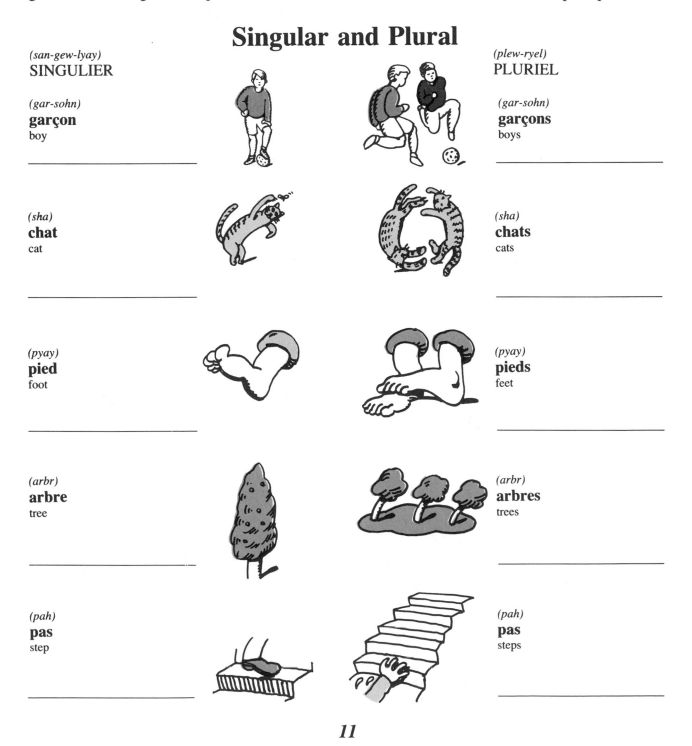

(san-gew-lyay) SINGULIER	*(plew-ryel)* PLURIEL
(gar-sohn) **garçon** boy ______	*(gar-sohn)* **garçons** boys ______
(sha) **chat** cat ______	*(sha)* **chats** cats ______
(pyay) **pied** foot ______	*(pyay)* **pieds** feet ______
(arbr) **arbre** tree ______	*(arbr)* **arbres** trees ______
(pah) **pas** step ______	*(pah)* **pas** steps ______

(nuh-vūh)
neveu
nephew

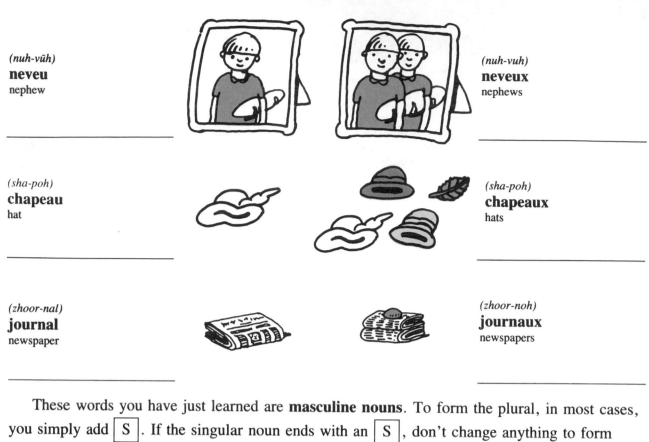

(nuh-vuh)
neveux
nephews

(sha-poh)
chapeau
hat

(sha-poh)
chapeaux
hats

(zhoor-nal)
journal
newspaper

(zhoor-noh)
journaux
newspapers

These words you have just learned are **masculine nouns**. To form the plural, in most cases, you simply add S. If the singular noun ends with an S, don't change anything to form the plural. If it ends with EU or EAU, add X instead of S. If the noun ends in AL, the ending becomes AUX in the plural.

Now look at the following nouns:

SINGULIER

(meh-zohn)
maison
house, home

PLURIEL

(meh-zohn)
maisons
houses, homes

(oh-toh-mo-beel)
automobile
automobile

(oh-toh-mo-beel)
automobiles
automobiles

(mehr)
mère
mother

(mehr)
mères
mothers

These new words are **feminine nouns**. Simply add an S to form the plural. If the noun ends with an S or an X or a Z in the singular, don't change anything to form the plural. (The final S, X, or Z is not pronounced.)

Test your knowledge of singular and plural by making these nouns all plural:

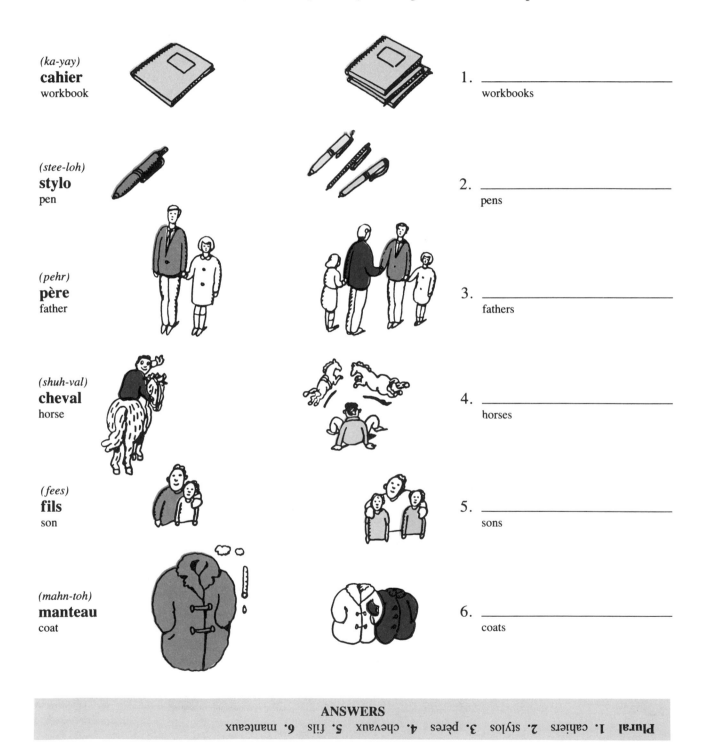

(ka-yay)
cahier
workbook

1. ______________________
workbooks

(stee-loh)
stylo
pen

2. ______________________
pens

(pehr)
père
father

3. ______________________
fathers

(shuh-val)
cheval
horse

4. ______________________
horses

(fees)
fils
son

5. ______________________
sons

(mahn-toh)
manteau
coat

6. ______________________
coats

ANSWERS

Plural 1. cahiers **2.** stylos **3.** pères **4.** chevaux **5.** fils **6.** manteaux

THREE EXCEPTIONS:

1. The following masculine nouns which end in **EU** take an **S** in the plural:

   (blūh) **bleus** (blue jeans), *(pnūh)* **pneus** (tires).

2. The following masculine nouns which end in **OU** take an **X** in the plural:

   (bee-zhoo) **bijoux** (jewels), *(ka-yoo)* **cailloux** (pebbles), *(shoo)* **choux** (cabbages), *(zhuh-noo)* **genoux** (knees), *(ee-boo)* **hiboux** (owls), *(zhoo-zhoo)* **joujoux** (toys).

3. The following masculine nouns which end in **AL** take an **S** in the plural:

   (bal) **bals** (balls), *(kar-na-val)* **carnavals** (carnivals), *(fehs-tee-val)* **festivals** (festivals).

(uhn) (ewn) (day)

Un, une, des

A (An), Some

When we name something—use a noun—we often precede it in English with the words *a* or *some*. The same is true in French, and here is how to say these words, depending on whether the noun is masculine or feminine.

WITH FEMININE NOUNS

SINGULIER

(ewn) (fee-y)
une fille
a girl

(ew) (na-mee)
une amie
a female friend

PLURIEL

(day)
des filles
some girls, girls

(day) (za-mee)
des amies
some female friends

WITH MASCULINE NOUNS

SINGULIER

(uhn nohnkl)
un oncle
an uncle

(uhn na-mee)
un ami
a male friend

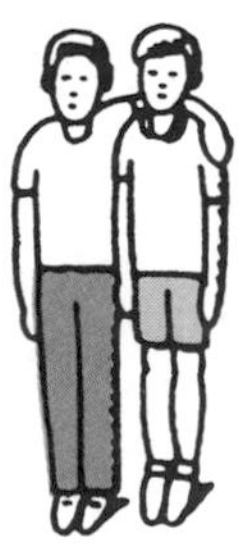

PLURIEL

(day zohnkl)
des oncles
some uncles

(day za-mee)
des amis
some friends

Note that in English, you often do not use **some** in the plural; you'll say: "I have friends in Paris." In French, you **must** say "I have **some** friends in Paris": **J'ai des amis à Paris.**

Now test yourself by putting the appropriate indefinite article in front of each noun.
Note: *m.* = masculine noun *f.* = feminine noun *pl.* = plural noun

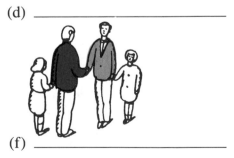

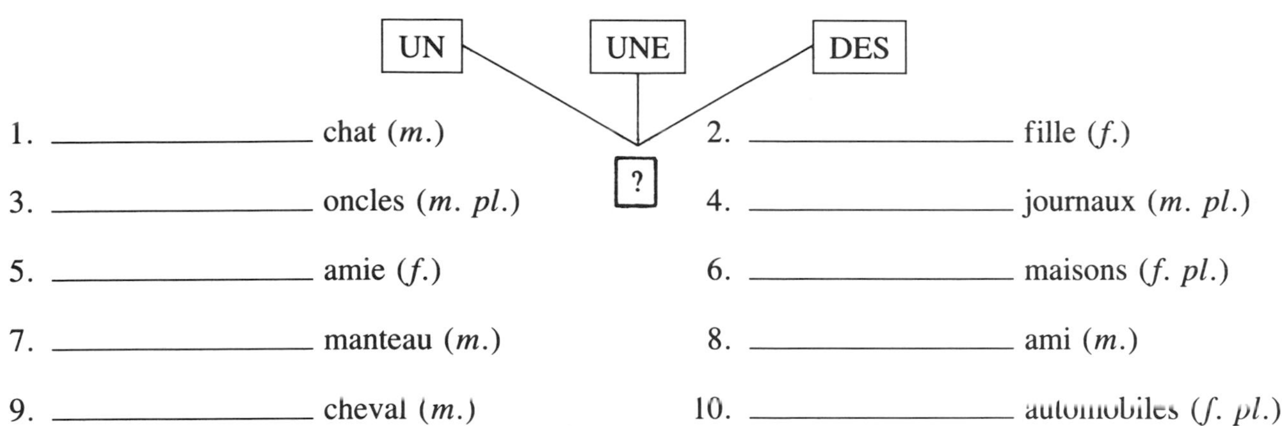

1. ______________ chat (*m.*)
2. ______________ fille (*f.*)
3. ______________ oncles (*m. pl.*)
4. ______________ journaux (*m. pl.*)
5. ______________ amie (*f.*)
6. ______________ maisons (*f. pl.*)
7. ______________ manteau (*m.*)
8. ______________ ami (*m.*)
9. ______________ cheval (*m.*)
10. ______________ automobiles (*f. pl.*)

Here's another chance to test yourself. Put the correct words on the lines below the pictures using the indefinite articles for "a" (an) and "some" and the French word for what is shown.

(kee) (ehs)
Qui est-ce?
Who is it?

(kehs) (kuh) (seh)
Qu'est-ce que c'est?
What is it?

(a) ______________

(b) ______________

(c) ______________

(d) ______________

(e) ______________

(f) ______________

ANSWERS

Indefinite article **1.** un chat **2.** une fille **3.** des oncles **4.** des journaux **5.** une amie **6.** des maisons **7.** un manteau **8.** un ami **9.** un cheval **10.** des automobiles

(a) un garçon **(b)** un chat **(c)** un pied **(d)** des journaux **(e)** une mère **(f)** des pères

(zhuh) (tew) (voo)

Je, tu et vous

"I" and "You"

It is also important to know how to say "I" and "you" in French. These words are called subject pronouns.

"I" is simply JE, (but j' before a vowel).
"You" is given in three ways:

TU	— When addressing one person: a friend, child, family member (familiar address).
VOUS	— When addressing anyone who is not a friend, child, family member.
VOUS	— Plural form of both TU and VOUS.

SUMMARY

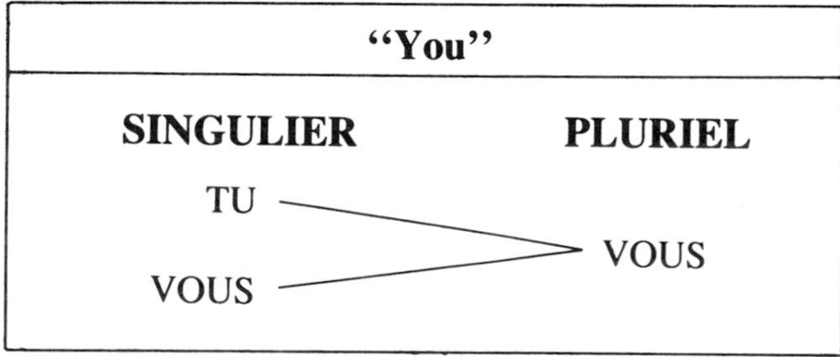

Which would you use—**tu** or **vous**—when speaking to the following? Write your answer in the space provided.

1. the doctor __________
2. your brother __________
3. your sisters __________
4. your child __________
5. the stewardess __________

ANSWERS

Tu or vous **1.** vous **2.** tu **3.** vous **4.** tu **5.** vous

(par-lohns) (mahn-bruh) (fa-mee-y)

PARLONS DES MEMBRES DE LA FAMILLE

Let's Talk about the Members of the Family

Henriette Dubois
(la) (grahn-mehr)
la grand-mère
grandmother

Pierre Dubois
(luh) (grahn-pehr)
le grand-père
grandfather

Jean-Pierre Dupont
le père
father

(ma-ree)
le mari
husband

Micheline Dupont
(née Dubois)
la mère
mother

(fam)
la femme
wife

Jean Dubois
(lohnkl)
l'oncle
uncle

Marie Dubois
(née Ogier)
(tahnt)
la tante
aunt

Michel Dupont
(frehr)
le frère
brother

le fils
son

Jeanine Dupont
(sūhr)
la soeur
sister

la fille
daughter

Philippe Dubois
(koo-zan)
le cousin
cousin (male)

Pierrette Dubois
(koo-zeen)
la cousine
cousin (female)

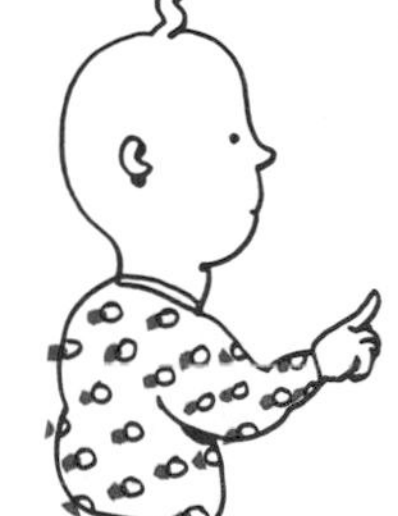

Note the members of Paul's family.

Identify the following members of the family:

1. **Henriette Dubois est la** ____________________.
2. **Jean est l'** ____________________.
3. **Pierrette est la** ____________________.
4. **Jean-Pierre est le** ____________________ **et le** ____________________.
5. **Michel est le** ____________________ **et le** ____________________.
6. **Jeanine Dupont est la** ____________________ **et la** ____________________.

Find the *plurals* of the following nouns hidden in the puzzle, write them down, and then circle them in the puzzle. We've done the first one for you, to show how easy it is.

1. **cousin** cousins
2. **cheval** ____________________
3. **fils** ____________________
4. **mère** ____________________
5. **chat** ____________________
6. **cousine** ____________________
7. **genou** ____________________
8. **fille** ____________________
9. **père** ____________________
10. **manteau** ____________________

C	O	U	S	I	N	S	J	E	S	U	F	I	L	L	E	S	X	A
H	U	L	A	L	G	M	A	N	T	E	A	U	X	S	O	U	P	U
E	E	N	M	M	E	O	E	C	H	A	T	S	I	E	O	T	O	P
V	A	U	C	E	D	R	U	N	A	M	D	E	S	N	T	A	I	E
A	L	A	I	R	R	A	C	O	U	S	I	N	E	S	P	O	U	R
U	N	M	O	T	M	E	A	C	H	A	N	G	P	L	U	M	E	E
X	J	A	I	T	U	A	S	I	L	A	N	O	F	I	L	S	O	S

ANSWERS

Family tree 1. grand-mère **2.** oncle **3.** cousine **4.** père . . . mari **5.** frère . . . fils **6.** soeur . . . fille
Word search 2. chevaux **3.** fils **4.** mères **5.** chats **6.** cousines **7.** genoux **8.** filles **9.** pères **10.** manteaux

Imagine you've begun your trip already. See how well you understand the following situation.

(sewr)
Monsieur Smith et la famille arrivent en France sur le vol 333 de New York. M. Smith
on

(dee)
dit "bonjour" à l'employé. M. Smith dit "merci" et l'employé dit "Je vous en prie."
says

(fee-nahl-mahn)
Finalement, M. Smith dit "Au revoir."
Finally

Are the following true or false?

1. **Monsieur Smith et la famille arrivent à New York.** T F

2. **Monsieur Smith dit "Je vous en prie" à l'employé.** T F

3. **Monsieur Smith et un ami arrivent en France.** T F

4. **Finalement, Monsieur Smith dit bonjour.** T F

ANSWERS

True or False 1. F 2. F 3. F 4. F

Have fun with the following crossword puzzle. The clues are English equivalents of French words.

DOWN
1. grandmother
2. some
4. girls, daughters
8. horse

ACROSS
3. I live
5. thank you
6. a, an (fem.)
7. I
9. sister

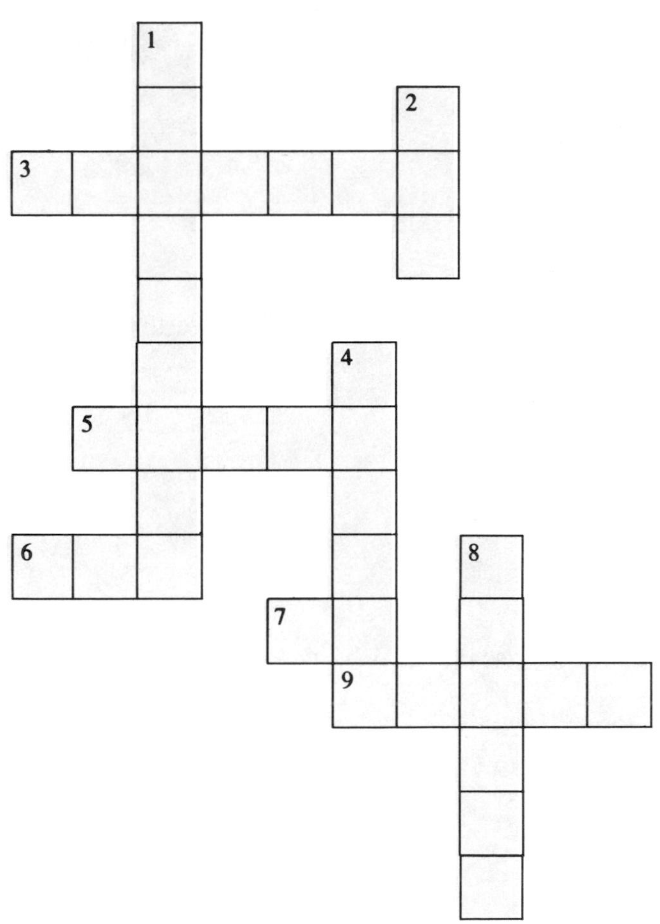

ANSWERS

Puzzle ACROSS **3.** j'habite **5.** merci **6.** une **7.** je **9.** soeur
DOWN **1.** grandmère **2.** des **4.** filles **8.** cheval

Now study and say aloud these parts of Paul's house.

UNE MAISON
A Home

(ray-free-zhay-rah-tūhr)
le réfrigérateur
refrigerator

(kwee-zeen)
la cuisine
kitchen

(kwee-zee-nyehr)
la cuisinière
stove

(ehs-ka-lyay)
l'escalier
stairway

(sahl) (duh) (ban)
la salle de bain
bathroom

(ay-vyay)
l'évier
sink

(twa-leht)
la toilette
toilet

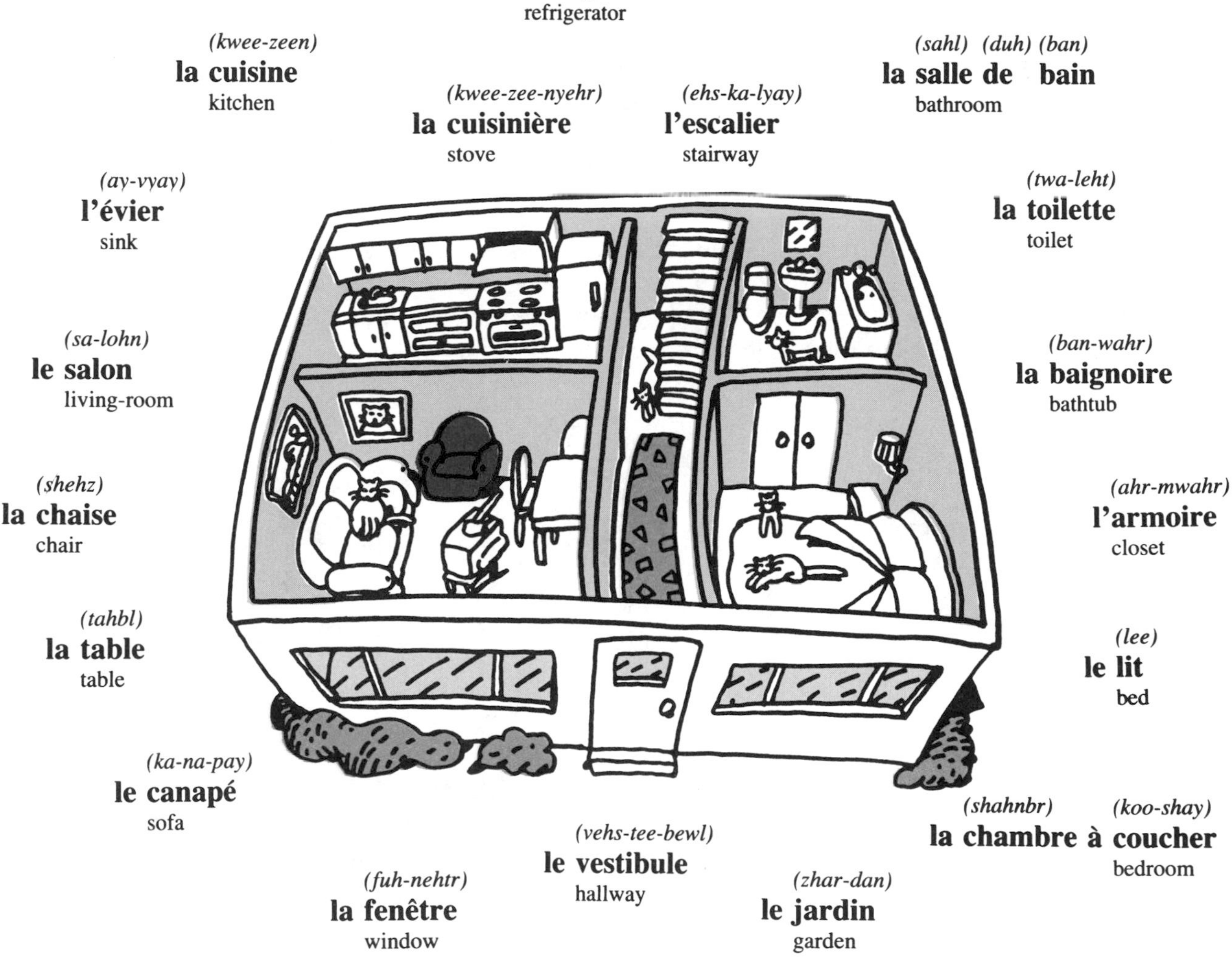

(sa-lohn)
le salon
living-room

(ban-wahr)
la baignoire
bathtub

(shehz)
la chaise
chair

(ahr-mwahr)
l'armoire
closet

(tahbl)
la table
table

(lee)
le lit
bed

(ka-na-pay)
le canapé
sofa

(shahnbr) (koo-shay)
la chambre à coucher
bedroom

(fuh-nehtr)
la fenêtre
window

(vehs-tee-bewl)
le vestibule
hallway

(zhar-dan)
le jardin
garden

(port)
la porte
door

ARRIVAL

(la-ree-vay)
L'arrivée

2 *(a)* À *(la)* la *(ruh-shehrsh)* recherche *(duhn)* d'un *(ahn-drwah)* endroit *(oo)* où *(pa-say)* passer *(la)* la *(nwee)* nuit

Finding a place to spend the night

You'll probably book your hotel room from home—at least for your first night in France. But whether you have a reservation or not, you'll want to know some basic words that describe the services and facilities you expect to find at your hotel. Learn these words first, and notice how they are used in the dialogue you will read later.

(oh-tehl)
l'hôtel
Hotel

(shahnbr)
la chambre
Room

(pree)
le prix
Price

(sahl) (duh) (ban)
la salle de bain
Bathroom

(ray-zehr-va-syohn)
la réservation
Reservation

(ray-zehr-vay)
réserver
To Reserve

(pahs-por)
le passeport
Passport

(ahn-plwa-yay)
l'employé/employée
Clerk (m.)/(f.)

(port)
la porte
Door

(fam) (duh) (shahnbr)
la femme de chambre
Maid

(fuh-nehtr)
la fenêtre
Window

Le, la, l', les

The Many Ways of Saying "The" in French

In English we use "the" to precede all nouns. In French, however, there are many ways of saying "the," depending on whether the noun is singular or plural, masculine or feminine.

SINGULIER	PLURIEL
WITH MASCULINE NOUNS	
Before a Consonant	
(luh) **Le père** father	**Les pères** fathers
Le garçon boy	**Les garçons** boys
Before a Vowel	
(lar-br) **L'arbre** tree	*(lay) (zarbr)* **Les arbres** trees
L'ami friend	*(lay) (zamee)* **Les amis** friends

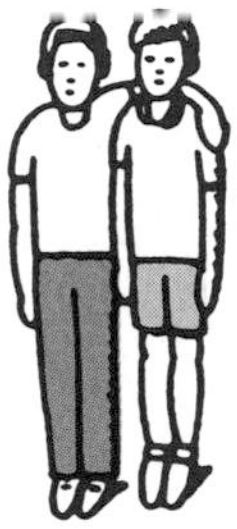

SINGULIER	PLURIEL
WITH FEMININE NOUNS	
Before a Consonant	
(la) **La maison** house	*(lay)* **Les maisons** houses
La fille girl	**Les filles** girls
La mère mother	**Les mères** mothers
Before a Vowel	
(lũhr) **L'heure** hour	*(lay) (zhũhr)* **Les heures** hours
(la-mee) **L'amie** girl friend	*(lay) (zamee)* **Les amies** girlfriends

Here's the same idea presented in a way that will make it easier for you to remember the forms of "the."

SUMMARY: "THE"	
WITH MASCULINE NOUNS	**WITH FEMININE NOUNS**
Singulier / **Pluriel**	**Singulier** / **Pluriel**
Before a Consonant: **LE** → **LES**	**Before a Consonant**: **LA** → **LES**
Before a Vowel: **L'** → **LES**	**Before a Vowel**: **L'** → **LES**

Let's practice. Put the appropriate form of "the" before each noun listed below. We've done the first for you as an example.

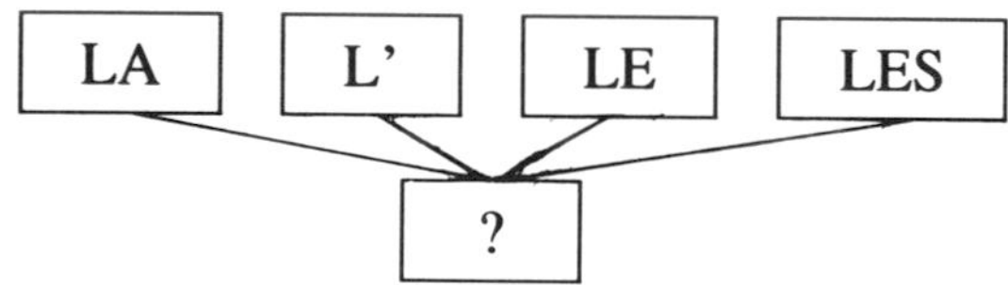

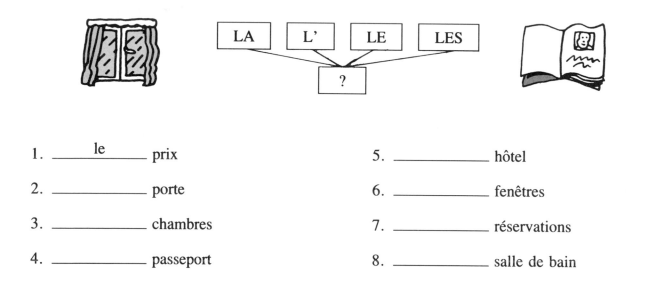

1. ___le___ prix
2. ______ porte
3. ______ chambres
4. ______ passeport
5. ______ hôtel
6. ______ fenêtres
7. ______ réservations
8. ______ salle de bain

ANSWERS

Definite article 1. le prix **2.** la porte **3.** les chambres **4.** le passeport **5.** l'hôtel **6.** les fenêtres **7.** les réservations **8.** la salle de bain

(pro-nohn) *(vehrb)*

Les pronoms et les verbes

Pronouns and verbs

You've already learned how to say "I" and "You" in French. Now it's time to move on to the forms for "he," "she," "we," and "they." Here are your new words:

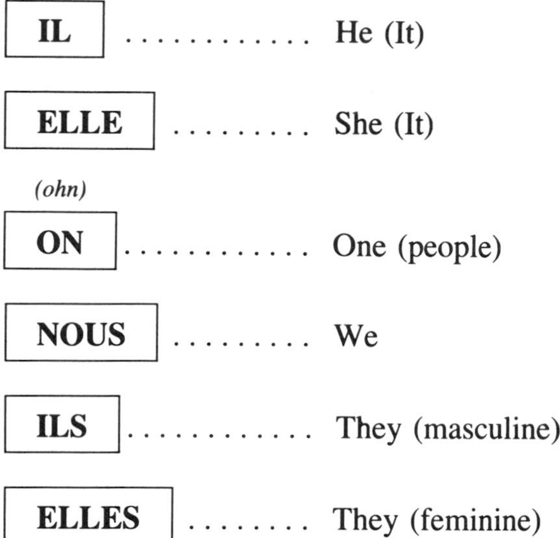

IL . . . . He (It)

ELLE . . . . She (It)

(ohn)
ON . . . . One (people)

NOUS . . . . We

ILS . . . . They (masculine)

ELLES . . . . They (feminine)

Do you remember how to say "I"? And "You"?

JE, **J'** . . . I

TU . . . . You (familiar, singular)

VOUS . . . . You (polite, singular)

VOUS . . . . You (plural)

Use this table to help you remember the French pronoun:

SUMMARY: PRONOUNS	
je, j'	I
tu	you (familiar)
il	he/it
elle	she/it
nous	we
vous	you (familiar) (pl.)
vous	you (polite)
ils	they (masculine)
elles	they (femine)
on	one

Now let's conjugate the verb **PARLER** *(par-lay)* (to speak). Conjugating the verb means changing the verb ending to agree with the subject. We do this automatically in English when we say "I speak" but "he speaks." Notice that the verb **PARLER** ends in **-ER**. **PARLER** is called the infinitive of the verb. The infinitive is the form of the verb corresponding to the English "to —" form. Many other verbs also end in **-ER**.: **CHANTER** (to sing), **ARRIVER** (to arrive). Watch how to conjugate them: drop the **-ER** and add the appropriate endings.

PARL <u>ER</u>

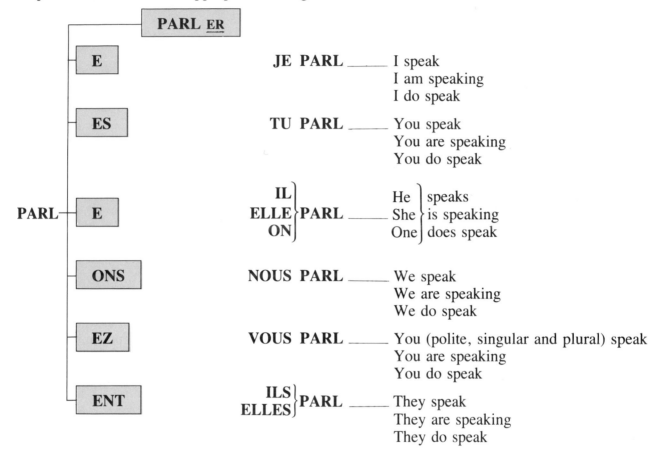

PARL	**E**	**JE PARL** ____	I speak I am speaking I do speak
PARL	**ES**	**TU PARL** ____	You speak You are speaking You do speak
PARL	**E**	**IL / ELLE / ON PARL** ____	He / She / One — speaks / is speaking / does speak
PARL	**ONS**	**NOUS PARL** ____	We speak We are speaking We do speak
PARL	**EZ**	**VOUS PARL** ____	You (polite, singular and plural) speak You are speaking You do speak
PARL	**ENT**	**ILS / ELLES PARL** ____	They speak They are speaking They do speak

NOTE: that the subject pronouns are **always** necessary, because after JE, TU, IL, ELLE, ON, ILS and ELLES, the verb sounds exactly the same:

je parle *(parl)*, tu parles *(parl)*, il/elle/on parle *(parl)*, ils/elles parlent *(parl)*:

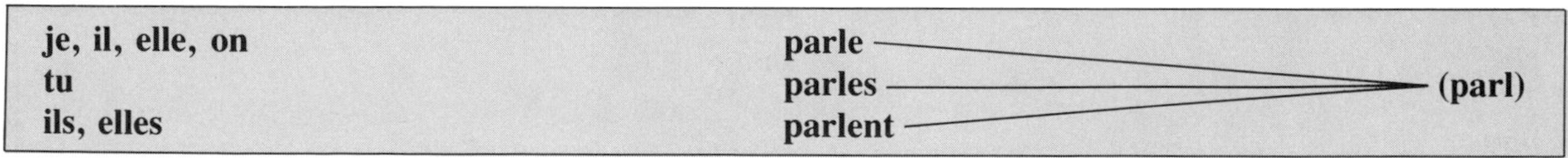

Notice that, exactly as in English, **Il, ELLE, ILS** and **ELLES** replace nouns:

LES GARÇONS (The boys) **PARLENT** (speak) **FRANÇAIS.** (French) **ILS** **PARLENT FRANÇAIS.** (They speak)

DON'T FORGET THAT **JE** becomes **J'** before a vowel sound.

Now try to put the right endings to CHANTER and ARRIVER:

Je chant ________	Nous chant ________	J'arriv ________	Nous arriv ________
Tu chant ________	Vous chant ________	Tu arriv ________	Vous arriv ________
Il chant ________	Ils chant ________	Il arriv ________	Ils arriv ________
Elle chant ________	Elles chant ________	Elle arriv ________	Elles arriv ________
On chant ________		On arriv ________	

Bon! (Good) Now put the right endings on the verbs:

Le garçon parl ____________ très bien.

Les oncles arriv ____________ demain.

Marie chant ____________ très bien.

Tu parl ________ et je chant ________.

Nous chant ________ et vous parl ________.

Negatives

NOTE: To make any verb negative, put NE (N' before a vowel sound) before the verb and PAS after the verb:

AFFIRMATIVE	NEGATIVE
JE PARLE I speak	**JE NE PARLE PAS** I don't speak

ANSWERS

Verb CHANTER

Je chante
Tu chantes
Il chante
Elle chante
On chante

Nous chantons
Vous chantez
Ils chantent
Elles chantent

Verb ARRIVER

J'arrive
Tu arrives
Il arrive
Elle arrive
On arrive

Nous arrivons
Vous arrivez
Ils arrivent
Elles arrivent

Verb PARLER, verb ARRIVER, verb CHANTER

Le garçon parle très bien.
Les oncles arrivent demain.
Marie chante très bien.
Tu parles et je chante.
Nous chantons et vous parlez.

(kee) (a-teel) (dahn) (zuhn) (nohn)

Qu'y-a-t-il dans un nom?

What's in a name?

When you are settled in your room, get to know the names of the items there. You might need another towel, or find that your lamp doesn't work. Ask the hotel staff to help you, and explain what you need.

(ewn) (shahnbr) (doh-tehl)

UNE CHAMBRE D'HOTEL

A Hotel Room

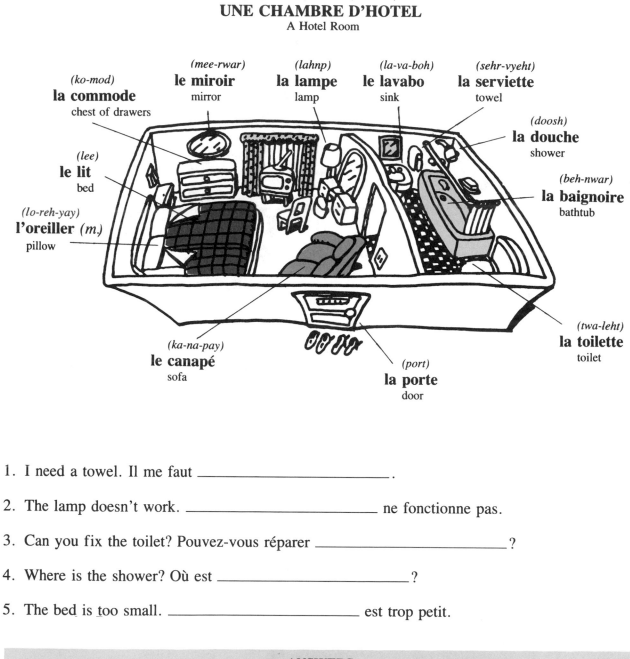

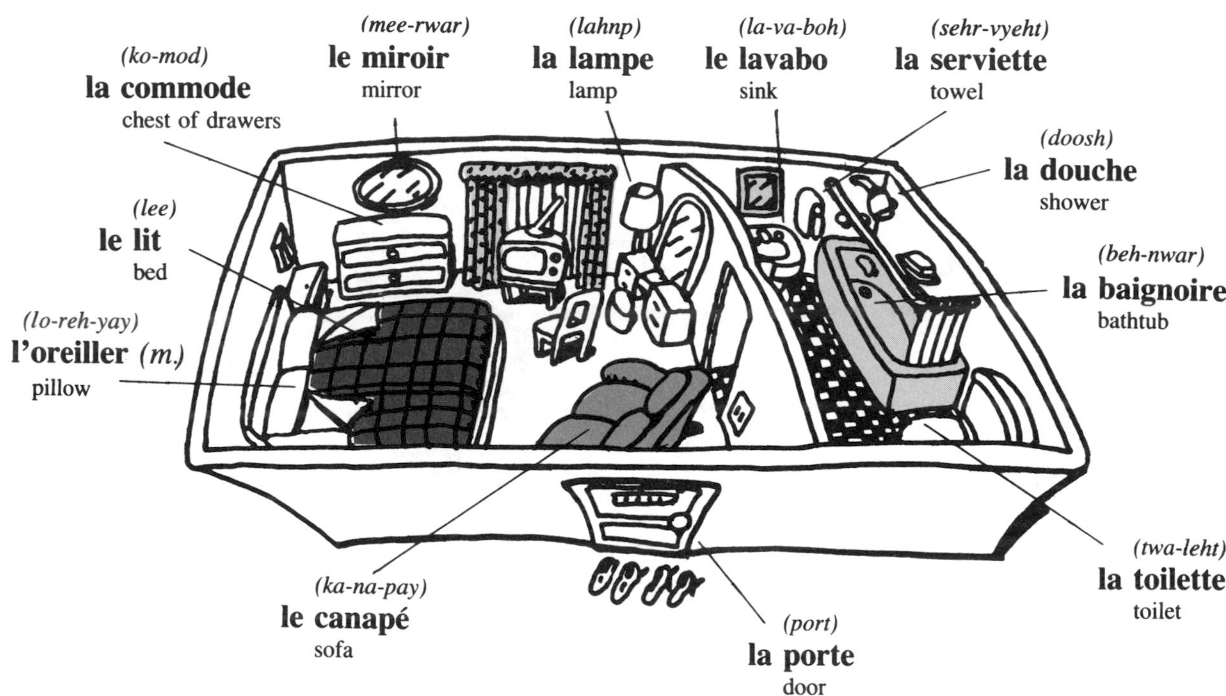

1. I need a towel. Il me faut ______________________.
2. The lamp doesn't work. ______________________ ne fonctionne pas.
3. Can you fix the toilet? Pouvez-vous réparer ______________________?
4. Where is the shower? Où est ______________________?
5. The bed is too small. ______________________ est trop petit.

ANSWERS

Hotel room 1. une serviette **2.** la lampe **3.** la toilette **4.** la douche **5.** le lit

Follow the adventures of the Smith family as they check into their hotel. Always read each line of dialogue out loud to practice your pronunciation.

MARC **Excusez-moi, monsieur. J'ai**	Excuse me, sir. I have
(ruh-tuh-new) *(shahnbr)*	
retenu deux chambres pour ce soir.	a reservation for 2 rooms for tonight.
Je m'appelle M. Smith.	My name is Smith.
EMPLOYÉ **Bonjour. Oui, nous avons votre**	Good afternoon. Yes, we have your
(ray-zehr-va-syohn)	
réservation pour deux chambres à	reservation for 2 double rooms
(lee) *(sahl)* *(duh) (ban)*	
deux lits avec salles de bain. Mais il	with bath. But there is
y a un problème.	a problem.
MARC **Qu'est-ce qu'il y a?**	What's the matter?
(doosh)	
EMPLOYÉ **Dans une chambre, la douche**	The shower in one room is broken.
ne marche pas.	
(nam-port)	
MARC **N'importe. Les enfants peuvent se**	It doesn't matter. The children can use our bath.
(beh-nyay)	
baigner chez nous.	
EMPLOYÉ **Bon. Mais il y a un autre**	Good. But there is another problem.
problème. Dans l'autre chambre, on	The window in the other room
(oo-vreer) *(fuh-nehtr)*	
ne peut pas ouvrir la fenêtre.	doesn't open.
MARC **(à Marie) Qu'est-ce que tu en**	What do you think?
(newl)	
penses? Il n'y a nulle part de	There are no rooms anywhere.
(fool)	
chambres. Il y a une foule de touristes	Paris is full of tourists now.
(man-tuh-nahn)	
à Paris maintenant.	

	(shoh)	
MARIE	**Il ne fait pas trop chaud. Prenons-**	The weather isn't too hot. Let's take them
	(kahn) (mehm)	
	les quand même.	anyway.
EMPLOYÉ	**Bon. Chaque chambre est à**	Fine. The rooms are
	(katr) (san) (fran)	
	400 francs par jour.	400 francs each per day.
	(puh-tee) (day-zhūh-nay)	
MARC	**Est-ce que le petit déjeuner est**	Is breakfast included?
	(kohn-pree)	
	compris?	
EMPLOYÉ	**Mais oui, monsieur.**	Oh yes, sir.
MARC	**Bon. Nous les prenons. Voici nos**	Okay, we'll take them. Here are our
	(pahs-por)	
	passeports.	passports.
	(vuh-yay) (rahn-pleer) (feesh)	
EMPLOYÉ	**Veuillez remplir cette fiche.**	Please fill out this form.
	(klay)	
	Voici votre clé. Les chambres sont	Here is your key. The rooms are
	(trwah-zee-ehm) (ay-tazh)	
	au troisième étage.	on the third floor.
	(a-sahn-sūhr)	
MARC	**Y a-t-il un ascenseur?**	Is there an elevator?
	(drwat)	
EMPLOYÉ	**Oui, monsieur. À droite.**	Yes. To the right.
MARC	**Merci beaucoup, monsieur.**	Thank you very much, sir.
	(pree)	
EMPLOYÉ	**Je vous en prie, monsieur.**	You're welcome, sir.
	(a-mew-zay)	
	Amusez-vous bien à Paris.	Have a good time in Paris.

Match these French expressions from the dialogue with their English equivalents:

1. J'ai retenu deux chambres pour ce soir.	a. It doesn't matter.
2. Il y a un problème.	b. What's the matter?
3. Qu'est-ce qu'il y a?	c. Have a good time in Paris.
4. N'importe.	d. The rooms are 400 francs each per day.
5. Chaque chambre est à 400 francs par jour.	e. There is a problem.
6. Est-ce que le petit déjeuner est compris?	f. Please fill out this form.
7. Veuillez remplir cette fiche.	g. I have a reservation for 2 rooms for tonight.
8. Amusez-vous bien à Paris.	h. Is breakfast included?

ANSWERS

Matching **1.** g **2.** e **3.** b **4.** a **5.** d **6.** h **7.** f **8.** c

(see) (duh-mahn-day) (kehl-kuh) (shohz)

SI VOUS VOULEZ DEMANDER QUELQUE CHOSE

If You Want to Ask for Something

You'll find yourself asking questions every day—of hotel clerks, tour guides, waitresses, and taxi drivers. To form a question from any statement, choose one of the three following methods:

TO FORM A QUESTION FROM ANY STATEMENT:

1. Just raise your voice in the normal way for questions:

(gar-sohn) (mahnzh) (krwah-sahn)
Le garçon mange le croissant.
The boy eats the croissant.

Le garçon mange le croissant?

2. Put the magical group of words *(es) (kuh)* **EST-CE QUE** (QU' before a vowel), which means literally "Is it that," at the beginning of a YES-NO question, or between the interrogative adverb and the rest of the question:

Le garçon mange le croissant.

(ehs-kuh)
Est-ce que le garçon mange le croissant?
Does the boy eat the croissant?

3. You can also invert the subject and the verb and put a hyphen between the two:

(voo) (poo-vay)
Vous pouvez.
You can.

(poo-vay) (voo)
Pouvez-vous?
Can you?

NOTICE: The previous inversion is rarely used after JE, which means "I." This is one of the times when **Est-ce que** comes in handy—and when the last letter of the verb and the first letter of the pronoun are vowels, you have to put -T- between them:

(eel)
Il mange.
he

(mahnzh) (teel)
Mange-t-il?

(el)
Elle mange.
she

(mahnzh) (tehl)
Mange-t-elle?

If the subject of the sentence is a noun or a name, the construction is as follows:

Le garcon mange le croissant.
Le garçon mange-t-il le croissant?

Marie mange le croissant.
Marie mange-t-elle le croissant?

BASIC QUESTION WORDS	
(kuh) **QUE, QU'** (+ vowel)	WHAT
(kee) **QUI**	WHO
(oo) **OÙ**	WHERE
(ko-mahn) **COMMENT**	HOW
(poor-kwa) **POURQUOI**	WHY
(kahn) **QUAND**	WHEN
(kohn-byan) **COMBIEN**	HOW MUCH, HOW MANY

NOTICE: When COMBIEN is followed by a noun, the noun is preceded by DE *(duh)*, or D' (before a vowel):

> **Combien d'argent?** *(dar-zhahn)* money
> **Combien de garçons?**
> **Combien de filles?**

These words can be used to form a question by following one of the two following formulas:

1. Interrogative + EST-CE QUE (EST-CE QU') + Subject + Verb

   Quand est-ce qu'ils arrivent?
   Où est-ce qu'ils habitent?

   Note: QUE becomes QU' before EST-CE QUE

   Qu'est-ce qu'ils cherchent?

2. Interrogative + verb (hyphen) subject (this is called *inversion*):

   Quand arrivent-ils?
   Où habitent-ils?

Try it yourself. Match up each question in the left column with its answer in the right column.

1. **Qu'est-ce que Marie mange?**
2. **Anne parle-t-elle français?** *(parl) (tehl)* speak
3. **Quand arrivent-ils?**
4. **Où arrivent-ils?**
5. **Est-ce que vous aimez les croissants?** *(e-may)* like

A. **Oui, j'aime les croissants.**
B. **Marie mange le croissant.**
C. **Oui, elle parle français.**
D. **Ils arrivent demain.** *(duh-mahn)* tomorrow
E. **Ils arrivent à l'aéroport.** *(a) (la-ay-ro-por)* at the airport

The phrase "there is" is useful to know in French. And it is the same in the singular and in the plural:
Il y a une chambre = There is a room.
Il y a des chambres = There are some rooms.

You can use this phrase in another way to ask a question. To form a question, you can either use the inversion or **EST-CE QUE:**

Y a-t-il une chambre? = Is there a room?
Y a-t-il des chambres? = Are there any rooms?

Est-ce qu'il y a encore une chambre?
Is there still a room? (Is there a room left?)

Il n'y a pas de chambre = There is no room.
Il n'y a plus de chambres = There are no rooms left.

Note: Un, une, des = de in a negative sentence.

(ee-lya) **IL Y A**	*(eel) (nya) (pah)* **IL N'Y A PAS**	*(ya-teel) (ya-teel) (pah)* **Y A-T-IL ou N'Y A-T-IL PAS?**
There is There are	There is not (no) There are not	Is there or Isn't there? Are there? Aren't there?

ANSWERS

Questions/Answers 1. B 2. C 3. D 4. E 5. A

Slow down! If you are getting confused, just ease up on your pace and review what you've learned so far. **Vous comprenez?** (Do you understand?)

See how much French you already know by doing the following "verb" crossword puzzle. These are verbs you have met so far: **parler** (to speak), **chanter** (to sing), **arriver** (to arrive), **habiter** (to live in a place).

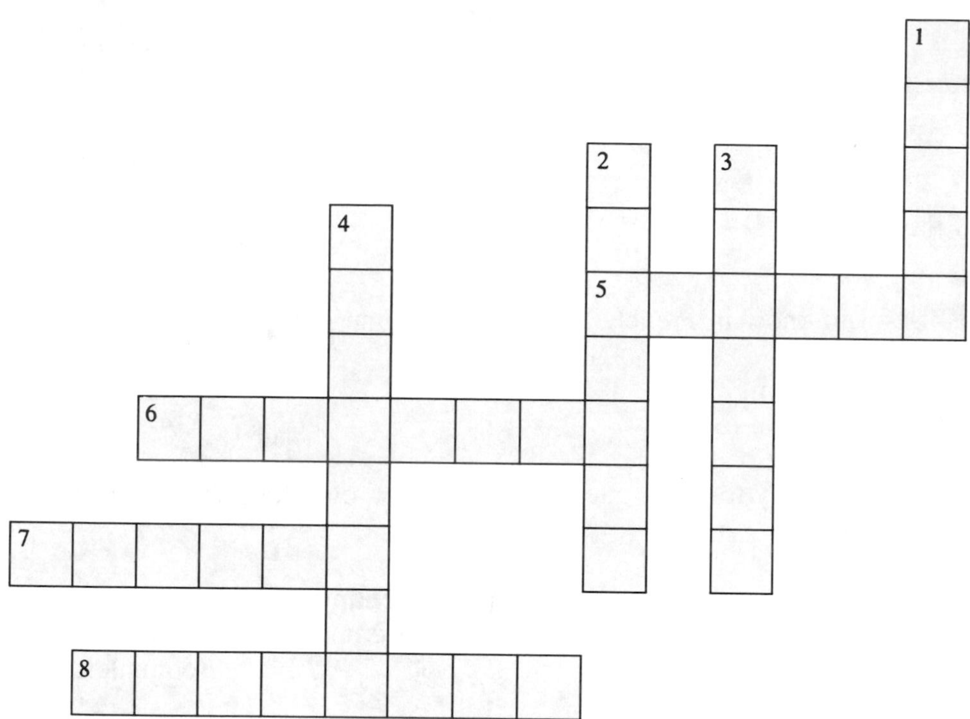

ACROSS

5. Elle (arrives)
6. Ils (arrive)
7. J' (live)
8. Nous (sing)

DOWN

1. On (speaks)
2. Tu (are singing)
3. Les garçons (speak)
4. Elles (live)

ANSWERS

Puzzle

ACROSS

5. arrive
6. arrivent
7. habite
8. chantons

DOWN:

1. parle
2. chantes
3. parlent
4. habitent

Now test your comprehension of what you have learned in this unit about requesting a room at a hotel.

Fill in the blanks:

1. M. Smith a une réservation pour ____________________ (two rooms).
2. ____________________ (The shower) ne marche pas.
3. On ne peut pas ____________________ (open the window).
4. Le petit déjeuner ____________________ (is included).
5. Les chambres sont ____________________ (on the third floor).

ANSWERS

Fill in blanks **1.** deux chambres **2.** La douche **3.** ouvrir la fenêtre **4.** est compris **5.** au troisième étage

SEEING THE SIGHTS

(kew-ree-oh-zee-tay)
Allons voir les curiosités

3 *(a-lohn-zee)* *(pyay)* Allons-y à pied
Let's Go on Foot

"How do I get to . . . ?" "Where is the nearest subway?" "Is the museum straight ahead?" You'll be asking directions wherever you travel. Acquaint yourself with words and phrases that will make getting around easier. Don't forget to read each line aloud several times to practice your pronunciation. Act out each part to be certain you understand these new words.

(Paul and Anne Smith set out on their first day to visit a museum.)

ANNE	*(duh-mahn-dohn) (la-zhahn)* **Paul, demandons à l'agent de** *(pol-lees) (e) (mew-zay)* **police où est le musée.**	Paul, let's ask the policeman where the museum is.
PAUL	*(sewr) (ray-ew-seer)* **Je ne suis pas sûr de réussir . . .**	I am not sure of succeeding . . .
	Excusez-moi, Monsieur l'agent,	Excuse me, Sir,
	(deer) **pouvez-vous nous dire où est le musée?**	can you tell us where the museum is?

(sehr-ten-mahn) (kohn-tee-new-ay) (too)
AGENT **Certainement. Continuez tout**
(drwah) (zhews-ka) (rew) (mo-lyehr)
droit jusqu'à la rue Molière et
(toor-nay) (drwat)
tournez à droite. Continuez jusqu'à
(vol-tehr) (ahn-sweet)
la rue Voltaire, ensuite tournez à
(gohsh) (ra-seen)
gauche et continuez sur la rue Racine
(zhews-koh) (fūh) (la) (a)
jusqu'aux feux. Le musée est là, à
(koh-tay) (lay-gleez)
côté de l'église.

Certainly. Continue straight ahead to Molière Street and turn right. Continue to Voltaire Street, then turn left and continue on Racine Street to the traffic lights. The museum is there, next to the church.

PAUL **Merci mille fois.**

Many thanks.

(ryan)
AGENT **De rien.**

You are welcome. (*lit.* of nothing.)

After having followed the directions:

(suh) (nay) (pas) (luh) (mew-zay)
ANNE **Ce n'est pas le musée.**

This building is not the museum.

(post)
C'est la poste.

It's the post office.

(troh) (tar)
PAUL **Patience, Anne. Il est trop tard**
(poor) (fee-neer) (notr)
pour finir notre sightseeing.
(ruh-toor-nohn)
Retournons à l'hôtel.

Be patient, Anne. It's too late to finish our sightseeing. Let's go back to the hotel.

Can you answer these true-false questions based on the dialogue? Write VRAI (true) next to each true statement. Correct any false statement.

_____ 1. Paul demande à l'agent où est *l'église*.
_____ 2. L'agent dit de tourner *à droite*.
_____ 3. Le musée est à côté de *l'école*.
_____ 4. Ce n'est pas *le musée*.
_____ 5. C'est *l'aéroport*.

ANSWERS

True-false **1.** le musée **2.** VRAI **3.** l'église **4.** VRAI **5.** la poste

(oo) (a-lay) (voo)
OÙ ALLEZ-VOUS?
Where Are You Going?

You'll find yourself *going to* a museum, or being *at* a bakery or *in* a theater often if you go abroad, so knowing the following words will come in very handy.

(lom)
L'homme est à Paris.
in

(va)
L'homme va à New York.
goes to

L'homme est ~~à + le~~ →
(oh)
AU cinéma.
at the

L'homme va ~~à + le~~ →
AU théâtre.
to the

Le garçon est à la
at the
boulangerie.
bakery

Le garçon va à la.
to the
boulangerie

Le garçon est à l'école.
at the school

Le garçon va à l'école.
to the

Madame Dubois est

~~à + les~~ → AUX États-Unis.
in the

Madame Dubois va
~~à + les~~ → AUX États-Unis.
to the

(deh) (puh-tee) (moh) (kee) (see-nee-fee) (boh-koo)

Des petits mots qui signifient beaucoup

Little words that mean a lot

The preposition **À** means "to" or "at" and is used before proper nouns:

Il parle à Jean.

The definite articles **LA** (used before feminine singular nouns beginning with a consonant) and **L'** (used before all singular nouns beginning with a vowel) can be placed after **À** to express "to the" or "at the":

Le garçon est À LA boulangerie. **Le garçon est À L' école.**

The definite articles **LE** (used before masculine singular nouns beginning with a consonant) and **LES** (used before all plural nouns) contract with **À** to form completely new words:

À + LE = AU (TO, AT THE)

À + LES = AUX (TO, AT THE)

Il parle AU garçon.

Il parle AUX garçons.

Try this exercise:

Jean va 1. __________ cinéma.

2. __________ école.

3. __________ États-Unis.

4. __________ Paris.

5. __________ boulangerie.

The same situation occurs with **DE**, which means "from," "of" or "about":

Il parle DE Jean.

Il parle DE la boulangerie.

Il parle DE l'école.

But note:

DE + LE = DU

DE + LES = DES

Il parle du garçon.
Il parle des garçons.

ANSWERS

Prepositions 1. au cinéma **2.** à l'école **3.** aux États-Unis **4.** à Paris **5.** à la boulangerie

Now do this exercise.

Jean parle 1. __________ école.

2. __________ théâtre.

3. __________ boulangerie.

4. __________ New-York.

5. __________ filles.

The other prepositions are easier. Some are followed by **DE** and the rule you just practiced applies.

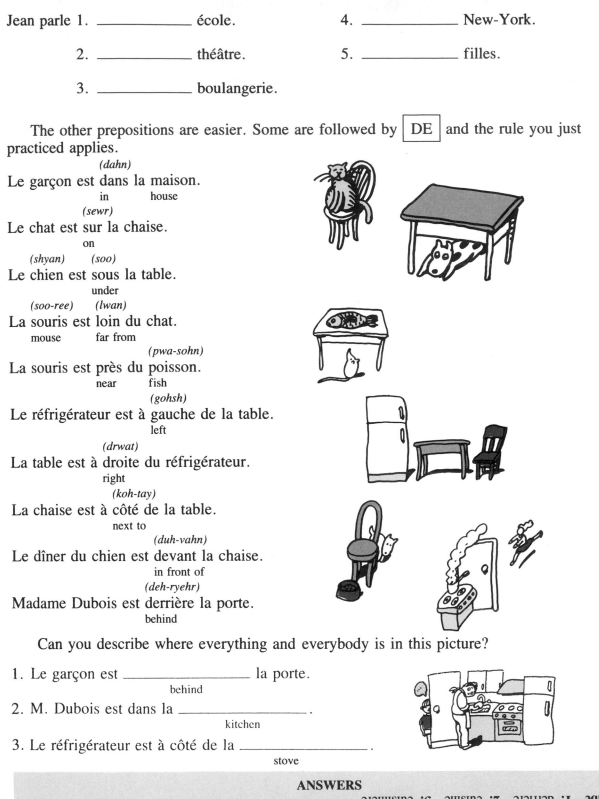

(dahn)
Le garçon est dans la maison.
in — house

(sewr)
Le chat est sur la chaise.
on

(shyan) *(soo)*
Le chien est sous la table.
under

(soo-ree) *(lwan)*
La souris est loin du chat.
mouse — far from

(pwa-sohn)
La souris est près du poisson.
near — fish

(gohsh)
Le réfrigérateur est à gauche de la table.
left

(drwat)
La table est à droite du réfrigérateur.
right

(koh-tay)
La chaise est à côté de la table.
next to

(duh-vahn)
Le dîner du chien est devant la chaise.
in front of

(deh-ryehr)
Madame Dubois est derrière la porte.
behind

Can you describe where everything and everybody is in this picture?

1. Le garçon est __________ la porte.
behind

2. M. Dubois est dans la __________.
kitchen

3. Le réfrigérateur est à côté de la __________.
stove

ANSWERS

About 1. de l'école **2.** du théâtre **3.** de la boulangerie **4.** de New-York **5.** des filles

Describe 1. derrière **2.** cuisine **3.** cuisinière

(ahn-kor)
Encore des verbes
Verbs again

In the previous unit you learned how to conjugate verbs ending in -ER. These are known as verbs of the first conjugation. Now you will learn how to conjugate some common verbs of the second conjugation. These end in -IR. Drop **IR** and add the endings:

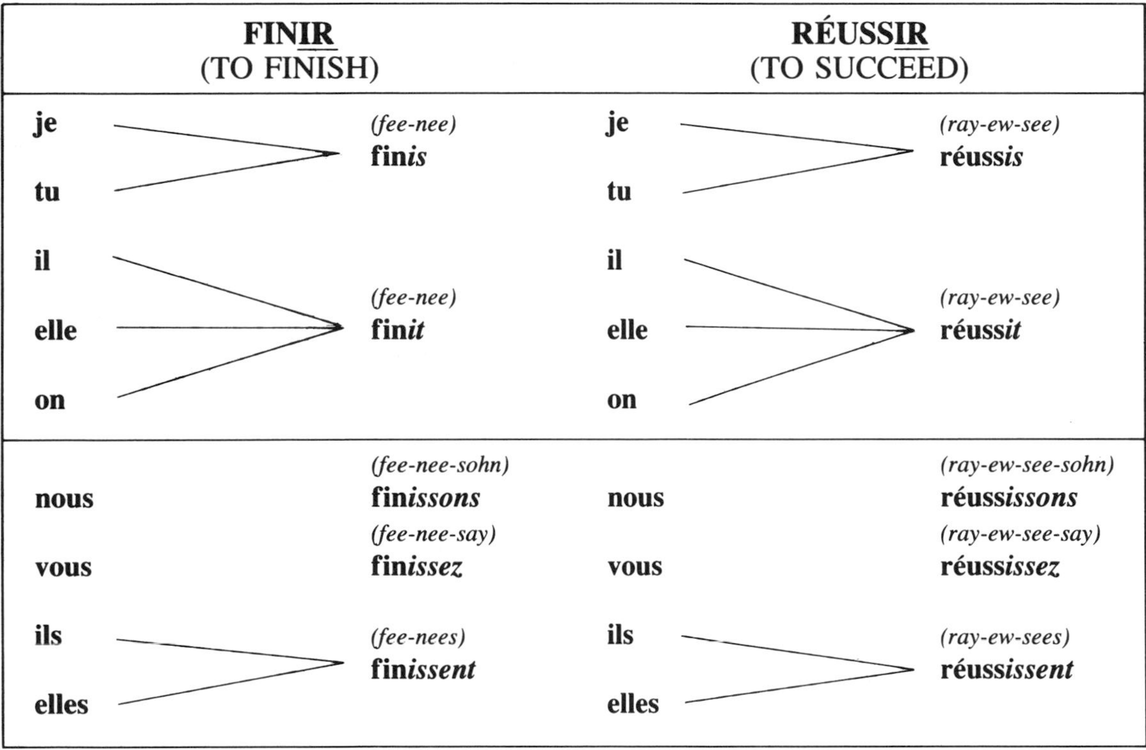

FINIR (TO FINISH)		**RÉUSSIR** (TO SUCCEED)	
je, **tu**	*(fee-nee)* **fin*is***	**je**, **tu**	*(ray-ew-see)* **réuss*is***
il, **elle**, **on**	*(fee-nee)* **fin*it***	**il**, **elle**, **on**	*(ray-ew-see)* **réuss*it***
nous	*(fee-nee-sohn)* **fin*issons***	**nous**	*(ray-ew-see-sohn)* **réuss*issons***
vous	*(fee-nee-say)* **fin*issez***	**vous**	*(ray-ew-see-say)* **réuss*issez***
ils, **elles**	*(fee-nees)* **fin*issent***	**ils**, **elles**	*(ray-ew-sees)* **réuss*issent***

Remember that to make verbs negative, you put NE (N') before the verb and PAS after.

Je ne finis pas. **Je ne réussis pas.**

Can you figure out each verb by unscrambling the letters? The only two verbs used are FINIR and RÉUSSIR.

a. Jean UÉRITSS ____________ à parler français.

b. Jean et Anne TNESSINIF ____________ leur *(lūhr)* (their) sightseeing.

c. Nous NFIISOSSN ____________ le dîner.

d. IRZEEUSSSS -vous à parler français?

e. Je NIFIS ce travail *(tra-va-y)*.

f. Tu RIÉUSSS ____________.

g. On TFINI ____________.

h. Vous EZNIFSSI ____________.

ANSWERS

Unscrambling IR verbs

a. Jean *réussit* à parler français.
b. Jean et Anne *finissent* leur sightseeing.
c. Nous *finissons* le dîner.
d. *Réussissez*-vous à parler français?
e. Je *finis* ce travail.
f. Tu *réussis*.
g. On *finit*.
h. Vous *finissez*.

(kel-kuh) (moh) (zew-teel)

Quelques mots utiles

Some useful words

(see-nay-mah) **le cinéma** movies

(ma-ga-zan) **le magasin** store

(mar-shay) **le marché** market

(bahnk) **la banque** bank

(lay-gleez) **l'église** church

(tro-twar) **le trottoir** sidewalk

(fehr) (koors) **faire des courses** to shop

(root) **la route** road

(day-zee-nyay) (shohz) (ahn)

Comment désigner les choses en français

How to point things out in French

Words like "this" and "that" are important to know, particularly when you go shopping, and want to buy that good-looking pair of gloves in the shop window. The French forms of these words vary, depending on whether the item is masculine or feminine, and whether you are pointing to one item or to many.

"THIS" or "THAT" and "THESE" or "THOSE"	
WITH FEMININE NOUNS	
Singulier	**Pluriel**
(set) **CETTE FILLE**	*(say)* **CES FILLES**
CETTE AMIE	**CES AMIES**
WITH MASCULINE NOUNS	
(suh)(bah-tee-mahn) **CE BÂTIMENT** this building	*(bah-tee-mahn)* **CES BÂTIMENTS** these buildings
(se tay-tew-dyahn) **CET ÉTUDIANT** this student—male	*(say zay-tew-dyahn)* **CES ÉTUDIANTS** these students

NOTE: CE becomes CET before masculine singular nouns which begin with a vowel.

(ee-see) *(la)*
ICI means "here" and LA means "there." So if you want to be more specific or to differentiate between this thing here and that thing over there, you simply add -CI or -LA to the noun.

"HERE" AND "THERE"

ICI	LÀ
cette fille-ci	**cette fille-là**
cette amie-ci	**cette amie-là**
ce garçon-ci	**ce garçon-là**
cet étudiant-ci	**cet étudiant-là**
ces filles-ci	**ces filles-là**
ces étudiants-ci	**ces étudiants-là**

Now, try the following: Put the appropriate form of "this" or "these" and "that" or "those" in each slot:

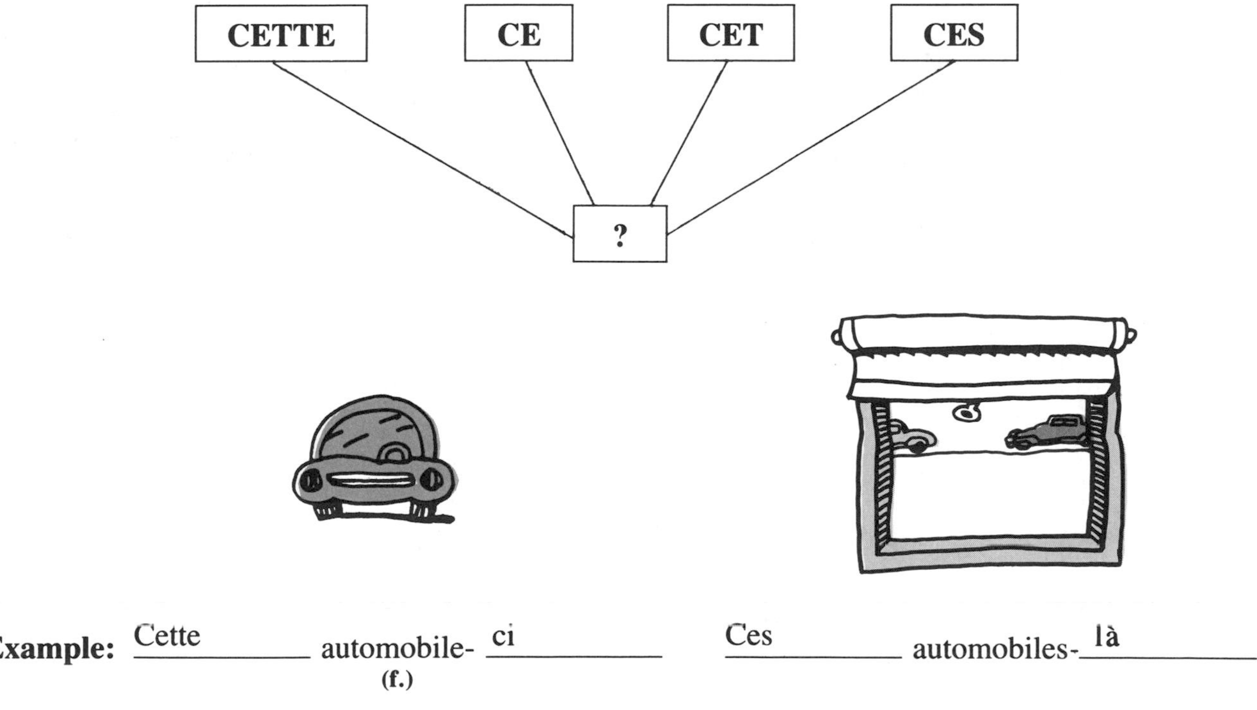

Example: Cette _____ automobile- ci _____ Ces _____ automobiles- là _____
(f.)

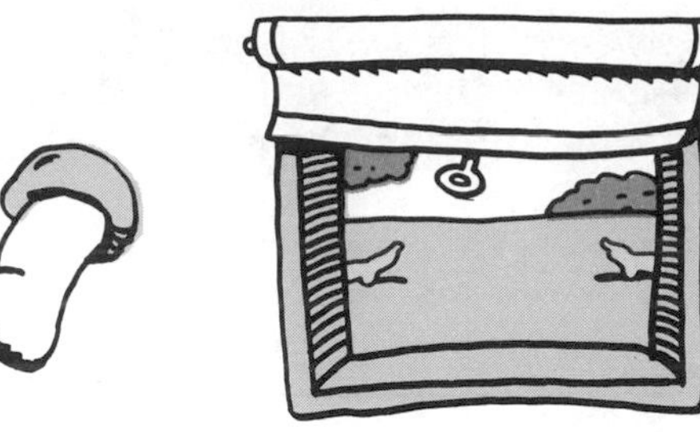

_______ chat- _______ _______ chats- _______
(**m.**)

_______ pied- _______ _______ pieds- _______
foot (**m.**)

_______ maison- _______ _______ maisons- _______
house (**f.**)

_______ étudiant- _______ _______ étudiants- _______

_______ église- _______ _______ églises- _______
church (**f.**)

(o-pay-rah)
_______ opéra- _______ _______ opéras- _______
opera (**m.**)

ANSWERS

Demonstrative adjectives

Ce chat-ci	Ces chats-là	Ce pied-ci	Ces pieds-là
Cette maison-ci	Ces maisons-là	Cet étudiant-ci	Ces étudiants-là
Cette église-ci	Ces églises-là	Cet opéra-ci	Ces opéras-là

Now have fun with the following crossword puzzle:

Across

3. Hotel
6. Behind
7. School
9. With
11. House
13. Foot
14. This (f.)
15. On

Down

1. She
2. Store
4. One, a (f.)
5. Movies
6. In front
7. Church
8. The (f.)
10. Cat
12. Under
14. This (m.)

ANSWERS

Across **3.** Hôtel **6.** Derrière **7.** École **9.** Avec **11.** Maison **13.** Pied **14.** Cette **15.** Sur
Down **1.** Elle **2.** Magasin **4.** Une **5.** Cinéma **6.** Devant **7.** Église **8.** La **10.** Chat **12.** Sous **14.** Ce

4 Les transports publics

(tran-spor) *(pew-bleek)*

Les transports publics
Public Transportation

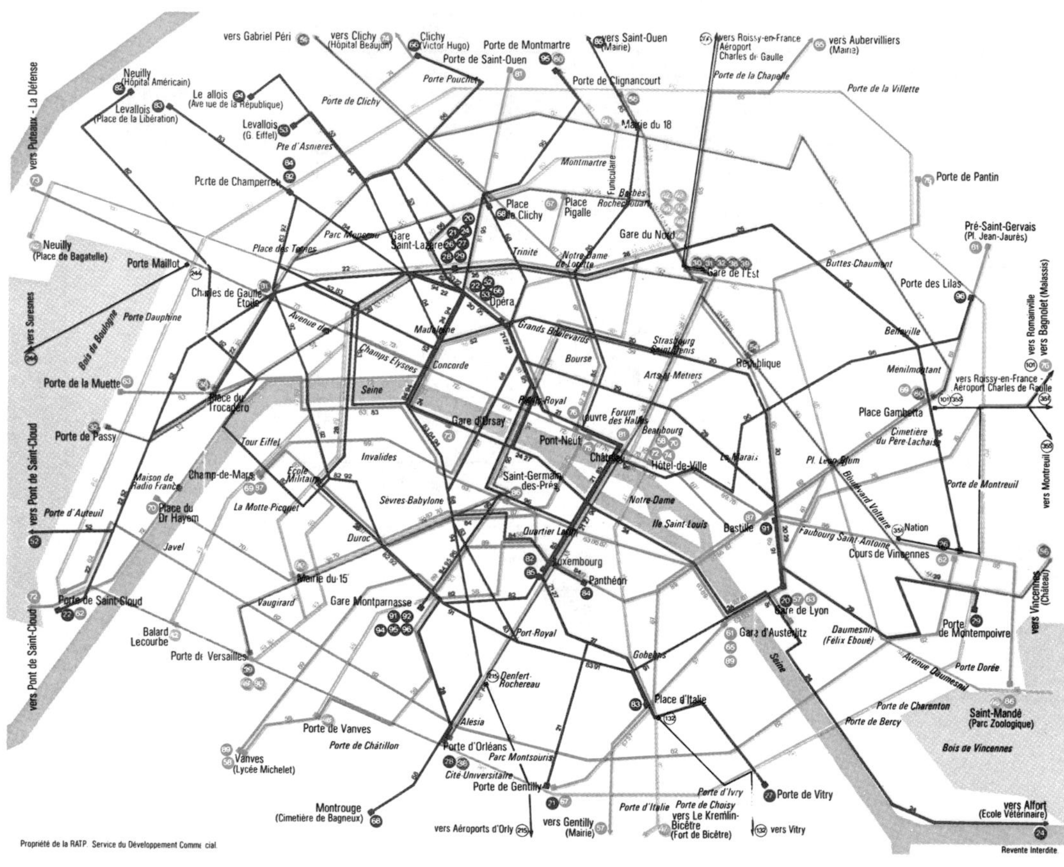

(From Barron's *Seeing the Real Paris,* © 1983)

You will certainly want to take public transportation when you are in a foreign city. The following dialogue contains some words and expressions that you will find useful in order to get around easily using public transportation. Always read the dialogue carefully several times out loud to familiarize yourself with the meaning and pronunciation of the words.

	(pruh-nohn) *(tak-see)* *(a-lay)*	
MARIE	**Prenons un taxi pour aller au cinéma.**	Let's take a taxi to go to the movies.
	(troh)	
MARC	**Non. C'est trop cher.**	No. It's too expensive.
MARIE	**Alors prenons le métro.**	Then let's take the metro.
	(vwa) *(vew)*	
MARC	**Non. On ne voit pas la vue.**	No. One doesn't see the view.

(keh) (lom) (ma-va) (ray) (dee-fee-seel)
MARIE **Quel homme avare et difficile!** — What a stingy and difficult man!

(o-to-bews)
Alors prenons l'autobus. — Then, let's take the bus.

(bee-yay) (too-reesm)
MARC **D'accord. Notre billet de tourisme** — Okay. Our tourist ticket

(bohn)
est bon pour le métro et l'autobus. — is good for the metro and the bus.

Dans l'autobus — On the Bus

(de-sahn-dohn)
MARC **Pardon Madame, où descendons-** — Excuse, me, Madam, where do we get off

nous pour aller au cinéma Broadway? — to go to the cinema "Broadway"?

(a-reh) (a-preh) (kohn-kord)
LA DAME **À l'arrêt après la Concorde.** — At the stop after the Concorde.

(kom) (sohn) (teh-mahbl)
MARC **Comme les Français sont aimables!** — How kind the French are!

Circle the best answer to each question.

1. Marie désire prendre un taxi pour aller
   a. au musée b. au cinéma c. à l'hôtel d. à Paris
2. L'autobus
   a. ne va pas au cinéma b. est trop cher
   c. va directement au cinéma d. ne va pas à la Concorde
3. Marie et Marc décident de prendre l'autobus et d'utiliser
   a. la carte de tourisme b. le billet de dix francs
   c. le passeport d. le billet de tourisme
4. Le cinéma Broadway est
   a. tout droit b. à la rue Racine c. à côté du musée
   d. à l'arrêt après la Concorde

Qu'est-ce que c'est?

a. un ______________________ b. un ______________________

ANSWERS

Multiple choice 1. b **2** c **3.** d **4.** d
Qu'est-ce que c'est? a. un taxi **b.** un autobus

c. un ________________________ d. une ________________________

Encore des verbes

More Verbs

Now, you will learn how to conjugate third conjugation verbs like *(de-sahndr)* DESCENDRE (to go down—to get off) and *(vahndr)* VENDRE (to sell) and the irregular verbs *(ehtr)* ÊTRE (to be), *(a-vwar)* AVOIR (to have) and *(prahndr)* PRENDRE (to take). Notice that third conjugation verbs end in **-RE**. Drop the **-RE** and add the endings.

VEND*RE* TO SELL		**DESCEND*RE*** TO GO DOWN, TO GET OFF	
je, **tu**	*(vahn)* **vend*s***	**je**, **tu**	*(deh-sahn)* **descend*s***
il, **elle**, **on**	*(vahn)* **vend**	**il**, **elle**, **on**	*(deh-sahn)* **descend**
nous	*(vahn-dohn)* **vend*ons***	**nous**	*(deh-sahn-dohn)* **descend*ons***
vous	*(vahn-day)* **vend*ez***	**vous**	*(deh-sahn-day)* **descend*ez***
ils, **elles**	*(vahnd)* **vend*ent***	**ils**, **elles**	*(deh-sahnd)* **descend*ent***

Remember that you are saying "I sell," "I am selling" or "I do sell." In other words, one French structure can express three different ideas in English.

ANSWERS

Qu'est-ce que c'est? **c.** un métro **d.** une automobile

It's wise now to review the conjugations of the three groups of regular French verbs.

SUMMARY: **ENDINGS FOR THREE TYPES OF REGULAR VERBS**			
	PARL-*ER*	FIN-*IR*	VEND-*RE*
je	**-E**	**-IS**	**-S**
tu	**-ES**	**-IS**	**-S**
il, elle, on	**-E**	**-IT**	**—**
nous	**-ONS**	**-ISSONS**	**-ONS**
vous	**-EZ**	**-ISSEZ**	**-EZ**
ils, elles	**-ENT**	**-ISSENT**	**-ENT**

Do you begin to see a pattern? Now conjugate DESCENDRE:

1. Je descend ____________________
2. Tu descend ____________________
3. Il descend ____________________
4. Nous descend ____________________
5. Vous descend ____________________
6. Ils descend ____________________
7. Le garçon descend ____________________
8. Les hommes descend ____________________

COMMENT PARLER AU CONTRÔLEUR . . .

How to Speak to the Conductor . . .

As a tourist in a French-speaking city, you may wish to communicate with the **conducteur** *(kohn-dewk-tūhr)* (driver) or the **contrôleur** *(kohn-troh-lūhr)* of the bus. Here are some typical questions.

ANSWERS

Descendre
1. Je descends **2.** Tu descends **3.** Il descend **4.** Nous descendons **5.** Vous descendez **6.** Ils descendent **7.** Le garçon descend **8.** Les hommes descendent

(pŭh) (ash-tay)
Est-ce que je peux acheter mon billet dans l'autobus? buy — Can I buy my ticket on the bus?

(foh) (mohn-tay)
Est-ce qu'il faut monter devant ou derrière? get on — Should one get on in the front or in the rear?

(koot)
Combien coûte le billet? — How much does the ticket cost?

Pouvez-vous me dire quand il faut descendre? — Can you tell me when to get off?

(day-zo-lay) (mo-ne)
Je suis désolé, je n'ai pas de monnaie. — I am very sorry, I don't have any change.

(lay) (vehrb) (kee) (nuh) (suh) (kohn-form) (pah) (zoh) (rehgl)

Les verbes qui ne se conforment pas aux règles

Verbs that don't follow the rules

You've learned how to use some common verbs that end in "er," "ir," and "re." Unfortunately, using verbs isn't that simple! *Naturellement!* There are exceptions to the rules, and we call them "irregular verbs." Here are two common irregular verbs. Notice how they take on different forms, depending upon the subject. It is hard work, but you just have to learn these well, because you will want to use them often.

(ehtr) **ÊTRE** TO BE		(a-vwar) **AVOIR** TO HAVE	
je	(swee) **suis**	**j'**	(zhay) **ai**
tu	(eh) **es**	**tu**	(a) **as**
il, elle, on	(eh) **est**	**il, elle, on**	(a) **a**
nous	(som) **sommes**	**nous**	(a-vohn) **avons**
vous	(eht) **êtes**	**vous**	(a-vay) **avez**
ils, elles	(sohn) **sont**	**ils, elles**	(zohn) **ont**

You may have noticed these verbs in the previous chapters:

Je ne suis pas sûr de réussir. I am not sure of succeeding.
Demandons à l'agent où est le musée. Let's ask the policeman where the museum is.
Comme les Français sont aimables! How friendly the French are!

Now, write down the meaning of the next short sentences in English.

1. Nous sommes à Paris. ______________________________

2. Vous avez une réservation. ______________________________

3. L'hôtel est loin de la banque. ______________________________

4. Marc et Marie n'ont pas de réservation. ______________________________

______________________________.

5. Est-ce que vous avez de la monnaie? ______________________________

______________________________?

There are a few more irregular verbs that you'll need to know. Take a look at **prendre** *(prahndr)* (to take), **apprendre** *(a-prahndr)* (to learn), and **comprendre** *(kohn-prahndr)* (to understand).

	PRENDRE TO TAKE	**APPRENDRE** TO LEARN	**COMPRENDRE** TO UNDERSTAND
je, j'	**prend*s***	**apprend*s***	**comprend*s***
tu	**prend*s***	**apprend*s***	**comprend*s***
il, elle, on	**prend**	**apprend**	**comprend**
nous	*(pruh-nohn)* **pren*ons***	*(a-pruh-nohn)* **appren*ons***	*(kohn-pruh-nohn)* **compren*ons***
vous	*(pruh-nay)* **pren*ez***	*(a-pruh-nay)* **appren*ez***	*(kohn-pruh-nay)* **compren*ez***
ils, elles	*(pren)* **pren*nent***	*(a-pren)* **appren*nent***	*(kohn-pren)* **compren*nent***

ANSWERS

English Translation **1.** We are in Paris. **2.** You have a reservation. **3.** The hotel is far from the bank. **4.** Mark and Mary have no reservation. **5.** Do you have any change?

This is how they would appear in context.

Prenons l'autobus! Let's take the bus! **J'apprends le français.** I am learning French.

(too) (ptee) (pūh)
Je comprends le francais un tout petit peu. I understand French a tiny little bit.

Write the meaning in English of the following sentences.

1. Marc et Marie comprennent le français. ______________________.
2. Est-ce que vous apprenez l'anglais? ______________________?
3. Jean ne comprend pas très bien le français. ______________________.
4. Prenons le métro! ______________________!
5. Prennent-ils un taxi? ______________________?

Now see if you can remember the regular and irregular verbs by writing in the appropriate forms on the blanks.

	ÊTRE	**AVOIR**	**PRENDRE**	**DESCENDRE**	**FINIR**
JE	______	______	______	______	______
TU	______	______	______	______	______
IL, ELLE, ON	______	______	______	______	______
NOUS	______	______	______	______	______
VOUS	______	______	______	______	______
ILS, ELLES	______	______	______	______	______

ANSWERS

English Translation

1. Mark and Mary understand French. **2.** Are you learning English? **3.** John does not understand French very well. **4.** Let's take the metro. **5.** Are they taking a taxi?

Verbs,	**être**	**avoir**	**prendre**	**descendre**	**finir**
je, j'	suis	ai	prends	descends	finis
tu	es	as	prends	descends	finis
il elle on	est	a	prend	descend	finit
nous	sommes	avons	prenons	descendons	finissons
vous	êtes	avez	prenez	descendez	finissez
ils elles	sont	ont	prennent	descendent	finissent

(ruh-vuh-nohn) *(pray-poh-zee-syohn)*

Revenons aux prépositions

Getting back to prepositions

Earlier we saw how the prepositions À ("to," "in") and DE ("of," "from," "about") contract with the definite articles LE and LES to become AU, AUX, and DU, DES. But we practiced them mostly before names of places (Paris, le cinéma, etc.). However,

À is the equivalent of "to" in a statement such as:

Je parle au garçon. I speak to the boy.

The indefinite article DES (plural of UN, UNE) could be considered a contraction of DE + LES, meaning "about the," "of the," "from the." However,

DE + definite article (or proper name) expresses possession:

Le livre du garçon — The boy's book
Le livre de Paul — Paul's book

and means "about" in sentences such as:

Nous parlons du professeur. We are talking about the teacher.

A little practice? Try these:

1. Le livre ________ (of the) garçon
2. Le cahier ________ (of the) fille
3. Les amis ________ (of the) étudiant
4. L'ami ________ (of the) étudiante *(ay-tew-dyant)* (fem. student)
5. Je parle ________ (about the) étudiant
6. Le professeur parle ________ (about the) livre ________ (to the) étudiants
7. J'ai ________ (some) amis ________ (in) Montréal
8. Je donne (*don*, give) le livre ________ (to the) garçon
9. Nous téléphonons *(tay-lay-fo-nohn)* ________ (to the) hôtel

ANSWERS

DE
1. du **2.** de la **3.** de l' **4.** de l' **5.** de l' **6.** du aux **7.** des à **8.** au **9.** à l'

The following brief passage will let you find out how well you have learned to answer questions and to get around town.

Monsieur Legros et sa femme prennent
his *(plew)*
l'autobus et descendent deux arrêts plus
two more
loin. Puis ils prennent le métro. Ils
(roo-soh)
descendent à la rue Rousseau. Ils arrivent
(a-shet) *(boh-koo)* *(shohz)*
au marché et achètent beaucoup de choses.
many things

1. Qu'est-ce que les Legros prennent ?

____

2. Où descendent-ils?

____

3. Et ensuite, qu'est-ce qu'ils prennent?

____

4. Où est-ce que les Legros arrivent?

____

5. Qu'est-ce qu'ils achètent?

____

ANSWERS

Questions 1. (Ils prennent) l'autobus. **2.** (Ils descendent) deux arrêts plus loin. **3.** (Ils prennent) le métro. **4.** (Ils arrivent) au marché. **5.** (Ils achètent) beaucoup de choses.

5 Exprimant l'heure et les nombres

(ehks-pree-mahn) *(lũhr)* *(nohmbr)*

Expressing Time and Numbers

Il est 9 heures du matin.	**Il est 1 heure du matin.**	**Il est 3 heures de l'après-midi.**	**Il est 8 heures du soir.**	**Il est 3 heures du matin.**

Expressing time is easy. Simply state the number of the hour, followed by the word **heure(s)**.

You use *du matin* *(ma-tan)* (A.M.) for the morning and *de* *(duh)* *l'après midi* *(la-preh-mee-dee)* (P.M.) for early afternoon; *du soir* *(swar)* (P.M.) is used for later afternoon and evening.

COMMENT COMPTER EN FRANÇAIS

(kohn-tay)

How to Count in French

Les nombres cardinaux 1–1000

(kar-dee-noh)

Cardinal numbers 1–1000

1	2	3	4	5	6	7	8
			(katr)	*(sank)*	*(sees)*	*(seht)*	*(weet)*
UN	**DEUX**	**TROIS**	**QUATRE**	**CINQ**	**SIX**	**SEPT**	**HUIT**

9	10	11	12	13	14	15
		(ohnz)	*(dooz)*	*(trehz)*	*(ka-torz)*	*(kanz)*
NEUF	**DIX**	**ONZE**	**DOUZE**	**TREIZE**	**QUATORZE**	**QUINZE**

16	17	18	19	20
(sehz)	*(dee-set)*	*(dee-zweet)*	*(deez-nuhf)*	*(van)*
SEIZE	**DIX-SEPT**	**DIX-HUIT**	**DIX-NEUF**	**VINGT**

Now it's easy . . . until we reach 70.

21 VINGT ET UN
22 VINGT-DEUX
23 VINGT-TROIS etc.
(trahnt)
30 TRENTE
31 TRENTE ET UN
32 TRENTE-DEUX
(ka-rahnt)
40 QUARANTE

(san-kahnt)
50 CINQUANTE
(swa-sahnt)
60 SOIXANTE
70 SOIXANTE-DIX
71 SOIXANTE ET ONZE
72 SOIXANTE-DOUZE etc.
80 QUATRE-VINGTS
81 QUATRE-VINGT-UN
82 QUATRE-VINGT-DEUX etc.

90 QUATRE-VINGT-DIX
91 QUATRE-VINGT-ONZE
92 QUATRE-VINGT-DOUZE etc.
(sahn)
100 CENT
200 DEUX CENTS etc.
(meel)
1000 MILLE

PRONUNCIATION NOTE: Six and ten are pronounced "sees" and "dees" if they are by themselves. When followed by a noun, they become "see" and "dee." Eight is pronounced "weet" by itself, "wee" when followed by a noun:

(see) **six garçons** *(dee)* **dix filles** *(wee)* **huit tables**

When these numbers are followed by a noun which begins with a vowel, one has to link:

(see) (zamee) **six amis** *(dee) (zay-kol)* **dix écoles** schools

And when nine is followed by a vowel sound, the final "F" sounds like a "V": **il est neuf heures** *(nuh) (vuhr)*

(or-dee-noh)

Les nombres ordinaux 1–10

Ordinal numbers 1–10

First

(Masculine) *(pruh-myay)* **PREMIER**

(Feminine) *(pruh-myer)* **PREMIÈRE**

Second *(duh-zyehm)* **DEUXIÈME**

Third *(trwah-zyehm)* **TROISIÈME**

Fourth *(ka-try-ehm)* **QUATRIÈME**

Fifth *(san-kyehm)* **CINQUIÈME**

Sixth *(see-zyehm)* **SIXIÈME**

Seventh *(se-tyehm)* **SEPTIÈME**

Eighth *(wee-tyehm)* **HUITIÈME**

Ninth *(nuh-vyehm)* **NEUVIÈME**

Tenth *(dee-zyehm)* **DIXIÈME**

ALARME **STOP**
9ème **10ème**
7ème **8ème**
5ème **6ème**
3ème **4ème**
1er **2ème**

(rayd) (shoh-say) **rez-de-chaussée**

NOTE: The "rez-de-chaussée" is the ground floor in the U.S.; the "premier étage" *(ay-tahzh)* is the second floor in the U.S.

(ke) (luh) (reh) (teel)

QUELLE HEURE EST-IL?

What time is it?

1. To add the minutes, simply add the number:

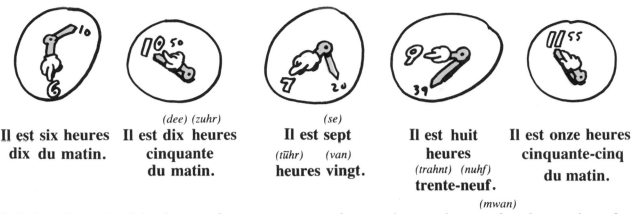

Il est six heures dix du matin.

(dee) (zuhr)
Il est dix heures cinquante du matin.

(se)
Il est sept
(tūhr) (van)
heures vingt.

Il est huit heures
(trahnt) (nuhf)
trente-neuf.

Il est onze heures cinquante-cinq du matin.

2. If the minute hand is close to the next, you can also say the next hour *(mwan)* **moins** (minus) the number of minutes to go:

(ohn) (zuhr) (mwan) (dees)
Il est onze heures moins dix.

3. Finally, the quarter hours and the half hours (although not in official time) can be replaced by the following expressions:

2:15—deux heures et *(kar)* **quart** (quarter)

3:30—trois heures et *(duh-mee)* **demie** (half—feminine because HEURE is feminine)

2:45—trois heures moins le **quart**.

12:30—midi (minuit) et **demi** (half—masculine because MIDI and MINUIT are masculine)

Easy? In France the 24-hour system is often used, especially in travel schedules and performance times; for example, *quatorze heures* (14 hours) is 2 P.M. To understand this system, subtract 12 from any number more than 12 and add P.M.

A few examples:
Le train part à 22 h 13 = The train leaves at 10:13 P.M.
Le concert commence à 20 h 30 = The concert begins at 8:30 P.M.
L'avion arrive à 17 h 35 = The plane arrives at 5:35 P.M.

Un moment. Now give the following times in French:

2:15	1:10
8:30	3:35
9:45	5:25
7:00	4:55

Express these numbers in French:

14	62
23	71
37	89
46	98
55	116

The following dialogue contains some useful expressions related to the telling of time. Read it out loud a few times.

MARC **Pardon, Monsieur, quelle heure est-il?**	Excuse me, Sir, what time is it?
UN MONSIEUR **Il est minuit.**	It's midnight.
MARC **Comment est-ce** *(ehs)* **possible?** *(po-seebl)* **Il fait** *(fay)* **encore** *(tahn-kor)* **jour.** *(zhoor)*	How can it be? It is still daytime.
UN MONSIEUR **Excusez-moi. Dans ce cas** *(kah)* **il est midi.**	Excuse me. In that case, it is noon.
MARC **Vous plaisantez?** *(play-zahn-tay)*	Are you joking?
UN MONSIEUR **Non. Je n'ai pas de montre.** *(mohntr)* **Vous êtes touriste?** *(too-reest)*	No. I don't have a watch. Are you a tourist?

ANSWERS

Time deux heures quinze, huit heures et demie, neuf heures quarante-cinq, sept heures, une heure dix, trois heures trente-cinq, cinq heures vingt-cinq, quatre heures cinquante-cinq.

Numbers quatorze, vingt-trois, trente-sept, quarante-six, cinquante-cinq, soixante-deux, soixante et onze, quatre-vingt-neuf, quatre-vingt-dix-huit, cent seize

MARC **Oui.** — Yes.

UN MONSIEUR *(voo-lay)* *(ash-tay)* **Voulez-vous acheter une montre? Soixante-dix francs.** — Do you want to buy a watch? Seventy francs.

MARC *(dee)* **Mais vous avez dit que vous n'avez pas de montre!** — But you said that you do not have a watch!

UN MONSIEUR **Quarante francs.** — Forty francs.

MARC **Non, merci.** — No, thanks.

UN MONSIEUR **Voilà votre montre. Je suis** *(peek-pō-keht)* *(oh-neht)* **un pickpocket honnête!** — Here is your watch. I am an honest pickpocket!

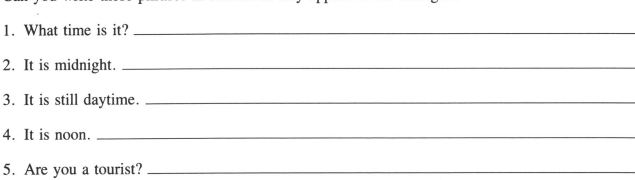

Can you write these phrases in French as they appear in the dialogue?

1. What time is it? ____________________
2. It is midnight. ____________________
3. It is still daytime. ____________________
4. It is noon. ____________________
5. Are you a tourist? ____________________
6. Here is your watch. ____________________

ANSWERS

Dialogue **1.** Quelle heure est-il? **2.** Il est minuit. **3.** Il fait encore jour. **4.** Il est midi. **5.** Vous êtes touriste? **6.** Voilà votre monte.

(uhn) UN *(mo-mahn)* MOMENT *(ahntr)* ENTRE *(ohtr)* AUTRES

A Place in Time

Remember the saying, "If it's Tuesday, I must be in . . ."

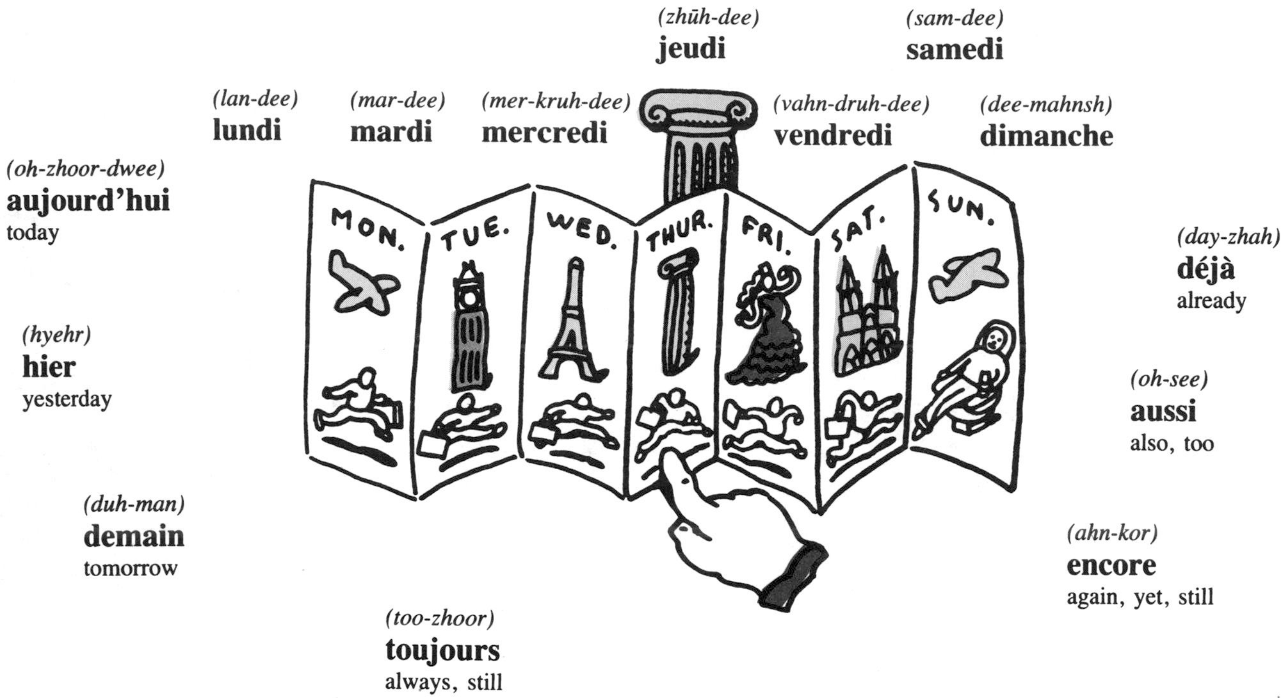

Now, see if you remember the meaning of the following adverbs by matching them up to their English equivalents.

1. **aujourd'hui**	A. today
2. **hier**	B. yesterday
3. **demain**	C. again
4. **toujours**	D. tomorrow
5. **encore**	E. always
6. **aussi**	F. already
7. **déjà**	G. also

ANSWERS

Matching adverbs 1. A 2. B 3. D 4. E 5. C 6. G 7. F

(ahn-kor) *(vehrb)* *(ee-reh-gew-lyay)*

Encore des verbes irréguliers

More irregular verbs

In a previous unit you learned to conjugate verbs of the second conjugation ending in **-IR**. There is a fairly large group of **-IR** verbs which follow a different pattern and are considered irregular. This table will help you remember these special verbs.

	(dor-meer) DORMIR to sleep		*(par-teer)* PARTIR to leave
je, **tu**	*(dor)* **DOR*S***	**je**, **tu**	*(par)* **PAR*S***
il, **elle**, **on**	*(dor)* **DORT**	**il**, **elle**, **on**	*(par)* **PART**
nous	*(dor-mohn)* **DORM*ONS***	**nous**	*(par-tohn)* **PART*ONS***
vous	*(dor-may)* **DORM*EZ***	**vous**	*(par-tay)* **PART*EZ***
ils, **elles**	*(dorm)* **DORM*ENT***	**ils**, **elles**	*(part)* **PART*ENT***

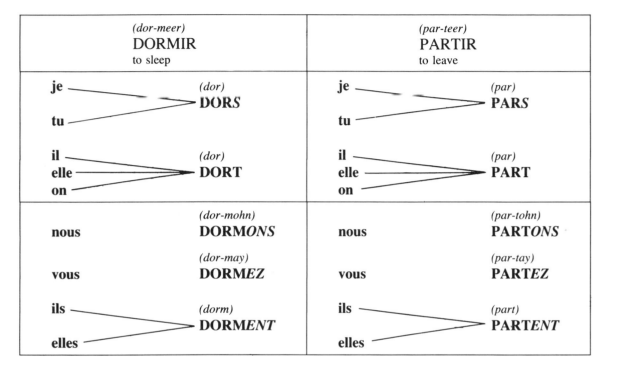

Some other verbs in this group are SORTIR *(sor-teer)* to go out, to exit, SERVIR *(ser-veer)* to serve, SENTIR *(sahn-teer)* to smell, to feel, MENTIR *(mahn-teer)* to lie. Unfortunately, you cannot predict which verbs belong to which group.

Add the endings to the verb stems in the following list.

1. Je sor ______________ 2. Tu dor ______________ 3. Il par ______________

4. Elle ser ______________ 5. On sen ______________ 6. Nous men ______________

7. Vous dor ______________ 8. Ils par ______________ 9. Elles sor ______________

ANSWERS

IR Verb **1.** Je sors **2.** Tu dors **3.** Il part **4.** Elle sert **5.** On sent **6.** Nous mentons **7.** Vous dormez **8.** Ils partent **9.** Elles sortent

How can you recognize a special **"-IR"** verb that takes these endings? You can't. **Je le regrette.** (I'm sorry!) Let's review all the regular and "semi-regular" verb forms. Now try to put the right endings in the blanks.

a. JE	parl________	b. TU	parl________	c. IL/ ELLE/ON	parl________
	fin ________		fin ________		fin ________
	ven ________		ven ________		ven ________
	dor ________		dor ________		dor ________
d. NOUS	parl________	e. VOUS	parl________	f. ILS/ ELLES	parl________
	fin ________		fin ________		fin ________
	ven ________		ven ________		ven ________
	dor ________		dor ________		dor ________

(mohn) *(ma)* *(may)*

Mon, ma, mes,

(tohn) *(ta)* *(tay)*

Ton, ta, tes

Mine and yours

What's "mine" or "yours"? Here's how to tell in French. Note that the forms of these words change, depending on the nouns they describe.

ANSWERS

Regular and Semi-Regular Verbs

a.	b.	c.	d.	e.	f.
Je parle	Tu parles	Il, parle	Nous parlons	Vous parlez	Ils, parlent
Je finis	Tu finis	Elle, finit	Nous finissons	Vous finissez	Elles finissent
Je vends	Tu vends	On vend	Nous vendons	Vous vendez	vendent
Je dors	Tu dors	dort	Nous dormons	Vous dormez	dorment

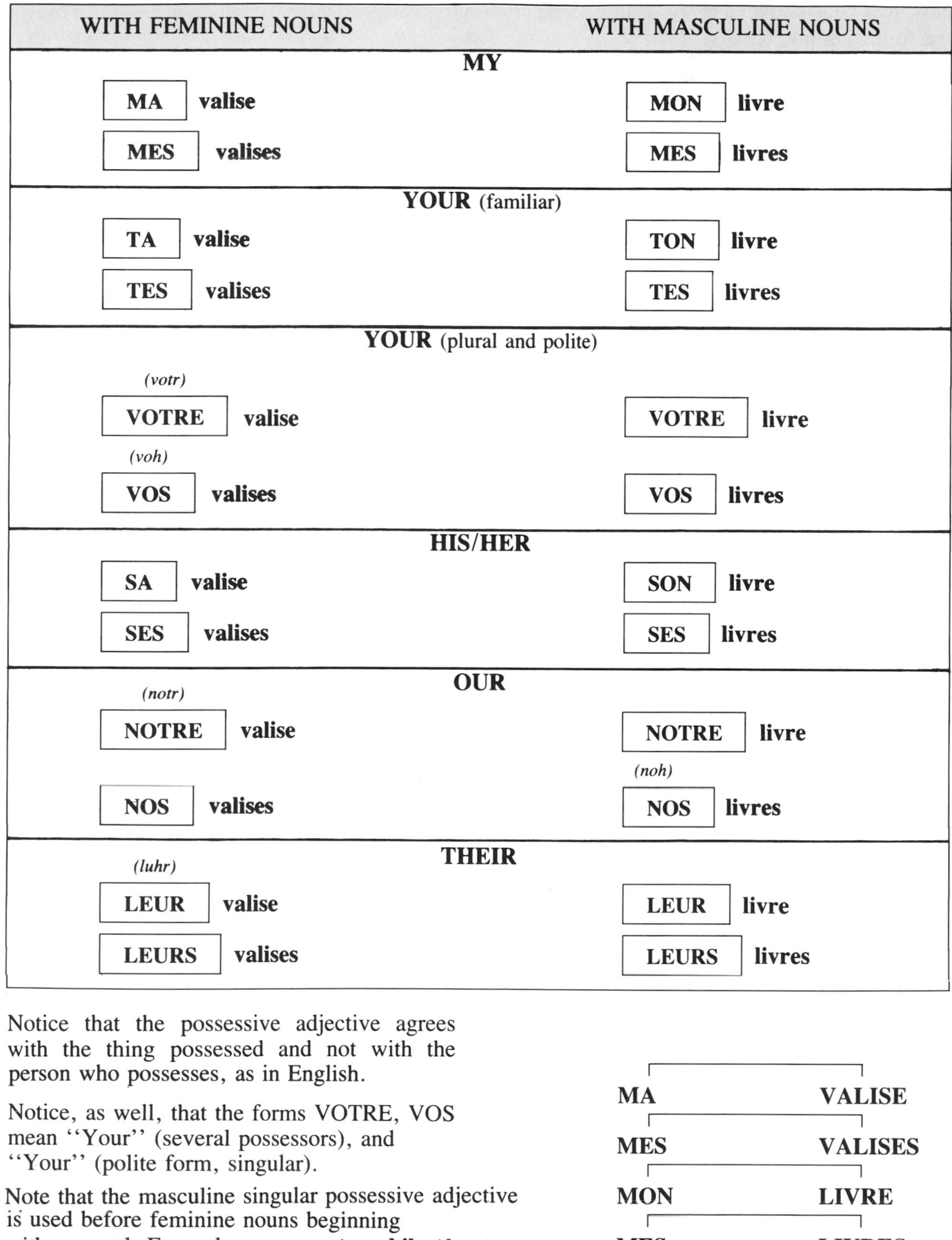

WITH FEMININE NOUNS		WITH MASCULINE NOUNS
	MY	
MA valise		**MON** livre
MES valises		**MES** livres
	YOUR (familiar)	
TA valise		**TON** livre
TES valises		**TES** livres
	YOUR (plural and polite)	
(votr) **VOTRE** valise		**VOTRE** livre
(voh) **VOS** valises		**VOS** livres
	HIS/HER	
SA valise		**SON** livre
SES valises		**SES** livres
	OUR	
(notr) **NOTRE** valise		**NOTRE** livre
NOS valises		*(noh)* **NOS** livres
	THEIR	
(luhr) **LEUR** valise		**LEUR** livre
LEURS valises		**LEURS** livres

Notice that the possessive adjective agrees with the thing possessed and not with the person who possesses, as in English.

Notice, as well, that the forms VOTRE, VOS mean "Your" (several possessors), and "Your" (polite form, singular).

Note that the masculine singular possessive adjective is used before feminine nouns beginning with a vowel. Example: **mon automobile** *(fem.)*.

MA — **VALISE**

MES — **VALISES**

MON — **LIVRE**

MES — **LIVRES**

Now test your knowledge by putting the appropriate possessive adjective in front of the following nouns:

1. ____________ mère (my)
2. ____________ maison (your (fam.))
3. ____________ chat (his)
4. ____________ chat (her (BE CAREFUL!!!))
5. ____________ ami (our)
6. ____________ automobile (your (polite))
7. ____________ valise (their)
8. ____________ soeurs (my)
9. ____________ maisons (your (fam.))
10. ____________ chats (his)
11. ____________ chats (her)
12. ____________ amis (our)
13. ____________ automobiles (your (polite))
14. ____________ valises (their)

If someone asks you, can you tell him or her the time in French? Read this passage and then answer the questions that follow.

"Quelle heure est-il?" demande (asks) le père à sa fille. "Il est trois heures," dit la fille. "A quelle heure pars-tu pour la France?" demande le père. "À dix-sept heures vingt," répond (*ray-pohn*) (answers) la fille. "Bon voyage!" "Au revoir, papa." (Goodbye)

1. Le père demande à sa fille:
   A. quelle heure il est en France;
   B. quelle heure il est;
   C. si (*see*) (if) elle part en voyage;
   D. quand le train de France arrive.

2. Quelle heure est-il?
   A. Il est deux heures.
   B. Il est six heures et quart.
   C. Il est trois heures.
   D. Il est neuf heures moins le quart.

ANSWERS

Possessive Adjectives
1. ma mère
2. ta maison
3. son chat
4. son chat
5. notre ami
6. votre automobile
7. leur valise
8. mes soeurs
9. tes maisons
10. ses chats
11. ses chats
12. nos amis
13. vos automobiles
14. leurs valises

Paragraph. 1. B **2.** C

6 Les trains

(tran)

Trains

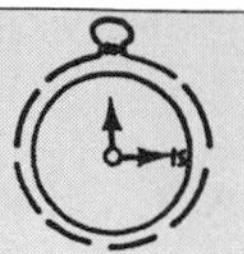

If you need to take the train, the following dialogue might prove useful to you. Don't forget to read it out loud.

MARIE **Nous voici à la gare.** *(gar)*	Here we are at the train station.
ANNE **Papa, prenons-nous le rapide pour aller à Cannes?** *(ra-peed)*	Dad, are we taking the express train to go to Cannes?
MARC **Non, c'est trop cher.**	No, it's too expensive.
ANNE **Alors, nous prenons l'express?** *(ehks-prehs)*	Then we are taking the fast train?
MARC **Oui. (à un employé): Pardon. Combien coûte un billet aller et retour pour Cannes pour quatre personnes?** *(a-lay) (ruh-toor)*	Yes. Excuse me, how much does a round-trip ticket to Cannes for four people cost?

L'EMPLOYÉ **Par l'express?** *(par)*	By fast train?
MARC **Oui.**	Yes.
L'EMPLOYÉ **Première ou seconde classe?** *(suh-gohnd)*	First or second class?
MARC **Seconde.**	Second.
L'EMPLOYÉ **Mil deux cent trente-deux francs par personne.**	1,232 francs per person.
MARC **C'est cher . . .**	It's expensive . . .
L'EMPLOYÉ **Il y a des billets de famille qui coûtent moins cher.** *(fa-mee-y)*	There are family tickets which cost less.
MARC **Bon.**	Good.
L'EMPLOYÉ **Compartiment fumeurs ou non-fumeurs?** *(kohn-par-tee-mahn) (few-mūhr) (oo)*	Smoking or nonsmoking compartment?
MARC **Non-fumeurs.**	Nonsmoking.
L'EMPLOYÉ **Trois mille cinq cent francs. Voilà vos billets.** *(meel)*	3,500 francs. Here are your tickets.
MARC **Merci. À quelle heure est-ce que le train part?**	Thank you. At what time does the train leave?
L'EMPLOYÉ **À quinze heures trente.**	At 3:30 P.M.

Match these French words or expressions from the dialogue with their English equivalents.

1. la gare
2. un billet aller et retour
3. première classe
4. des billets de famille
5. compartiment non-fumeurs

a. first class
b. family tickets
c. nonsmoking compartment
d. the station
e. a round-trip ticket

European trains are excellent. The **T.E.E. (Trans-Europe-Express)** and the **T.G.V. (Trains à Grande Vitesse)** are two very popular high-speed trains. Here are some examples of the **T.E.E.**:

L'Etoile du Nord: Paris/Bruxelles/Amsterdam in 5 hours (547 km.)
Le Parsifal: Paris/Liège/Cologne/Dortmund/Hambourg in 9¼ hours (954 km.)
Le Cisalpin: Paris/Lausanne/Milan in 7 hours 53 minutes (822 km.)

These trains are more expensive and you must reserve your seat ahead of time. In order to make a reservation or to obtain information, go to any travel agency. You can even put your car on the train and check your bags.

To help you read the *Chaix* (*sheh*) (official train schedule) here is the explanation for a few signs:

(zhoor) (oo-vrahbl)
jours ouvrables
week days

(va-gohn) (lee)
wagon-lit

(vwa-tewr) (bar)
voiture-bar

(dee-mahnsh)
dimanches et
Sundays
(feht) *(sühl-mahn)*
fêtes **seulement**
holidays only

(rehs-to-rahn)
wagon-restaurant

ANSWERS

Matching 1. d 2. e 3. a 4. b 5. c

Here is a train schedule. Plan a trip from Paris to Nice. Figure out the cities you would like to visit along the way and the timetable you would follow. (Note: each timetable indicates: (1) in left columns, the departure times from the first station, then arrival time; (2) in right columns, departure times, then arrival times at the end of the line; (3) in italics, the schedule that requires changing trains).

SUD-EST

×	×	×	×	×	×	×	↓ ↑	×	×	×	×	×	×	×
6 55	7 44	10 16	11 42	15 10	17 46	18 40	PARIS-Gare de Lyon*	11 33	12 54	13 54	16 58	18 51	21 43	23 33
	9 12						LE CREUSOT TGV*			12 25				22 04
9 48	10 45		14 35	18 05	20 41	21 37	VALENCE*	8 34	9 57	10 51	13 59		18 44	20 28
10 46	11 45	14 12	15 33	19 05	21 43	22 37	AVIGNON*	7 34	8 59	9 49	12 59	14 55	17 44	19 28
11 17	12 13	14 39	16 04	19 33	22 11	23 08	NIMES	7 04	8 27	9 20	12 29	14 27	17 14	18 58
11 42	12 39	15 05	16 29	19 59	22 36	23 34	MONTPELLIER*	6 39	8 02	8 55	12 04	14 02	16 49	18 33
12 41	*13 29*	*15 30*	*17 17*	*20 51*	*23 05*	*0 51*	SÈTE*	*6 01*	*7 05*	*8 24*	*11 06*	*12 59*	*16 15*	*17 43*
13 18	*13 55*	*15 58*	*17 21*	*21 19*	*23 35*	*1 21*	BÉZIERS*	*5 29*	*6 31*	*7 59*	*10 41*	*12 25*	*15 45*	*17 12*
13 43	*14 12*	*16 16*	*17 39*	*21 39*	*23 52*	*1 41*	NARBONNE* (A)	*5 12*	*6 16*	*7 42*	*10 24*	*12 10*	*15 27*	*16 50*
...	*14 47*	*17 08*	*18 14*	*22 42*	...	...	PERPIGNAN* (A)	...	*5 35*	*6 40*	*9 22*	*11 22*	*14 24*	*16 03*

×	×	×	×	×	×	×	↓ ↑					×	×	×
6 55	7 44	10 10	11 42	12 48	15 10	16 49	PARIS-Gare de Lyon*	6 21	6 25	7 42	8 14	9 29	11 33	12 54
9 48	10 45	13 05	14 35	15 41	18 05	19 52	VALENCE*		0 08			*6a15*	8 34	9 57
10 46	11 45	14 05	15 33	16 39	19 05	20 52	AVIGNON*		23 01	23 59		*5a14*	7 34	8 59
11 48	12 51	15 07	16 35	17 40	20 11	21 54	MARSEILLE*		21 47	22 35		...	6 29	7 58
13 16	*14 00*	*16 03*	*17 29*	*18 37*	*21 13*	*22 45*	TOULON*	21 48	20 46	*21 32*	23 03	...	*4 35*	*6 52*
14 50	*14 50*	*16 56*	*18 14*	*19 29*	*22 01*	*23 32*	ST-RAPHAEL	20 52	19 25	*20 33*	22 15	...	...	...
15 17	*15 17*	*17 22*	*18 37*	*19 53*	*22 24*	*23 56*	CANNES	20 26	18 58	*20 08*	21 49	...	...	...
15 31	*15 31*	*17 38*	*18 47*	*20 03*	*22 36*	*0 07*	ANTIBES	20 13	18 40	*19 51*	21 32	...	...	...
15 48	*15 48*	*18 00*	*19 02*	*20 18*	*22 52*	*0 23*	NICE*	19 55	18 19	*19 30*	21 15	...	...	...

×	×	×					↓ ↑	×	×	×	×	×	×	×
17 46	18 40	20 00	20 45	21 46	22 17	22 36	PARIS-Gare de Lyon*	13 54	16 58	18 56	19 50	21 43	22 32	23 33
20 41	21 37	*23a13*					VALENCE*	10 51	13 59		16 51	18 39	19 33	20 28
21 43	22 37	*0a15*				5 35	AVIGNON*	9 49	12 59	15 00	15 51	17 39	18 29	19 28
22 48	23 40	...	5 06			7 20	MARSEILLE*	8 45	11 54	14 00	14 51	16 39	17 29	18 23
...	*1 22*	...	6 14		7 00	*8 33*	TOULON*	*7 47*	*10 53*	*12 59*	*13 55*	*15 31*	*16 21*	*16 46*
...	...	...	7 16	6 50	8 03	*9 27*	ST-RAPHAEL	*6 52*	*9 48*	*12 12*	*13 06*	*14 37*	*15 34*	...
...	...	...	7 42	7 16	8 29	*9 50*	CANNES	*6 27*	*9 21*	*11 49*	*12 43*	*14 13*	*15 10*	...
...	...	...	8 00	7 35	8 46	*9 59*	ANTIBES	*6 16*	*9 05*	*11 39*	*12 30*	*14 03*	*15 00*	...
...	...	...	8 21	7 55	9 10	*10 14*	NICE*	*6 00*	*8 47*	*11 24*	*12 10*	*13 48*	*14 45*	...

(A) *Voir aussi tableau PARIS-TOULOUSE-BARCELONA.*
(a) *Changement de train à Lyon Part-Dieu.*

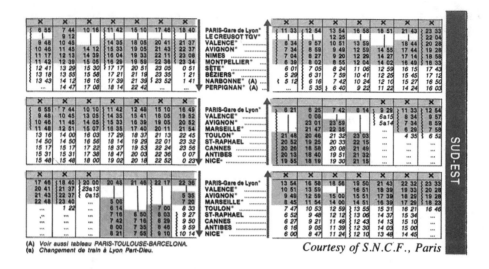

Courtesy of S.N.C.F., Paris

(voo-lwar) *(poo-vwar)*

Vouloir c'est pouvoir

To want is to be able to

"To want" and "to be able to" are very useful verbs when requesting and asking for things. The French verbs are VOULOIR and POUVOIR. They are both irregular, but follow a similar pattern.

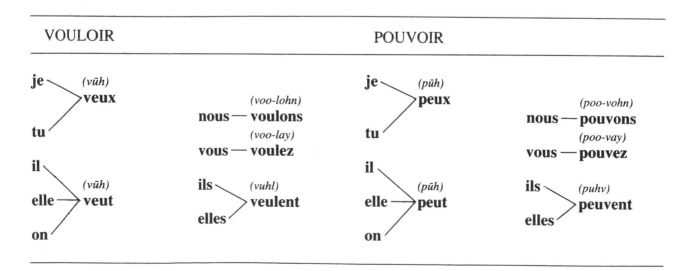

VOULOIR		POUVOIR	
je, **tu** → *(vūh)* **veux**	**nous** — *(voo-lohn)* **voulons**	**je**, **tu** → *(pūh)* **peux**	**nous** — *(poo-vohn)* **pouvons**
	vous — *(voo-lay)* **voulez**		**vous** — *(poo-vay)* **pouvez**
il, **elle**, **on** → *(vūh)* **veut**	**ils**, **elles** → *(vuhl)* **veulent**	**il**, **elle**, **on** → *(pūh)* **peut**	**ils**, **elles** → *(puhv)* **peuvent**

If you want to be really polite—"I would like"—"Could you," the forms are:

(voo-dreh)
JE VOUDRAIS ______________________________ I would like

(poo-ryay)
POURRIEZ-VOUS ______________________________ Could you

Now fill in the blanks with the appropriate form of the verb.

1. ____________ -vous *(meh-day)* m'aider?
   (could) ... (help)

2. Je ____________, *(dohnk)* donc je ____________.
   (want) ... (therefore) ... (can)

3. ____________ -vous du *(ka-fay)* café?
   (want)

4. Je ____________ une *(om-leht)* omelette, *(seel)(voo) (pleh)* s'il vous plaît.
   (would like)

5. ____________ -nous prendre le rapide?
   (can, may)

6. Anne et Jean ne ____________ pas prendre le rapide.
   (can)

NOTE: You may have noticed that there is only one verb in French for "can" and "may."

ANSWERS

Fill ins

1. Pourriez **2.** veux... peux **3.** Voulez **4.** voudrais **5.** Pouvons **6.** peuvent

(ahn) (vwa-tewr) EN VOITURE!

All Aboard!

(pa-sa-zhehr) **une passagère** passenger	*(a-swar)* **s'asseoir** to sit down	*(suh-luh-vay)* **se lever** to get up

(sahl) (da-tahnt) **la salle d'attente** waiting room	*(o-rehr)* **l'horaire** *(m.)* schedule	*(kay)* **le quai** railway platform	*(sha-reht)* **la charrette** luggage cart	*(par-tūhr)* **le porteur** porter	*(tran)* **le train** train

(feht) *(luh)* *(voo)* *(mehm)*
Faites-le vous-même
Do it yourself

(ruh-gard) *(ta-bloh)*
Il regarde le tableau.

Il se regarde.

Reflexive verbs express actions people do "to themselves": to get up, to sit down, to get dressed, to go to bed, to wake up, to get married, to have fun, to be bored. For example, "to get washed" is a reflexive verb because you wash yourself or "reflect back" the action of the verb upon yourself. This is done by means of reflexive pronouns, like "myself" and "yourself." Here are the reflexive pronouns in French.

REFLEXIVE PRONOUNS	
(muh) **ME**, **M'** (before vowel)	Myself
(tuh) **TE**, **T'** (before vowel)	Yourself (familiar)
SE, **S'** (before vowel)	Himself, Herself, Oneself
NOUS	Ourselves
VOUS	Yourselves, Yourself (polite)
SE, **S'** (before vowel)	Themselves

Now let's conjugate a reflexive verb: LAVER *(la-vay)* can become reflexive "To wash oneself" (SE LAVER) as follows:

JE	**ME**	**LAVE**	I wash myself, I am washing myself, I do wash myself
TU	**TE**	**LAVES**	You wash yourself, etc.
IL, ELLE, ON	**SE**	**LAVE**	He/She/One washes himself/herself/oneself
NOUS	**NOUS**	**LAVONS**	We wash ourselves
VOUS	**VOUS**	**LAVEZ**	You wash yourselves/yourself (polite)
ILS, ELLES	**SE**	**LAVENT**	They wash themselves

Now you try it with the verb AMUSER *(a-mew-zay)*, which in its reflexive form means "To enjoy oneself, to have fun." It begins with a vowel, so the reflexive pronouns become m', t', and s'.

1. je ________________ amuse.
2. tu ________________ amuses.
3. il, elle ________________ amuse.
4. nous ________________ amusons.
5. vous ________________ amusez.
6. ils, elles ________________ amusent.

ANSWERS

Reflexive verbs **1.** je m'amuse **2.** tu t'amuses **3.** il, elle s'amuse **4.** nous nous amusons **5.** vous vous amusez **6.** ils, elles s'amusent

The following passage is about train travel. Read about Marc and Marie, then answer the questions that follow.

(vohn) *(eel)(za-sheht)*

Marc et Marie vont à la gare. Ils achètent un billet aller-retour Paris-Marseille. Ils voyagent par le T.G.V. de Paris à Lyon. Ensuite, de Lyon à Marseille ils prennent un rapide. Ils arrivent à cinq heures.

1. Où vont Marc et Marie?

____

2. Qu'est-ce qu'ils achètent?

____

3. Qu'est-ce que c'est que le T.G.V.?

____

ANSWERS

Reading **1.** Ils vont à la gare. **2.** Ils achètent un billet. **3.** C'est le Train à Grande Vitesse.

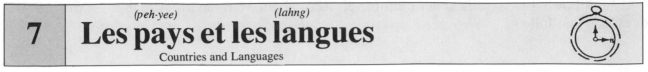

7 Les pays et les langues

(peh-yee) (lahng)

Countries and Languages

Je parle un peu français. I speak a little French. And so do you! By now you've learned quite a bit of French. Take a look at the rest of the world, too, and learn how to say the names of other countries in French. Note that in French the article "the" is used with the name of a country, a city, or a language.

COUNTRIES

Masculine

(bray-zeel)
le Brésil

(ka-na-dah)
le Canada

(shee-lee)
le Chili

(dan-mark)
le Danemark

(zha-pohn)
le Japon

(por-tew-gal)
le Portugal

(vay-nay-zew-ay-lah)
le Vénézuéla

(mehk-seek)
le Mexique

Plural

(ay-ta) (zew-nee)
les États-Unis

Feminine

(al-ma-nyuh)
l'Allemagne
Germany

(a-may-reek)
l'Amérique

(ahn-gluh-tehr)
l'Angleterre
England

(grahnd) (bruh-ta-nyuh)
la Grande Bretagne

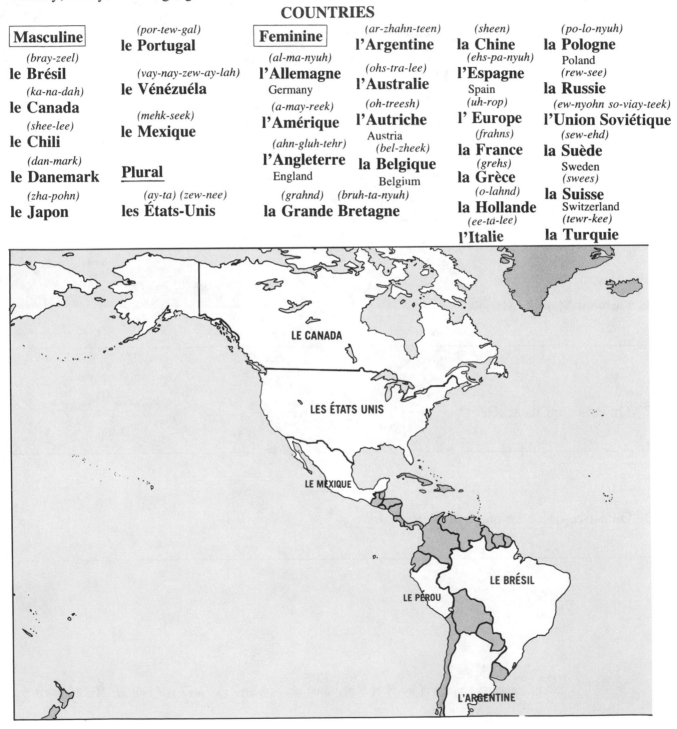

(ar-zhahn-teen)
l'Argentine

(ohs-tra-lee)
l'Australie

(oh-treesh)
l'Autriche
Austria

(bel-zheek)
la Belgique
Belgium

(sheen)
la Chine

(ehs-pa-nyuh)
l'Espagne
Spain

(uh-rop)
l' Europe

(frahns)
la France

(grehs)
la Grèce

(o-lahnd)
la Hollande

(ee-tä-lee)
l'Italie

(po-lo-nyuh)
la Pologne
Poland

(rew-see)
la Russie

(ew-nyohn so-viay-teek)
l'Union Soviétique

(sew-ehd)
la Suède
Sweden

(swees)
la Suisse
Switzerland

(tewr-kee)
la Turquie

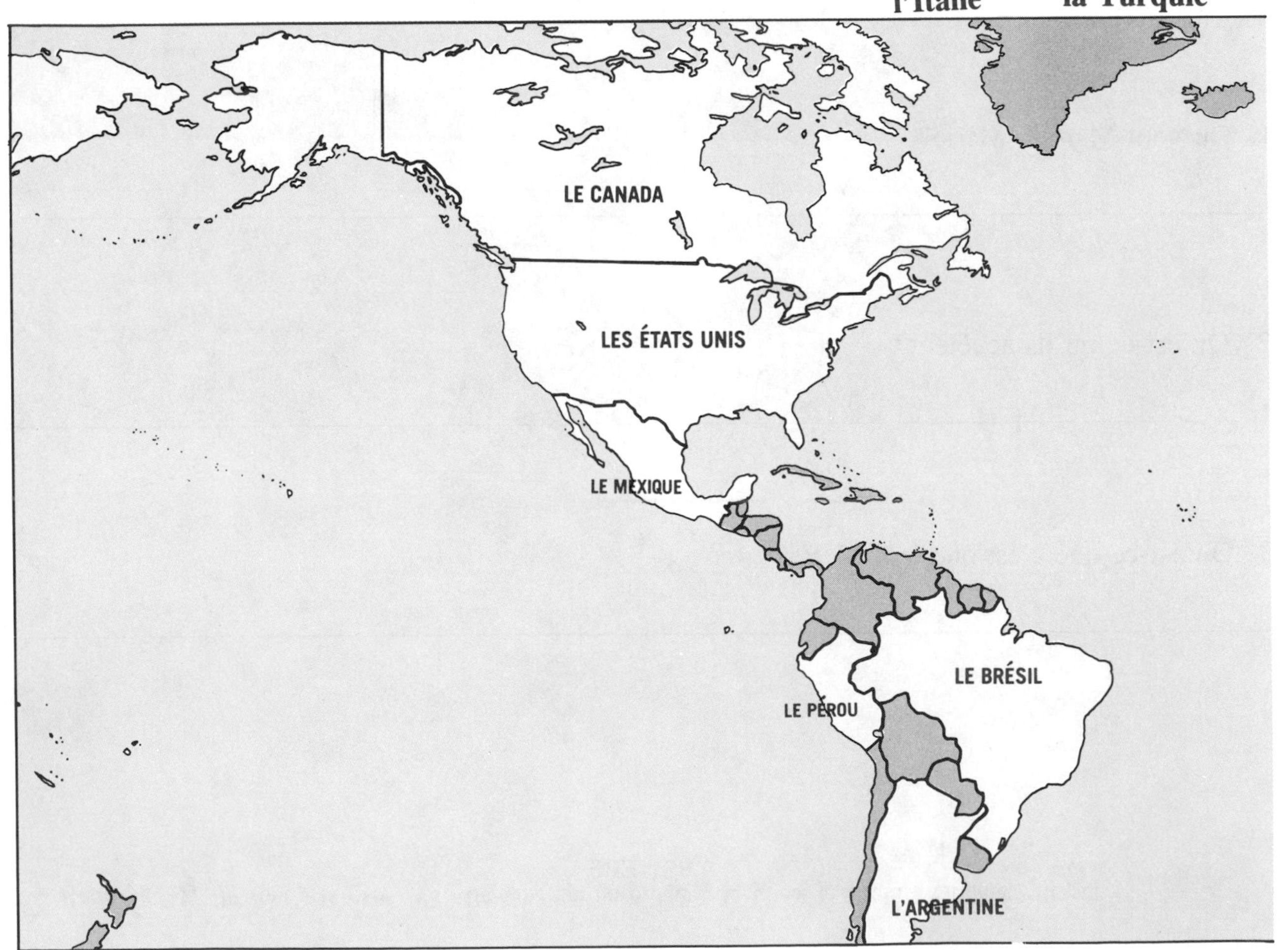

Je parle
I speak

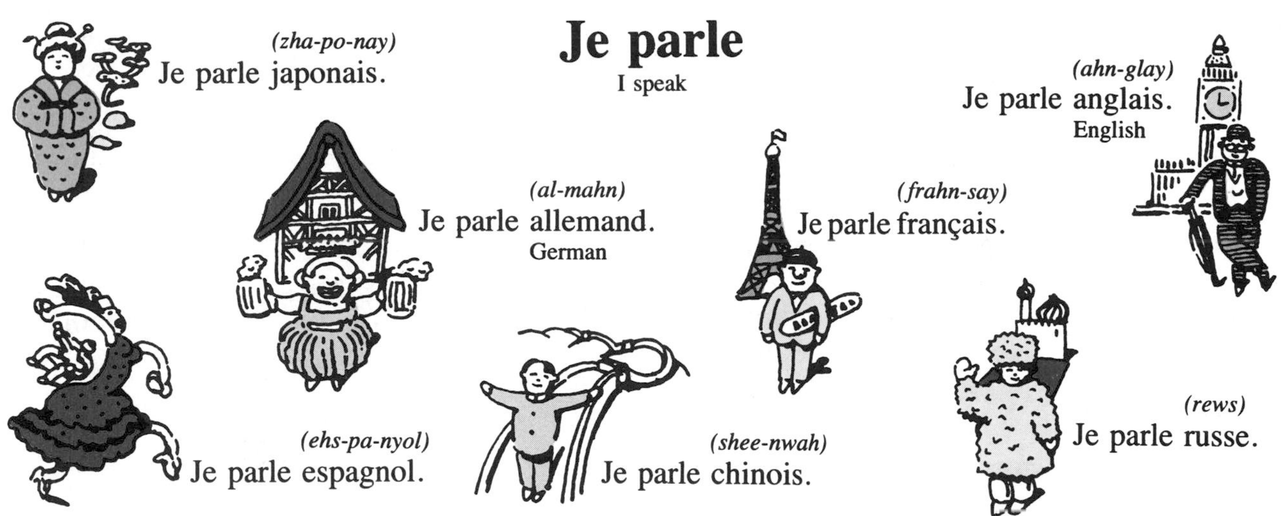

(zha-po-nay)
Je parle japonais.

(ahn-glay)
Je parle anglais.
English

(al-mahn)
Je parle allemand.
German

(frahn-say)
Je parle français.

(rews)
Je parle russe.

(ehs-pa-nyol)
Je parle espagnol.

(shee-nwah)
Je parle chinois.

Names of languages are masculine and are not capitalized. After verbs other than parler (comprendre, apprendre, aimer (*eh-may*, to like, love), and so on), the definite article LE is used: J'aime le français!

Nationalities are not capitalized when they are used as adjectives. They *are* capitalized when used as nouns. Example: **un homme français arrive,** but **le Français arrive.**

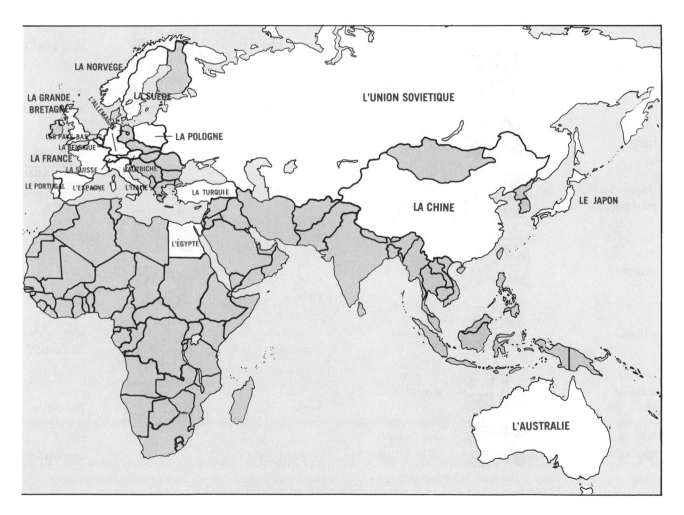

LA NORVÈGE
LA GRANDE BRETAGNE
LA SUÈDE
L'ALLEMAGNE
L'UNION SOVIETIQUE
LES PAYS-BAS
LA POLOGNE
LA BELGIQUE
LA FRANCE
LA SUISSE
L'AUTRICHE
LE PORTUGAL
L'ESPAGNE
L'ITALIE
LA TURQUIE
LA CHINE
LE JAPON
L'ÉGYPTE
L'AUSTRALIE

(zhuh) (swee)

Je suis

I am

Many of us are combinations of several nationalities. Which are you? Use **Je suis** . . . (I am . . .)

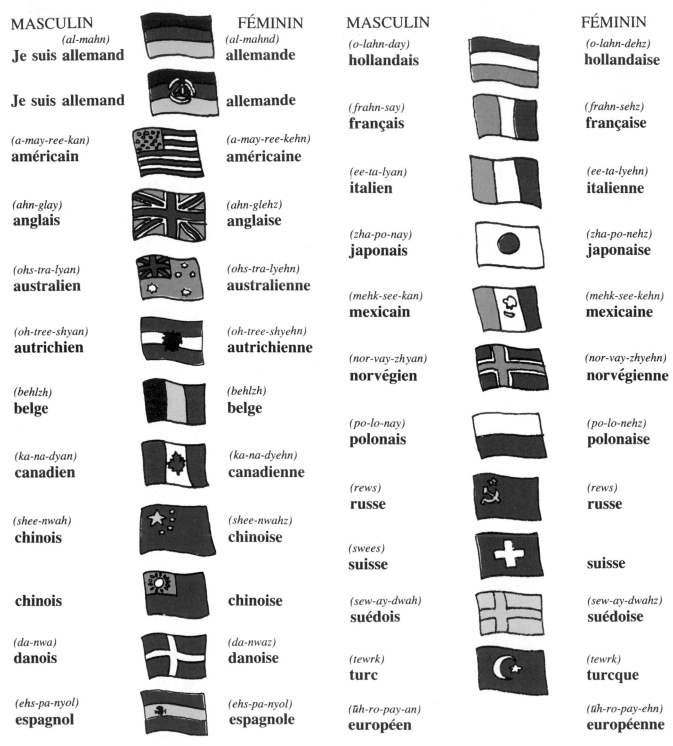

MASCULIN	FÉMININ
(al-mahn) **Je suis allemand**	 *(al-mahnd)* **allemande**
Je suis allemand	 **allemande**
(a-may-ree-kan) **américain**	 *(a-may-ree-kehn)* **américaine**
(ahn-glay) **anglais**	 *(ahn-glehz)* **anglaise**
(ohs-tra-lyan) **australien**	 *(ohs-tra-lyehn)* **australienne**
(oh-tree-shyan) **autrichien**	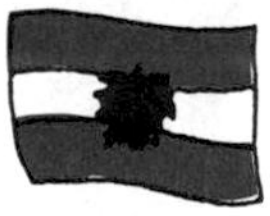 *(oh-tree-shyehn)* **autrichienne**
(behlzh) **belge**	 *(behlzh)* **belge**
(ka-na-dyan) **canadien**	 *(ka-na-dyehn)* **canadienne**
(shee-nwah) **chinois**	 *(shee-nwahz)* **chinoise**
chinois	 **chinoise**
(da-nwa) **danois**	 *(da-nwaz)* **danoise**
(ehs-pa-nyol) **espagnol**	 *(ehs-pa-nyol)* **espagnole**

MASCULIN	FÉMININ
(o-lahn-day) **hollandais**	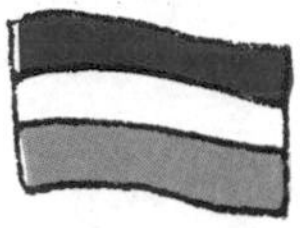 *(o-lahn-dehz)* **hollandaise**
(frahn-say) **français**	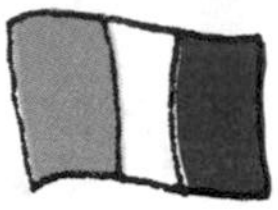 *(frahn-sehz)* **française**
(ee-ta-lyan) **italien**	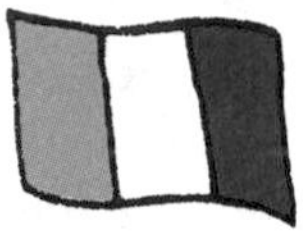 *(ee-ta-lyehn)* **italienne**
(zha-po-nay) **japonais**	 *(zha-po-nehz)* **japonaise**
(mehk-see-kan) **mexicain**	 *(mehk-see-kehn)* **mexicaine**
(nor-vay-zhyan) **norvégien**	 *(nor-vay-zhyehn)* **norvégienne**
(po-lo-nay) **polonais**	*(po-lo-nehz)* **polonaise**
(rews) **russe**	 *(rews)* **russe**
(swees) **suisse**	 **suisse**
(sew-ay-dwah) **suédois**	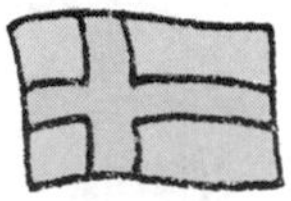 *(sew-ay-dwahz)* **suédoise**
(tewrk) **turc**	 *(tewrk)* **turcque**
(ūh-ro-pay-an) **européen**	*(ūh-ro-pay-ehn)* **européenne**

Notice that in French, languages and nationalities are not capitalized.

(zhuh) (vay)
Je vais
I am going to

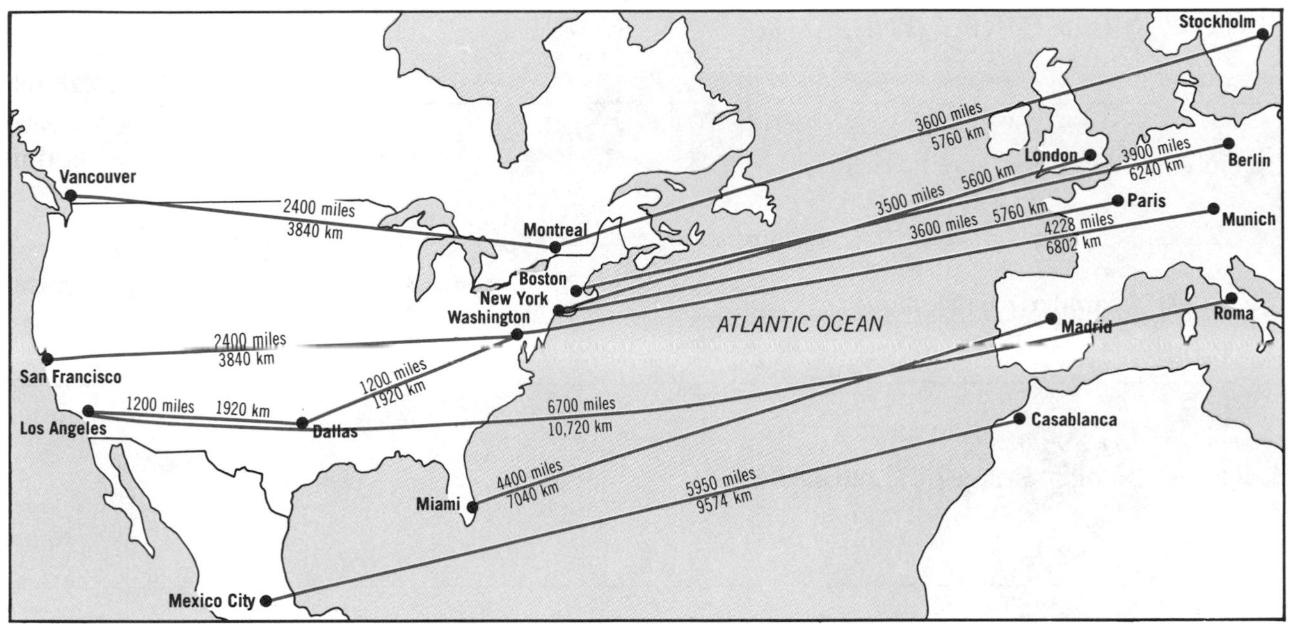

à + CITIES	en + FEMININE COUNTRIES & COUNTRIES STARTING WITH A VOWEL*	au + MASCULINE COUNTRIES	aux + PLURAL COUNTRIES
(pa-ree) **Paris**	**France**	**Canada**	
(ma-dreed) **Madrid**	**Espagne**	**Portugal**	
(ber-lan) **Berlin**	**Allemagne**	**Chili**	**États-Unis**
(rom) **Rome**	**Italie**	**Brésil**	
(brew-sel) **Bruxelles**	**Belgique**		
(zhuh-nehv) **Genève**	**Suisse**		
	(ee-rahn) **Iran**		
	Alaska		

*En *is also used with continents, and subdivisions, such as states and provinces.*

Now, **répondez aux questions**, using the correct **préposition** as in the following example:

(ark)(duh)(tree-yohnf)
Où est l'Arc de Triomphe? *L'arc de Triomphe est à Paris.*

(toor) (eh-fehl)
1. Où est la Tour Eiffel? (Paris)

____

2. Où est New York? (États-Unis)

____

3. Où est Acapulco? (Mexique)

____

(bah-tohn) (roozh)
4. Où est Bâton Rouge? (Louisiane)
red stick

____

5. Où est Berlin? (Allemagne)

____

(ko-lee-zay)
6. Où est le Colisée? (Rome, Italie)

____

(prah-doh)
7. Où est le Prado? (Madrid, Espagne)

____

(ran)
8. Où est le Rhin? (Allemagne)

____

ANSWERS

Prepositions: 1. à Paris **2.** aux États-Unis **3.** au Mexique **4.** en Louisiane **5.** en Allemagne **6.** à Rome, en Italie **7.** à Madrid, en Espagne **8.** en Allemagne

(zhuh) (kohn-prahn)

Je comprends

I understand

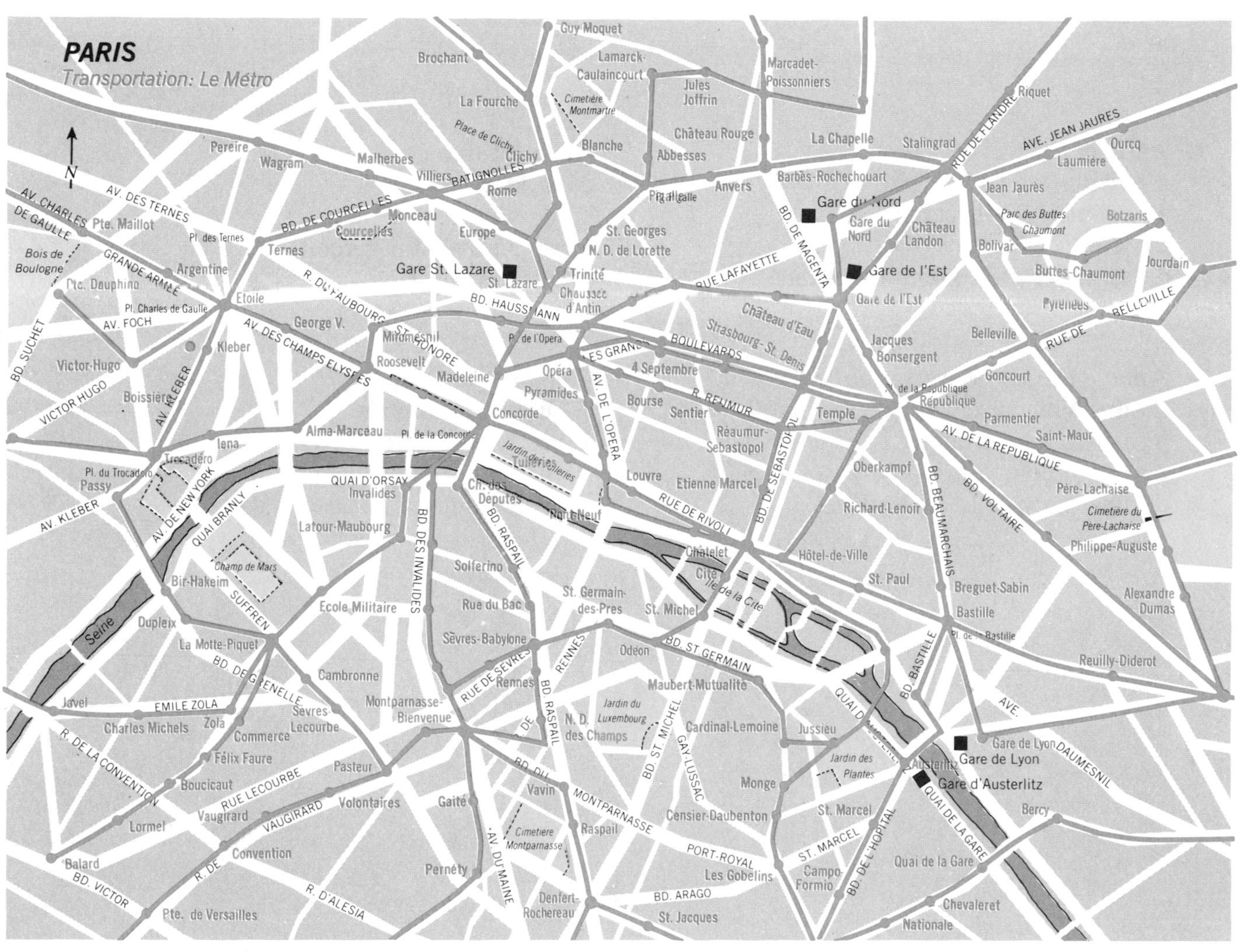

Read the following brief passage and try answering the questions.

(gar) *(lyohn)* *(sahntr)* *(pohn-pee-doo)*
Anne part de son hôtel près de la Gare de Lyon pour aller au Centre Pompidou. À la

(shah-tlay)
station du Châtelet, une jeune fille française commence à lui parler. Elle dit qu'elle désire

(a-kohn-pa-nyay) *(sor)* *(oh)* *(ahl)*
l'accompagner voir l'exposition d'art. Quand elle sort du métro aux Halles, Anne est très
leaves

(kohn-tahnt) *(ofr)*
contente d'avoir une amie. La jeune fille française offre aussi de lui montrer quelques
some

(kew-ryo-zee-tay)
curiosités de la belle capitale et elle l'invite à prendre chez elle un déjeuner typiquement
lunch

français.

1. Anne désire
   a. visiter les jardins.
   b. écouter un concert.
   c. aller à un centre d'art.
   d. déjeuner à un grand restaurant.

2. Anne entre en conversation avec
   a. une Française.
   b. un homme étranger.
   c. un garçon.
   d. une jeune fille américaine.

3. Anne est très contente
   a. d'aller à Nice.
   b. de voyager en métro.
   c. de parler à un garçon.
   d. d'avoir une amie.

4. Anne va prendre
   a. un avion anglais.
   b. un déjeuner français.
   c. une photo de la jeune fille.
   d. une montre française.

ANSWERS

Multiple choice 1. c 2. a 3. d 4. b

(vwa-tewr) *(grahnd)* *(puh-teet)*

8 Les voitures, grandes et petites

Cars, big and small

(see-nya-lee-za-syohn) *(roo-tyehr)*

La signalisation routière

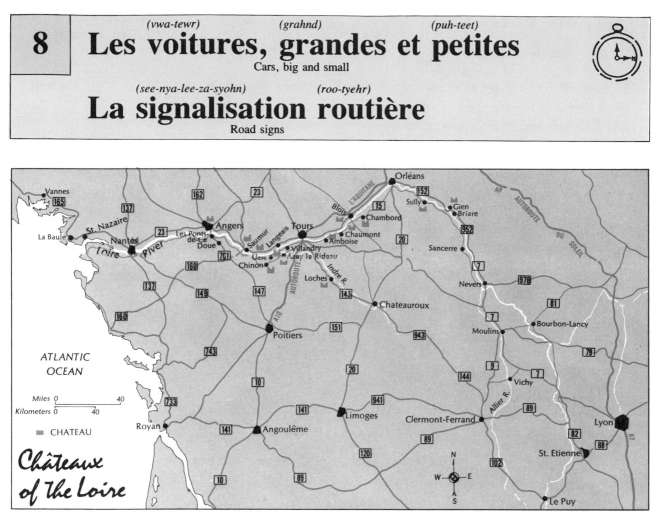

Road signs

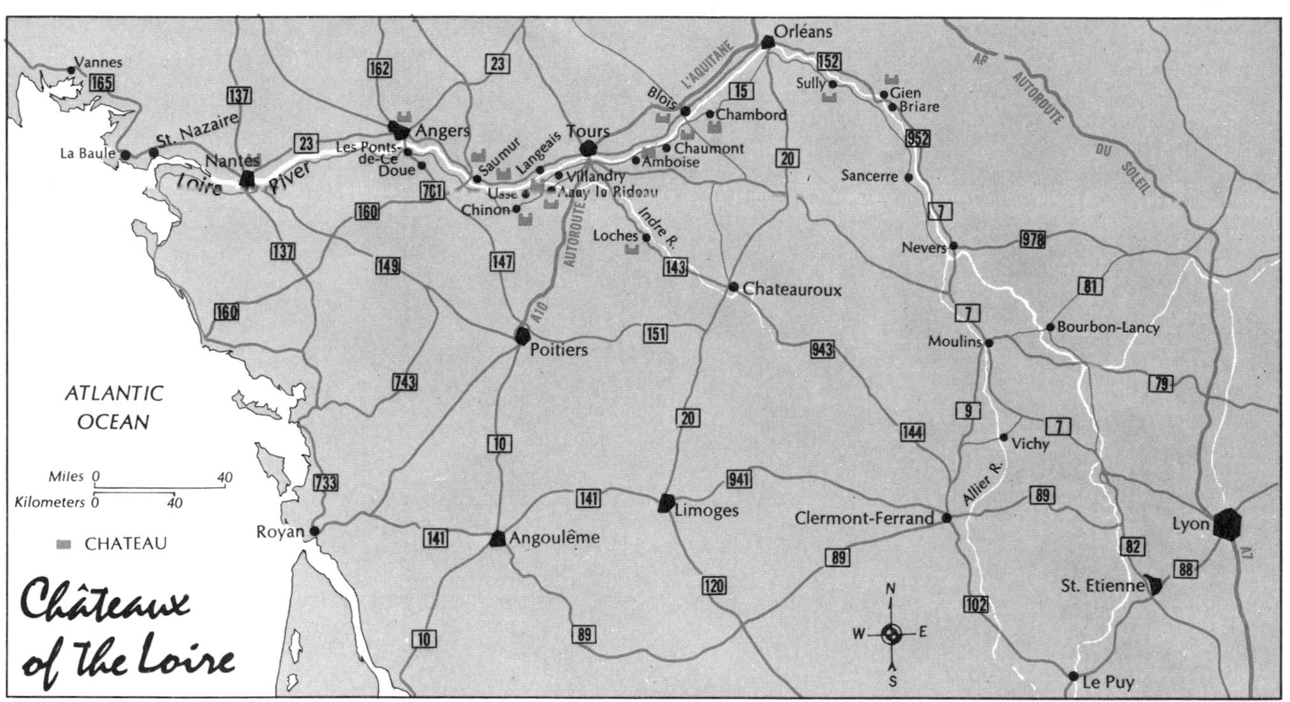

© *Fisher Annotated Travel Guides. Reprinted by permission.*

Mark has decided to rent a car and take his family for an excursion into the French countryside. You may want to rent a car and see the country close up yourself!

(a-zhahns) *(lo-ka-syohn)*

À L'AGENCE DE LOCATION DE VOITURES

At the Car Rental Office

MARC	**Bonjour, Monsieur. Je voudrais** *(loo-ay)* **louer une voiture.** (rent)	Good morning, Sir. I would like to rent a car.
L'EMPLOYÉ	**Pour combien de temps?** *(tahn)*	For how long?
MARC	**Deux semaines. Ça coûte combien?** *(suh-mehn)*	Two weeks. How much does that cost?
L'EMPLOYÉ	**Voyons . . . Une Peugeot** *(vwa-yohn)* *(pŭh-zhoh)*	Let's see . . . A Peugeot

pour deux semaines;	for two weeks;
mille neuf cent quatre-vingt	1,995 francs,
(eh-sahns) (a-sew-rahns)	
quinze francs, essence et assurance	gas and insurance
(kohn-preez) (pay-yay) (plews)	
comprises. Vous payez en plus une	included. You also pay a
(poor-sahn)	
taxe de trente-trois pour cent.	tax of 33%.
MARC **C'est cher. Est-ce que vous avez**	That's expensive. Do you have
une voiture plus petite?	a smaller car?
(ruh-noh)	
L'EMPLOYÉ **Oui, une Renault: mille**	Yes, a Renault:
trois cent quatre-vingt quinze francs.	1,395 francs.
(kee-lo-may-trahzh)	
MARC **Est-ce que le kilométrage est**	Is the mileage included?
(kohn-pree)	
compris?	
(mehm)	
MARIE (à elle-même) **Comme il est avare!** to herself	How stingy he is!
(a-lay) (ay-trahn-zhay)	
L'EMPLOYÉ **Oui. Allez-vous à l'étranger?**	Yes. Are you going abroad?
(a-lohn)	
MARC **Non. Nous allons voir les Châteaux**	No. We are going to see the castles
de la Loire.	of the Loire valley.
(ram-nay)	
L'EMPLOYÉ **Allez-vous ramener la voiture**	Are you going to bring the car back
à Paris?	to Paris?
(pro-bah-bluh-mahn) (see-nohn)	
MARC **Probablement. Sinon, est-ce que**	Probably. If not,
nous pouvons la laisser à votre agence	can we leave it at your agency
(or-lay-ahn)	
à Orléans ?	in Orléans?
(byan) (sewr)	
L'EMPLOYÉ **Bien sûr.**	Of course.
(mohn-tray)	
MARC **Pouvez-vous me montrer comment**	Can you show me how
(vee-tehs)	
marchent le changement de vitesse et	the gear shift and the
(far)	
les phares?	lights work?

L'EMPLOYÉ *(na-tew-rehl-mahn)* **Naturellement. Voilà la clé et les papiers de la voiture. Je viens** *(vyan)* **avec vous.**	Of course. Here are the key and the car's papers. I'm coming with you.
PAUL **Mon Dieu!** *(dyūh)* **Il va conduire** *(kohn-dweer)* **une voiture non automatique!** *(oh-toh-ma-teek)*	My God! He is going to drive a nonautomatic car!
(koo-rahzh) **Courage, Anne!**	Be brave, Anne!

Pretend that you wish to rent a car. How would you respond to these questions and statements based on the dialogue?

	Vous:	Je voudrais louer une voiture.
	L'employé:	Pour combien de temps?
1.	Vous:	______________________
	L'employé:	Quelle voiture prenez-vous?
2.	Vous:	______________________
	L'employé:	Ça coûte mille neuf cent quatre-vingt quinze francs.
3.	Vous:	______________________
	L'employé:	Allez-vous à l'étranger?
4.	Vous:	______________________
	L'employé:	Òu allez-vous ramener la voiture?
5.	Vous:	______________________
	L'employé:	Bon. Merci. Voici les clés de la voiture.

ANSWERS

Dialogue 1. Pour deux semaines. **2.** Une Peugeot. **3.** C'est cher. **4.** Non. Nous allons voir les Châteaux de la Loire. **5.** à Orléans.

The procedure for renting a car in France and other European countries is the same as in the U.S. You can rent the car on a daily, weekly, two-week or monthly basis. The insurance is usually included but there is a 33% tax. If you rent from the larger companies, you can drop the car off at another location at no extra charge. As in the U.S., smaller cars are less expensive.

(a-lay) *(vuh-neer)*

Aller et venir

To go and to come

While traveling, you will do a lot of "coming" and "going." Study carefully these two very important irregular verbs.

ALLER		VENIR	
je	*(vay)* **vais**	**je**	*(vyan)* **viens**
tu	*(va)* **vas**	**tu**	**viens**
il / elle / on	*(va)* **va**	**il / elle / on**	*(vyan)* **vient**
nous	*(a-lohn)* **allons**	**nous**	*(vuh-nohn)* **venons**
vous	*(a-lay)* **allez**	**vous**	*(vuh-nay)* **venez**
ils / elles	*(vohn)* **vont**	**ils / elles**	*(vyehn)* **viennent**

ALLER is also used when inquiring about somebody's health:

(ko-mahn) *(ta-lay) (voo)* **Comment allez-vous?**	How are you? How do you feel?
Je vais très bien, merci.	Very well, thank you.
Je vais pas mal, merci.	Not bad, thank you.
Je vais assez bien, merci.	Fairly well, thank you.
(kom) *(see) (kom)* *(sa)* **Je vais comme-ci comme-ça, merci.**	So-so, thank you.
Je vais mal, merci.	Not well, thank you.
Et vous?	And you?

Try to answer the questions:

1. Comment allez-vous?

   Je ____________________

2. Comment va votre mère?

   Elle ____________________

3. Comment va votre mari?

   Il ____________________

4. Comment vont vos enfants? *(ahn-fahn)* children

   Ils ____________________

A simple way of expressing an idea in the future is to use **ALLER** + infinitive:
Je vais prendre un bateau-mouche. I'm going to take a bateau-mouche.

In the negative, **NE** and **PAS** are around the conjugated form of **ALLER**:
Je ne vais pas prendre de bateau-mouche. I'm not going to take a bateau-mouche.

With reflexive verbs, the reflexive pronoun comes before the infinitive:
Je vais me lever. I'm going to get up.

And with negative reflexive constructions, **NE** and **PAS** are around the conjugated form of **ALLER**:
Je ne vais pas me lever. I'm not going to get up.

ANSWERS

Verb ALLER (for health) **1.** Je vais bien, merci, (et vous?) **2.** Elle va. . . . **3.** Il va. . . . **4.** Ils vont. . . .

Quelques expressions essentielles

(e-sahn-syehl)

Some essential expressions

(pehr-dew) **Je suis perdu(e).**	I am lost.
(ga-rahzh) **Est-ce qu'il y a un garage près d'ici?**	Is there a garage near here?
Qu'est-ce qu'il y a?	What's the matter?
(seer-kew-la-syohn) **Il y a beaucoup de circulation.**	There is a lot of traffic.
(ray-zohn) **Vous avez raison.**	You are right.
(tor) **Vous avez tort.**	You are wrong.
(deesk) **le disque**	the disk (record)
(pehr-mee) (kohn-dweer) **le permis de conduire**	driver's license
l'essence	gasoline
(kwan) **au coin de**	at the corner of
(boo) **au bout de**	at the end of
(nor) **le nord**	north
(sewd) **le sud**	south
(lehst) **l'est**	east
(loo-ehst) **l'ouest**	west
(no) (rehst) **le nord-est, etc.**	northeast, etc.
(fūh) **Les feux**	traffic lights
*(zohn) (blūh)** **la zone bleue**	the blue zone

* In large cities, you get *un disque* which enables you to park in the blue zone (downtown).

(see-nya-lee-za-syohn) *(roo-tyehr)*
LA SIGNALISATION ROUTIÈRE
Road Signs

If you're planning to drive while you're abroad, spend some time memorizing the meanings of these signs.

Dangerous intersection

Danger!

Stop

Speed Limit
(in km/hr)

Minimum
Speed

End of limited
Speed

No Entrance

Yield right-of-way

Two-way
traffic

Dangerous curve

Entrance to expressway

Expressway Exit
(road narrows)

Customs

No Passing

End of
No Passing Zone

One-way Street

Detour

Road Closed

Parking

No Parking
(or waiting)

Roundabout

No Parking

No Parking
(or waiting)

No Cyclists

Pedestrian Crossing

Railroad Crossing
(no gate)

Guarded Railroad
Crossing

(sta-syohn) *(sehr-vees)*

À LA STATION SERVICE

At the Service Station

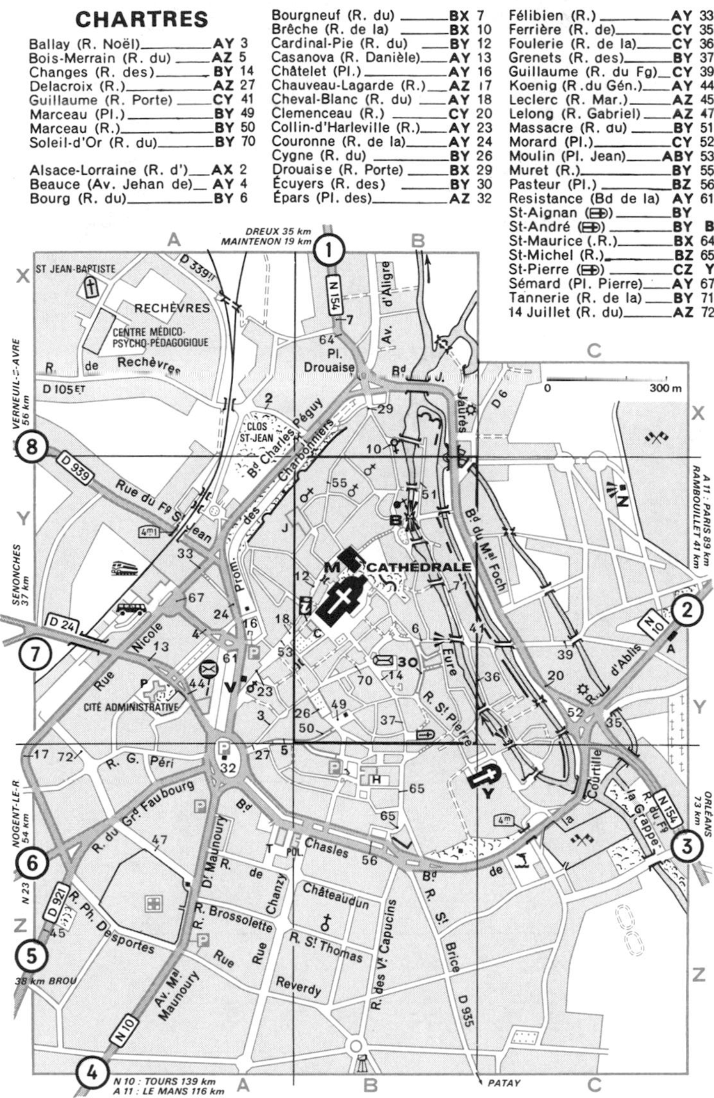

From Michelin Guide, Environs de Paris, *20th Edition. Reprinted with permission.*

MARC **Pardon. Pourriez-vous faire le** *(fehr)* **plein?** *(plan)* — Excuse me. Could you fill 'er up?

LE POMPISTE (gas pump attendant) **Ordinaire ou super?** *(or-dee-nehr)* *(sew-pehr)* — Regular or super?

MARC **Ordinaire. Et pourriez-vous aussi vérifier la pression des pneus, et le niveau d'huile et d'eau?** *(vay-ree-fyay)* *(preh-syohn)* *(pnūh)* *(weel)* *(oh)* — Regular. And could you also check the tire pressure and the level of the oil and water?

(ah) (nordr)
LE POMPISTE **Tout est en ordre.** — Everything is okay.

(ka-tay-drahl)
MARC **Nous allons a la Cathédrale de**
(shahrtr)
Chartres. Quelle est la route la plus
(koort)
courte? — We are going to the Chartres Cathedral. Which is the shortest way?

LE POMPISTE **Regardez. Vous êtes ici. Allez**
(drwah) (gohsh)
tout droit, tournez à gauche, puis à
(swee-vay) (ay-kree-toh)
droite. Ensuite suivez les écriteaux. — Look. You are here. Go straight ahead, turn left, then right. Then follow the signs.

Now write these important words and phrases from the dialogue.

1. Could you fill 'er up? ______________________
2. Could you also check the level of the oil and the water? ______________________

____
3. Everything is O.K. ______________________
4. Which is the shortest way? ______________________
5. To the left ______________________
6. To the right ______________________
7. Follow the signs. ______________________

ANSWERS

Dialogue
1. Pourriez-vous faire le plein? **2.** Pourriez-vous aussi vérifier le niveau d'huile et d'eau? **3.** Tout est en ordre. **4.** Quelle est la route la plus courte? **5.** À gauche **6.** À droite **7.** Suivez les écriteaux.

(vwa-tewr)
LA VOITURE (L'AUTOMOBILE)
The Car

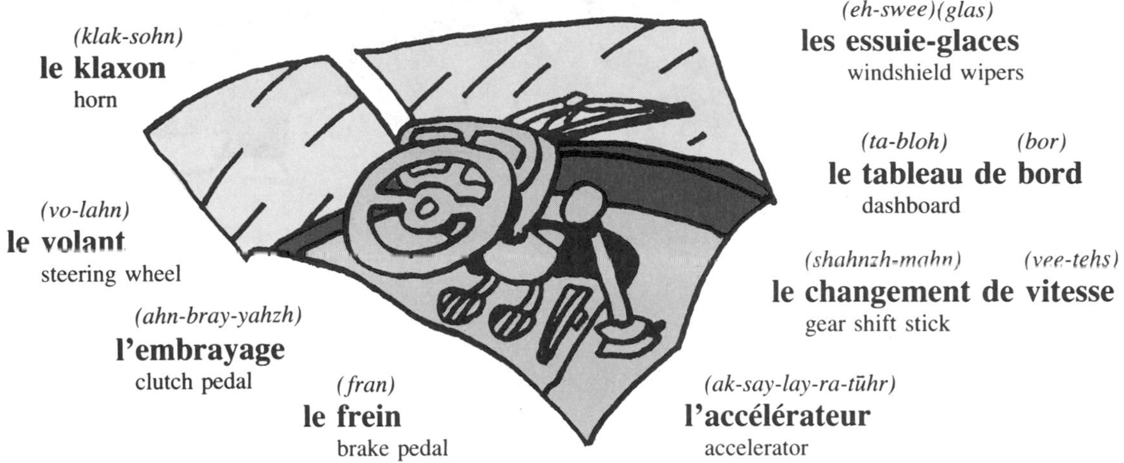

(klak-sohn)
le klaxon
horn
(vo-lahn)
le volant
steering wheel
(ahn-bray-yahzh)
l'embrayage
clutch pedal
(fran)
le frein
brake pedal
(eh-swee)(glas)
les essuie-glaces
windshield wipers
(ta-bloh) (bor)
le tableau de bord
dashboard
(shahnzh-mahn) (vee-tehs)
le changement de vitesse
gear shift stick
(ak-say-lay-ra-tũhr)
l'accélérateur
accelerator

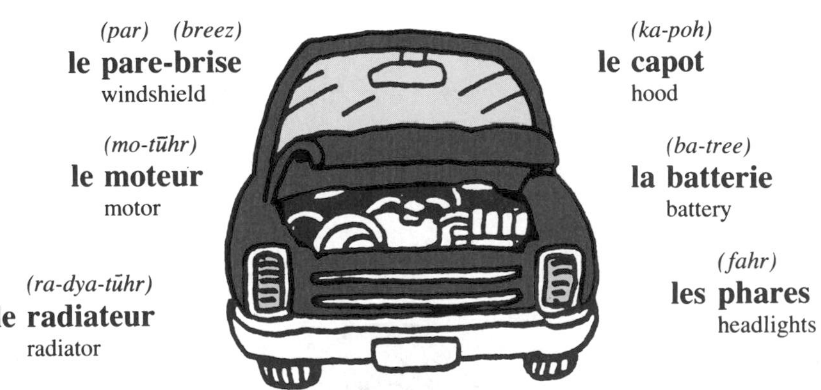

(par) (breez)
le pare-brise
windshield
(mo-tũhr)
le moteur
motor
(ra-dya-tũhr)
le radiateur
radiator
(ka-poh)
le capot
hood
(ba-tree)
la batterie
battery
(fahr)
les phares
headlights

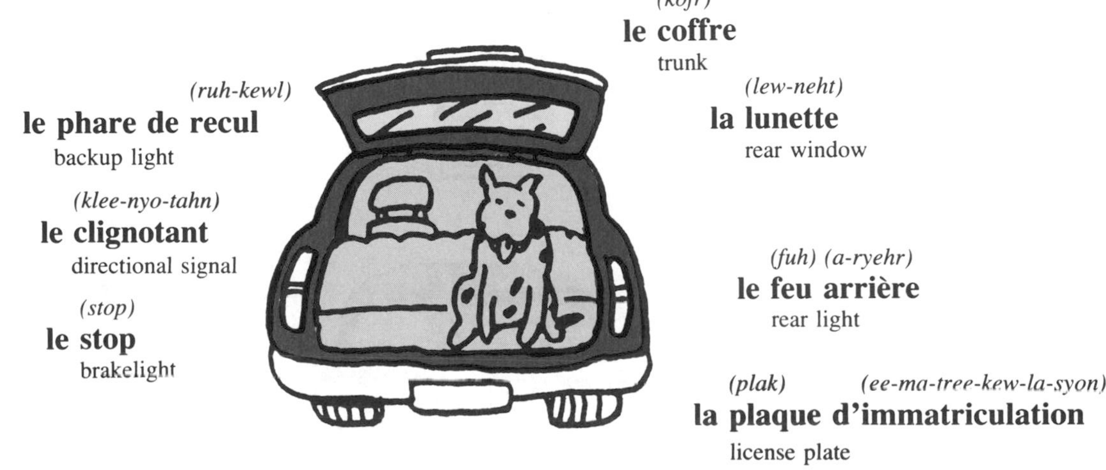

(kofr)
le coffre
trunk
(ruh-kewl)
le phare de recul
backup light
(klee-nyo-tahn)
le clignotant
directional signal
(stop)
le stop
brakelight
(lew-neht)
la lunette
rear window
(fuh) (a-ryehr)
le feu arrière
rear light
(plak) (ee-ma-tree-kew-la-syon)
la plaque d'immatriculation
license plate

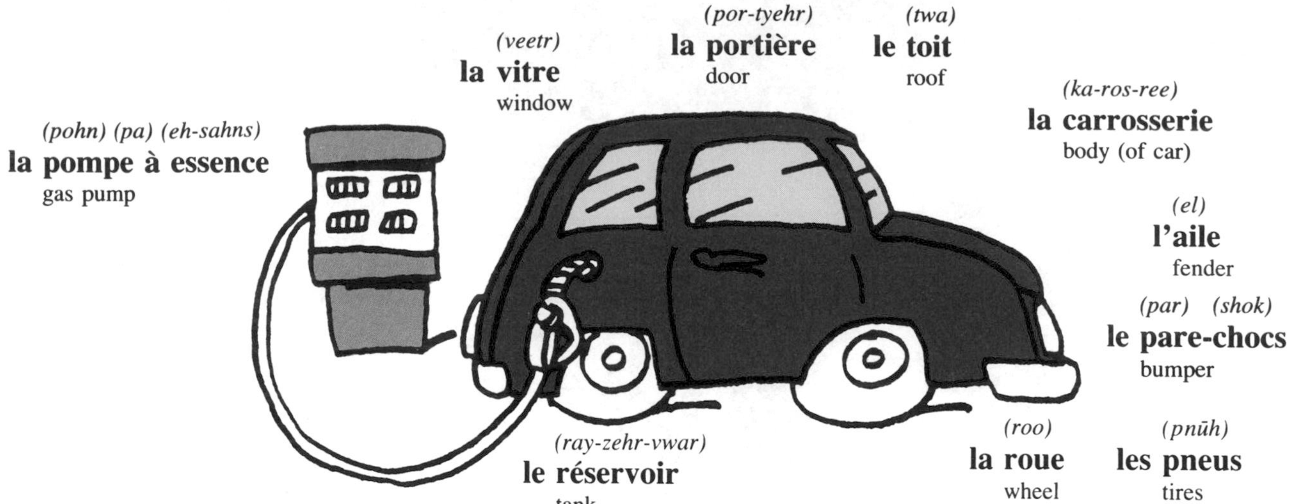

Now fill in the names for the following auto parts.

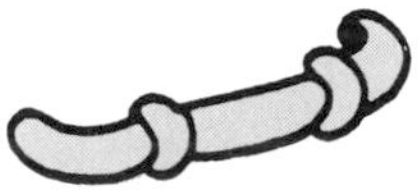

Quelques expressions utiles en cas de difficulté

(ew-teel) *(kah)* *(dee-fee-kewl-tay)*

Some phrases useful in case of problems

(meh-day) **Pouvez-vous m'aider?**	Can you help me?
(kruh-vay) **J'ai un pneu crevé.**	I have a flat tire.
(pan) **Ma voiture est en panne.**	My car has broken down.
(day-mar) **Ma voiture ne démarre pas.**	My car won't start.
Je suis en panne d'essence.	I've run out of gas.
(marsh) **Mes freins ne marchent pas.**	My brakes don't work.
Ma voiture chauffe.	My car is overheating.
(ra-tay) **Mon moteur fait des ratés.**	My engine is misfiring.
(day-pah-nūhz) **J'ai besoin d'une dépanneuse.**	I need a tow truck.
(kool) **Le radiateur coule.**	The radiator is leaking.
(trahns-mee-syohn) *(kah-say)* **La transmission est cassée.**	The transmission is broken.
(pla) **La batterie est à plat.**	The battery is dead.
(klee-nyo-tahn) **Les clignotants ne marchent pas.**	The signal lights don't work.
(weel) **L'huile coule.**	The oil is leaking.
(klee-ma-tee-za-syohn) **La climatisation (le chauffage) ne marche pas.**	The air conditioning (heater) doesn't work.

Fill in the blanks by referring to the dialogue and these new expressions.

1. Je voudrais ______________ une voiture.
   (to rent)
2. Pourriez-vous ______________ ______________ ______________, s'il vous plaît?
   (fill 'er up)
3. Mes freins ne ______________ pas.
   (work)
4. Quelle est la route la plus ______________?
   (short)
5. Est-ce qu'il y a un ______________ près d'ici?
   (garage)

(fehr)

Faire

To do, to make

Now, here is another common—and irregular—verb:

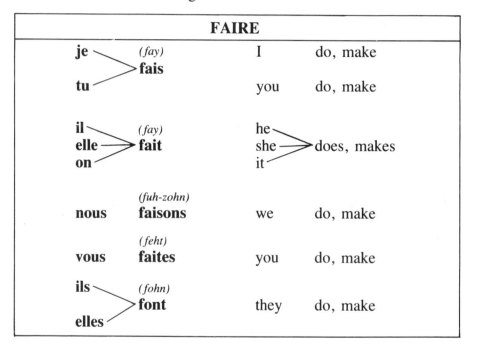

FAIRE			
je	*(fay)* **fais**	I	do, make
tu		you	do, make
il / **elle** / **on**	*(fay)* **fait**	he / she / it	does, makes
nous	*(fuh-zohn)* **faisons**	we	do, make
vous	*(feht)* **faites**	you	do, make
ils / **elles**	*(fohn)* **font**	they	do, make

Fill in the correct form of the verb FAIRE.

1. Je ______________ la liste.
2. Que ______________-vous?
3. Nous ______________ une promenade.
4. Qu'est-ce qu'il ______________?
5. Elles ______________ la queue.
   (line)

ANSWERS

Fill in the blanks **1.** louer **2.** faire le plein **3.** marchent **4.** courte **5.** garage

FAIRE **1.** fais **2.** faites **3.** faisons **4.** fait **5.** font

(see) (voo) (voo-lay) (ko-mahn-day)

Si vous voulez commander . . .

If you want to give orders . . .

In order to get people to do things for you, you will have to know how to use verbs in a "command" or "imperative" way. The following chart shows you how to form the imperative of regular verbs. Just keep in mind that the subject of a command is "YOU" (understood). So, simply use the TU form of the verb to be familiar and the VOUS form to be polite, without using the subject pronouns.

THE IMPERATIVE

	Parler	**Finir**	**Attendre**
Familiar	**Parle***	**Finis**	**Attends**
Polite	**Parlez**	**Finissez**	**Attendez**

*Drop the final -s from the "TU" form for -er verbs only.

To say "Let's," use the NOUS form command:

Parlons! Let's speak!
Finissons! Let's finish!
Attendons! Let's wait!

ÊTRE and **AVOIR** have irregular command forms:

	Être	**Avoir**
Familiar	**Sois**	**Aie**
Polite	**Soyez**	**Ayez**
(NOUS)	**Soyons**	**Ayons**

Don't get discouraged. With a little practice, you will become familiar and quite proficient with these verb forms. To make a command negative, put **NE** before the verb and **PAS** after the verb:

Ne parlez pas! Don't speak!
Ne finis pas! Don't finish!
N'attendons pas. Let's not wait.

Now try the following. You are speaking to a person you meet in your travels. Tell him the following:

1. (speak) ______________________ anglais.
2. (wait for) ______________________-moi.
3. (finish) ______________________ vite. (quickly)
4. (be) ______________________ prudent.
5. (have) ______________________ du courage.

ANSWERS

Commands **1.** Parlez **2.** Attendez **3.** Finissez **4.** Soyez **5.** Ayez

Attention! (Watch out!) Driving in a foreign country means watching the road even when the scenery is breathtaking. **Très beau!** Yes, very beautiful! Read the following passage and determine what happened on the trip. Then answer the questions.

(ak-see-dahn)
UN ACCIDENT
An Accident

PREMIER CHAUFFEUR **Sacrebleu!** *(sakr-blūh)* **Vous ne pouvez pas faire attention?** *(a-tahn-syohn)* **Vous êtes aveugle?** *(a-vūhgl)* **J'ai** *(ay)* **la priorité!**	For heaven's sake! Can't you be careful? Are you blind? I have the right of way!
DEUXIÈME CHAUFFEUR **Je le sais!** *(say)* **Mais vous faites du 150 kilomètres à l'heure et la limite de vitesse** (speed) **est 60 kilomètres à l'heure!**	I know! But you are driving at 150 km per hour and the speed limit is 60 km per hour!
TROISIÈME CHAUFFEUR **Est-ce que je peux vous aider?**	May I help you?
PREMIER CHAUFFEUR **Oui. Demandez à l'agent là-bas de venir examiner** *(ehg-za-mee-nay)* **les dégâts.** *(day-gah)*	Yes. Ask the policeman over there to come and look at the damage.
L'AGENT **Qu'est-ce qui se passe?**	What's happening?

(ee-dyoh) (tahn-po-nay) PREMIER CHAUFFEUR **Cet idiot a tamponné**	This idiot hit
ma voiture. Il a tort.	my car. He is in the wrong.
(vreh) DEUXIÈME CHAUFFEUR **Ce n'est pas vrai.**	It's not true.
(teep) (foo) **Ce type conduit comme un fou.**	This guy drives like a madman.
(troh) (veet) **Il est allé trop vite.**	He was speeding.
(pehr-son) (bleh-say) L'AGENT **Personne n'est blessé? Bon. Vos**	Nobody is hurt? Good. Your
permis de conduire, s'il vous plaît.	driver's licenses, please.
(au deuxième chauffeur): Est-ce que	(To the second driver): Is this
c'est une voiture de location?	a rented car?
DEUXIÈME CHAUFFEUR **Oui.**	Yes.
(foh) (prayv-neer) L'AGENT **Alors il faut prévenir l'agence et**	Then it's necessary to notify the agency and
(kohn-pa-nyee) (a-sew-rahns) **aussi votre compagnie d'assurance.**	also your insurance company.
DEUXIÈME CHAUFFEUR **Est-ce qu'il y a un**	Is there a
garage près d'ici?	garage near here?
(pro-shen) L'AGENT **Oui, au coin de la prochaine**	Yes, at the corner of the next
(ee) **route. Vous pouvez y aller à pied.**	road. You can walk there.

(Au garage)

DEUXIÈME CHAUFFEUR **Est-ce que vous**	Could you repair
(ray-pa-ray) **pourriez réparer vite ma voiture?**	my car quickly?
Je suis touriste.	I am a tourist.
(may-ka-nee-syan) (shahns) LE MÉCANICIEN **Vous avez de la chance.**	You are lucky.
(vwah-lay) **La roue arrière est voilée et le**	The rear wheel is bent and the
(ka-bo-say) **pare-choc est cabossé, c'est tout.**	bumper is dented, that's all.
Téléphonez demain après-midi.	Telephone tomorrow afternoon.

Mon numéro est quarante quatre cinquante-et-un dix sept. — My number is 44-51-17.

DEUXIÈME CHAUFFEUR **Merci mille fois. (à lui-même): Ah, les conducteurs** *(kohn-dewk-tũhr)* **français!** — Many thanks. (to himself): Ah, the French drivers!

Circle the statements which might be appropriate if you had a car accident in France:

1. Je voudrais faire le plein.
2. Demandez à l'agent de venir examiner les dégâts.
3. Je voudrais louer une voiture.
4. Votre permis de conduire, s'il vous plaît.
5. Est-ce qu'il y a un garage près d'ici?
6. Je cherche une agence de location.

Should you get into an accident, do the same things you would do in this country: get the name, address and telephone number of the other person. If you are traveling in a rented car, notify the rental agency. Ask someone to notify the police and, if necessary, to call an ambulance. If it's a minor accident and both persons can drive away, be especially careful to have all the information needed by the insurance company. And try to keep calm!

ANSWERS

Circle statements 2. 4. 5.

9 Le Camping

(kahn-peng) **Le Camping** — Camping

LE NÉCESSAIRE

(nay-seh-sehr) — Essentials

(mat-la) (pnūh-ma-teek) **le matelas pneumatique** — air mattress

(a-bee) **les habits** — clothes

(bwaht) (kohn-sehrv) **les boîtes de conserve** — cans

(pa-gay) **les pagaies** — paddles

(koo-vehr-tewr) **la couverture** — blanket

(tahnt) **la tente** — tent

(arbr) **un arbre** — tree

(soh-leh-y) **le soleil** — sun

(rwee-soh) **le ruisseau** — brook

(sak) (duh) (koo-shahzh) **le sac de couchage** — sleeping bag

(lahnp) (duh) (posh) **la lampe de poche** — flashlight

(pa-nyay) **un panier** — basket

(bwaht) **une boîte** — box

(ka-noh-ay) **le canoé** — canoe

(soh) **un seau** — bucket

(kan) (pehsh) **une canne à pêche** — rod fishing

(teer) (boo-shohn) **le tire-bouchon** — corkscrew

(ews-tahn-seel) (kwee-zeen) **les ustensiles de cuisine** — cooking utensils

(bot) **des bottes** — boots

(ar-teekl) (twa-leht) **les articles de toilette** — toilet articles

(tehr-mohs) **le thermos**

(ra-dyoh) (por-ta-teev) **la radio portative** — portable radio

(a-lew-meht) **des allumettes** — matches

If you are planning to go camping in France, a good idea would be to get hold of the *Michelin Guide to Camping and Caravaning*, available in many American bookstores. Conditions and regulations vary from region to region. In general, they are similar to those in the U.S. Road signs tell you which camping grounds arc for tcnts only, for vans only or for both.

(san-dee-ka) (dee-nee-sya-teev)
In many cities, a good source of information is the Syndicat d'Initiative, the local Tourism Office. If your first stop is Paris, you can go to the Fédération Française de Camping et Caravaning, 78 rue de Rivoli, Paris 75004.

(root) (teh-ran)

EN ROUTE POUR LE TERRAIN DE CAMPING

On the Way to the Campground

Now read the following dialogues, which contain some useful words, expressions, and information on camping. Read them aloud, repeating each line several times, so you know how to pronounce the new words.

MARC **Excusez-moi, Monsieur. Est-ce que**	Excuse me, Sir.
(poo-ryohn) (kahn-pay) **nous pourrions peut-être camper sur**	Could we perhaps camp on
(pro-pree-yay-tay) **votre propriété?**	your property?
(fehr-myay) LE FERMIER (farmer) **Je suis désolé, mais c'est**	I am sorry, but it's
(tan-po-seebl) (kahn-pūhr) **impossible. Les campeurs font trop de**	impossible. Campers make
(ko-shon-ree) **cochonneries.**	too much of a mess.
MARC **Je comprends. Est-ce qu'il y a un**	I understand. Is there a
terrain de camping près d'ici?	campground near here?
LE FERMIER **Oui. À vingt kilomètres.**	Yes. Twenty kilometers from here.
(pa-noh) (see-nya-lee-za-syohn) **Suivez les panneaux de signalisation.**	Follow the signs.
(mee-lyūh) **Il y a une tente au milieu.**	There is a tent in the middle of the signs.
MARC **Savez-vous s'il y a des douches?**	Do you know if there are showers?
(mwandr) (ee-day) LE FERMIER **Pas la moindre idée.**	Not the slightest idea.
On va vous le dire au camping.	They'll tell you at the campground.
(pray-fay-ray) **Ou si vous préférez, vous pouvez vous**	Or if you prefer, you can
(a-reh-tay) (san-dee-ka) (dee-nee-sya-teev) **arrêter au Syndicat d'Initiative au**	stop at the Tourist Office in
(mee-lyūh) (vee-lahzh) **milieu du village.**	the middle of the village.

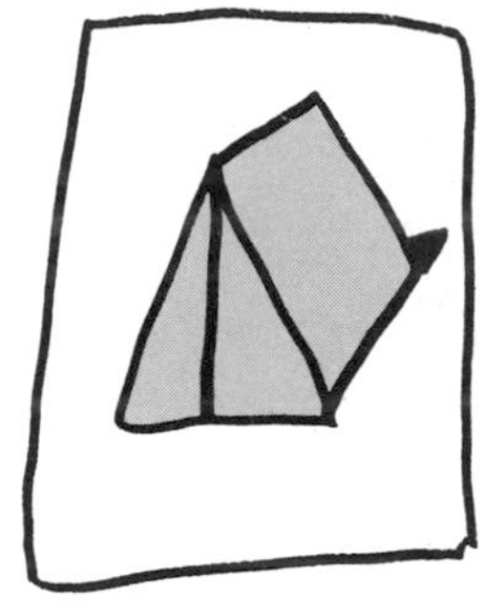

(teh-ran)

SUR LE TERRAIN DE CAMPING

At the Campground

MARC	*(plas)* **Est-ce que vous avez de la place pour nous?**	Do you have room for us?
LE DIRECTEUR *(dee-rek-tühr)* manager	*(tahn)* *(kohn-tay)* *(rehs-tay)* **Oui. Combien de temps comptez-vous rester?**	Yes. How long are you planning to stay?
MARC	*(nwee)* **Deux ou trois nuits. Est-ce qu'il y a des douches?**	Two or three nights. Are there any showers?
DIRECTEUR	**Oui.**	Yes.
ANNE	*(oof)* *(teht)* **Ouf! Je vais pouvoir me laver la tête.**	Oh! I am going to be able to wash my hair!
MARC	**C'est combien par jour?**	How much is it per day?
DIRECTEUR	*(ay-lehk-tree-see-tay)* *(pran-see-pal)* *(swar)* *(dees-ko-tehk)* *(oo-vehrt)* *(a)* *(par-teer)* **Pour quatre personnes, cent soixante francs. Il y a l'électricité dans le bâtiment principal. Le soir, la discothèque est ouverte à partir de vingt et une heures.** (ouverte = open)	For four people, 160 francs. There is electricity in the main building. In the evening, the discothèque is open from 9 P.M. on.

Fill in the missing word in French:

1. Est-ce qu'il y a ______________________ près d'ici? (a campground)
2. Savez-vous s'il y a des ______________________? (showers)
3. Vous pouvez vous arrêter au ______________________. (tourist office)
4. Combien de temps comptez-vous ______________________? (to stay)

ANSWERS

Fill in **1.** un terrain de camping **2.** douches **3.** syndicat d'initiative **4.** rester

(buh-zwan)

J'ai besoin de . . .

I need

Study the vocabulary on page 99, then make a list of items you need to go camping.

EX.: **Pour aller camper, j'ai besoin d'une tente, d'un matelas pneumatique, d'allumettes, etc.** (If the noun is plural, you don't need to use an article; only DE or D'.)

The following puzzle contains seven camping terms in addition to the one circled. Try to find these words: boots, bucket, stream, sun, basket, tree, blankets.

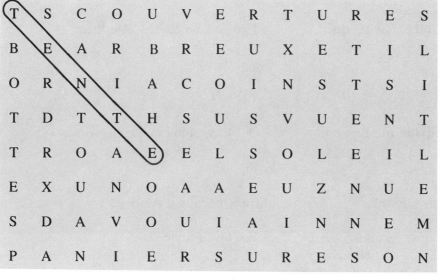

T	S	C	O	U	V	E	R	T	U	R	E	S
B	E	A	R	B	R	E	U	X	E	T	I	L
O	R	N	I	A	C	O	I	N	S	T	S	I
T	D	T	T	H	S	U	S	V	U	E	N	T
T	R	O	A	E	E	L	S	O	L	E	I	L
E	X	U	N	O	A	A	E	U	Z	N	U	E
S	D	A	V	O	U	I	A	I	N	N	E	M
P	A	N	I	E	R	S	U	R	E	S	O	N

(ay-pees-ree)

À L'ÉPICERIE

At the Grocery Store

(leevr) (noo-y) MARIE **Je voudrais une livre de nouilles,**	I would like a pound of noodles,
(gram) (bŭhr) **cent grammes de beurre, quatre**	100 grams of butter, four
(trahnsh) (zhahn-bohn) (leetr) (leh) **tranches de jambon, un litre de lait,**	slices of ham, one liter of milk,
(sel) (boo-teh-y) (van) **du sel et une bouteille de vin rouge**	some salt and a bottle of ordinary red wine . . .
ordinaire . . . et aussi une boîte	and also a box
d'allumettes.	of matches.

ANSWERS

Puzzle (Camping) BOTTES SEAU RUISSEAU SOLEIL PANIER ARBRE COUVERTURES

(lay-pee-syehr) *(kahn-pūhr)* *(fūh)*

L'ÉPICIÈRE (fem. grocer) **Vous êtes campeurs? Vous savez qu'il est interdit de faire du feu?** — You are campers? You know it's forbidden to light fires?

(gahz)

MARC **Oui, nous avons un réchaud à gaz.** — Yes. We have a gas heater.

(dwa)

MARIE **Je vous dois combien?** — How much do I owe you?

L'ÉPICIÈRE **Quatre-vingt dix francs.** — 90 francs.

(fee-leh)

Vous avez un filet? — Do you have a string bag?

MARIE **Non.** — No.

(tahn) *(pee)*

L'ÉPICIÈRE **Tant pis. Je vais vous trouver un sac en papier.** — Never mind. I'm going to find a paper bag for you.

MARC (à l'épicière) **Merci. Au revoir, Madame. Bonne journée!** — Thank you. Good-bye, Madam! Have a good day!

Match these French expressions with their English equivalents.

1. une livre	a. a slice
2. cent grammes	b. a bottle
3. une tranche	c. a liter
4. un litre	d. 100 grams
5. une bouteille	e. a pound

ANSWERS

Matching 1. e 2. d 3. a 4. c 5. b

Vous avez besoin de savoir les verbes *savoir* (sa-vwar) (to know) et *connaître* (ko-nehtr) (to know)

SAVOIR implies acquired knowledge; to know how to do something; to know a fact.

Je sais le français. I know French.

Je sais où se trouve Paris. I know where Paris is.

Je sais nager. I know how to swim.

(may)
Mais
But

CONNAÎTRE—to know, to be acquainted with, a person, place, or thing.

Je connais Paris. I know Paris (because I was there).

Je connais Robert. I know Robert (I have met him).

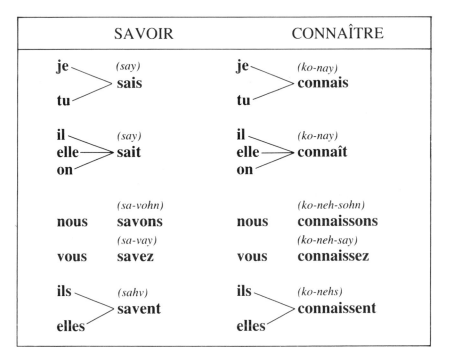

SAVOIR		CONNAÎTRE	
je, tu	*(say)* **sais**	**je, tu**	*(ko-nay)* **connais**
il, elle, on	*(say)* **sait**	**il, elle, on**	*(ko-nay)* **connaît**
nous	*(sa-vohn)* **savons**	**nous**	*(ko-neh-sohn)* **connaissons**
vous	*(sa-vay)* **savez**	**vous**	*(ko-neh-say)* **connaissez**
ils, elles	*(sahv)* **savent**	**ils, elles**	*(ko-nehs)* **connaissent**

To practice the new verbs, fill in the blanks:

1. Je ______________ (know) Londres.
2. Tu ______________ (know) qui est le Président de la République française.
3. Il ______________ (knows) Brigitte Bardot.
4. Nous ______________ (know (how)) parler français.

ANSWERS

New Verbs **1.** connais **2.** sais **3.** connaît **4.** savons

(ko-mahn) (dee) (tohn)

Comment dit-on

How do you say

In English, you say: I am hot, you are hungry, she is cold, he is afraid, we are thirsty, they are sleepy. In French, the tendency is to say I have heat, you have hunger, and so forth.

Ils ont chaud.
They are hot.

(frwah)
Nous avons froid.
We are cold.

(pūhr)
Les garçons ont peur.
The boys are afraid.

(fan)
Le chien a faim.
The dog is hungry.

(ohnt)
Le garçon a honte.
The boy is ashamed.

(so-meh-y)
L'homme a sommeil.
The man is sleepy.

Can you match up the pictures and sentences below?

1. Ils ont froid.
2. La dame a chaud.
3. Il a sommeil
4. Les enfants ont peur.
5. Le garçon a faim.
6. La fille a honte.

ANSWERS

Match up sentences 1. d 2. a 3. f 4. e 5. b 6. c

Très bien! (Very good!) Now practice your irregular verbs, some old, some new, and adjective agreement.

1. Je suis ici.

   Tu ______________________ ici.

   Elle ______________________ ici.

   On ______________________ ici.

   Nous ______________________ ici.

   Vous ______________________ ici.

   Ils ______________________ ici.

2. Je ne sais pas.

   Ils ne ______________________ pas.

   Nous ne ______________________ pas.

   Vous ne ______________________ pas.

   On ne ______________________ pas.

   Il ne ______________________ pas.

   Tu ne ______________________ pas.

3. Nous pouvons aller à Paris.

   Je ______________________ aller à Paris.

   On ______________________ aller à Paris.

   Vous ______________________ aller à Paris.

   Elles ______________________ aller à Paris.

   Il ______________________ aller à Paris.

4. Vous avez faim.

   J'______________________ faim.

   Il ______________________ faim.

   On ______________________ faim.

   Nous ______________________ faim.

   Ils ______________________ faim.

ANSWERS

Irregular Verbs

1. Tu es
Elle est
On est
Nous sommes
Vous êtes
Ils sont

2. Ils ne savent pas
Nous ne savons pas
Vous ne savez pas
On ne sait pas
Il ne sait pas
Tu ne sais pas

3. Je peux
On peut
Vous pouvez
Elles peuvent
Il peut

4. J'ai
Il a
On a
Nous avons
Ils ont

10 Le temps, les saisons, les mois, et les jours

(tahn) (seh-zohn) (mwah) (zhoor)

The weather, the seasons, months and days,

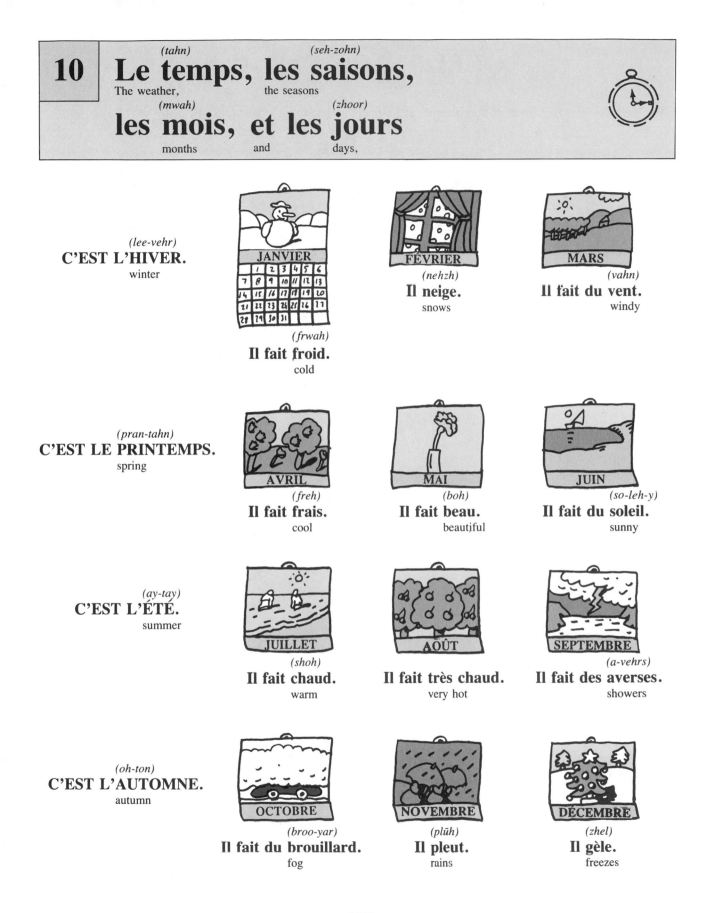

(lee-vehr)
C'EST L'HIVER.
winter

(frwah)
Il fait froid.
cold

(nehzh)
Il neige.
snows

(vahn)
Il fait du vent.
windy

(pran-tahn)
C'EST LE PRINTEMPS.
spring

(freh)
Il fait frais.
cool

(boh)
Il fait beau.
beautiful

(so-leh-y)
Il fait du soleil.
sunny

(ay-tay)
C'EST L'ÉTÉ.
summer

(shoh)
Il fait chaud.
warm

Il fait très chaud.
very hot

(a-vehrs)
Il fait des averses.
showers

(oh-ton)
C'EST L'AUTOMNE.
autumn

(broo-yar)
Il fait du brouillard.
fog

(plūh)
Il pleut.
rains

(zhel)
Il gèle.
freezes

(kehl) (tahn) (fay) (teel)

QUEL TEMPS FAIT-IL?

How Is the Weather?

As you noticed, the French don't say "It IS cold." They say "It MAKES cold," *"Il fait froid."*

Il fait

. . . beau

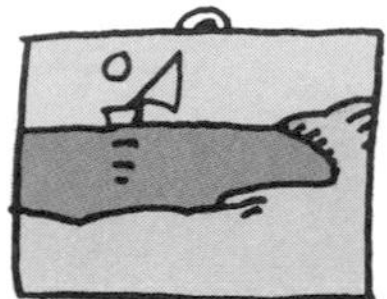

(sew-pehrb)
. . . un temps superbe

. . . chaud

(o-reebl)
. . . un temps horrible

(mehr-veh-yūh)
. . . un temps merveilleux
marvelous

(frwah)
. . . froid
cold

(a-frūh)
. . . un temps affreux
awful

(ew-meed) (loor) **Il fait humide, lourd,**	It is humid, heavy,
(o-ra-zhūh) **orageux.**	stormy.
(vahn) **Il fait du vent.**	It is windy.

Note these exceptions:

Il neige.	It is snowing.
Il pleut.	It is raining.
(vers) **Il pleut à verse.**	It is pouring.

Can you describe the weather in the pictures below?

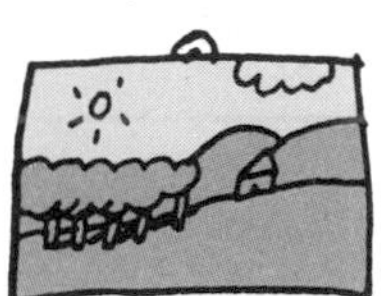

1. Il fait ______________________

2. ______________________

3. ______________________

4. ______________________

ANSWERS

Weather **1.** un temps merveilleux **2.** Il fait chaud. **3.** Il neige. **4.** Il fait un temps horrible.

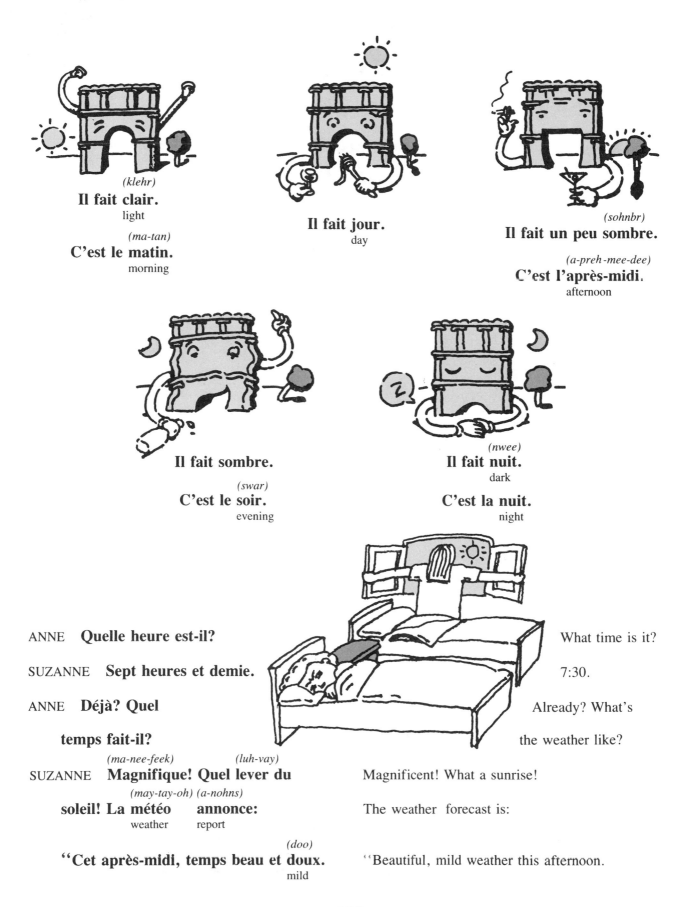

(klehr)
Il fait clair.
light

(ma-tan)
C'est le matin.
morning

Il fait jour.
day

(sohnbr)
Il fait un peu sombre.

(a-preh-mee-dee)
C'est l'après-midi.
afternoon

Il fait sombre.

(swar)
C'est le soir.
evening

(nwee)
Il fait nuit.
dark

C'est la nuit.
night

ANNE **Quelle heure est-il?** — What time is it?

SUZANNE **Sept heures et demie.** — 7:30.

ANNE **Déjà? Quel temps fait-il?** — Already? What's the weather like?

SUZANNE **Magnifique!** *(ma-nee-feek)* **Quel lever** *(luh-vay)* **du soleil! La météo** *(may-tay-oh)* (weather) **annonce:** *(a-nohns)* (report) — Magnificent! What a sunrise! The weather forecast is:

"Cet après-midi, temps beau et doux. *(doo)* (mild) — "Beautiful, mild weather this afternoon.

(ahntr) **Température entre quinze et dix-huit** between	Temperature between 15 and 18°C.
(duh-gray) *(new-a-zhuh)* **degrés centigrades. Ce soir, nuageux** cloudy	This evening, cloudy
(behs) *(tahn-pay-ra-tewr)* **à couvert avec baisse de température.** lowering	and overcast with temperatures dropping.
(par-syehl-mahn) **Mercredi, partiellement couvert.** partially	Wednesday, partly cloudy.
Température entre dix-sept	Temperatures between 17
et vingt degrés centigrades.''	and 20°C.''
ANNE **Levons-nous! J'ai faim!**	Let's get up! I am hungry!

Choose the correct answer:

1. Cet après-midi, il va faire
   A. très chaud B. très froid
   C. mauvais D. beau

2. C'est la météo pour un jour
   A. d'août B. de janvier
   C. de février D. d'avril

Temperature conversions

Centigrade Degrés Fahrenheit

Thermomètre

To change Fahrenheit to Centigrade: Subtract 32 and multiply by $\frac{5}{9}$.

To change Centigrade to Fahrenheit: Multiply by $\frac{9}{5}$ and add 32.

ANSWERS

Multiple choice 1. D 2. D

(ka-lahn-dree-yay)

LE CALENDRIER

The Calendar

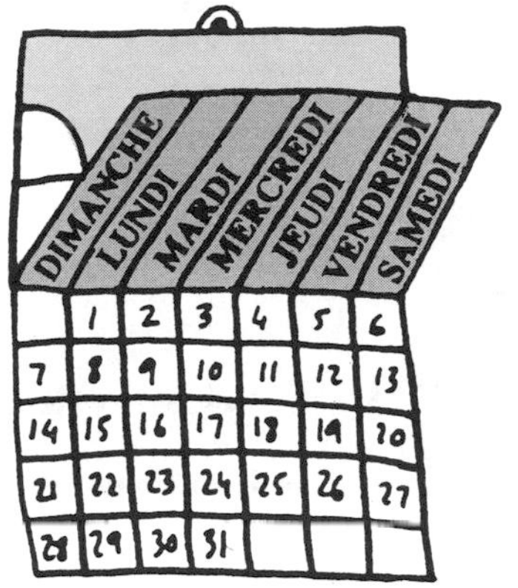

(mwah)

THE MONTHS OF THE YEAR—LES MOIS DE L'ANNÉE

(zhahn-vyay) **janvier** January	*(ah-vreel)* **avril** April	*(zhwee-yeh)* **juillet** July	*(ok-tobr)* **octobre** October
(fay-vree-yay) **février** February	*(may)* **mai** May	*(oot)* **août** August	*(no-vahnbr)* **novembre** November
(mars) **mars** March	*(zhwan)* **juin** June	*(sehp-tahnbr)* **septembre** September	*(day-sahnbr)* **décembre** December

(suh-men)

THE DAYS OF THE WEEK—LES JOURS DE LA SEMAINE

(dee-mahnsh) **dimanche** Sunday	*(luhn-dee)* **lundi** Monday	*(mar-dee)* **mardi** Tuesday	*(mehr-kruh-dee)* **mercredi** Wednesday	*(zhūh-dee)* **jeudi** Thursday	*(vahn-druh-dee)* **vendredi** Friday	*(sam-dee)* **samedi** Saturday

Si c'est mardi, je dois	If it's Tuesday, I must
(vee-zeet) rendre visite à ma mère, parce que (pay a visit)	pay a visit to my mother, because
le mardi, je vais toujours visiter ma mère.	I always go to visit my mother on Tuesdays.

Use LE with days of the week when describing a habit, but if you want to say, "On Tuesday, (this particular Tuesday) I am going to visit my mother," it is **Mardi, je vais rendre visite à ma mère.**

(ehk-spree-may) (dat)

Comment exprimer la date

How to express the date

To express the date in French use:

LE + number + month + year

C'est le six avril mille neuf cent quatre-vingt-cinq (1985)
It is

Use this formula to express all dates, except for the first of the month:

C'est le premier mai.
first

(feht)
La fête nationale américaine est le 4 juillet.

La fête nationale française est le 14 juillet.

(noh-ehl)
Noël est le 25 décembre.

Pâques est en avril.

La Saint-Sylvestre est le trente-et-un décembre.

La fête nationale suisse est le premier août. **La fête nationale belge est le 21 juillet.**

Comment exprimer les mois

How to express the months

Use EN with months to express "in":

En janvier, je fais du ski. In January, I ski.

With seasons, use AU before a consonant. Use EN before a vowel to express "in the":

au printemps, en été, en automne, en hiver.

Complete the following sentences, using the correct form:

1. Quel jour est-ce aujourd'hui? *(oh-zhoor-dwee)* (today)

   C'est ____________________

2. Quelle est la date?

   C'est ____________________

3. Quelle est la date de votre anniversaire? *(a-nee-vehr-sehr)*

   C'est ____________________

4. Quand est la fête nationale française?

   C'est ____________________

5. Quand est la fête nationale américaine?

   C'est ____________________

ANSWERS

Date **1.** C'est aujourd'hui lundi. (example) **2.** C'est aujourd'hui le onze juillet. (example) **3.** C'est le douze janvier. (example) **4.** C'est le quatorze juillet. **5.** C'est le quatre juillet.

(ad-zhehk-teef)
Les adjectifs
Adjectives

Throughout your trip you will notice many wonderful things that you will want to describe. In order to do this, you will have to know how to use French adjectives.

Adjectives agree in gender (masculine or feminine) and number (singular or plural) with the nouns they modify.

In most instances, add **−E** to the masculine form of the adjective to obtain the corresponding feminine form:

un garçon intelligent	**une fille intelligente**
un dîner parfait	**une maison parfaite**

LE DÎNER EST . . .

(noo-ree-tewr)
LA NOURRITURE EST . . .
food

Masculine		Feminine
(preh) **prêt** ready		*(preht)* **prête**
(loor) **lourd** heavy		*(loord)* **lourde**
(par-feh) **parfait** perfect		*(par-feht)* **parfaite**

If the masculine form of the adjective already ends in **−E**, add nothing to obtain the feminine form.

More examples.

MON HÔTEL EST . . .
My Hotel Is . . .

(shahnbr)
MA CHAMBRE EST . . .
My Room Is . . .

Masculine		Feminine
(brwee-yahn) **bruyant** noisy		*(brwee-yahnt)* **bruyante**
(klehr) **clair** bright		*(klehr)* **claire**
(grahn) **grand** big		*(grahnd)* **grande**
(puh-tee) **petit** small		*(puh-teet)* **petite**

BUT

(sahl) **sale** dirty		*(sahl)* **sale**
(pūh) (kohn-for-tahbl) **peu confortable** not very comfortable	 	*(pūh) (kohn-for-tahbl)* **peu confortable**

When a masculine adjective ends in **−É**, the adjective is considered regular. The feminine form, therefore, is simply obtained by adding another **−E**: *(ahn-shan-tay)* **enchanté, enchantée.** delighted

JE SUIS
I am . . .

Masculine	Feminine
(sa-tees-fay) **satisfait** satisfied	*(sa-tees-feht)* **satisfaite**
(kohn-tahn) **content** pleased, glad	*(kohn-tahnt)* **contente**
(puh-tee) **petit** small	*(puh-teet)* **petite**
(zho-lee) **joli** pretty, handsome	*(zho-lee)* **jolie** pretty

AND

Masculine	Feminine
(fa-tee-gay) **fatigué** tired	**fatiguée**
(fa-shay) **fâché** angry	**fâchée**

Masculine	Feminine
(a-zhay) **âgé** old	**âgée**
(ee-ree-tay) **irrité** annoyed	**irritée**

(poor) (shahn-zhay)(oh) (plew-ryehl)
Pour changer au pluriel
To change to the plural

Add **−S** to the masculine or feminine singular form of the adjective to obtain the corresponding plural forms of most adjectives. Add nothing to form the plural of an adjective that ends in **−S** or **−X**. The **−AL** ending of a masculine singular adjective becomes **−AUX** in the plural;

des garçons intelligents	**des filles intelligentes**
des dîners parfaits	**des maisons parfaites**
des garçons surpris	**des filles surprises**
des problèmes nationaux	**des fêtes nationales** holidays

Fill in the correct form of the adjective in parentheses:

1. (content) Les garçons ____________________________.
2. (parfait) La voiture ____________________________.
3. (satisfait) La mère ____________________________.

ANSWERS

Adjectives **1.** contents, **2.** parfaite, **3.** satisfaite,

4. (prêt) L'homme ________________________.

5. (lourd) Les livres ________________________.

6. (intelligent) Les filles ________________________.

7. (général) Les problèmes (m.) ________________________.

8. (surpris) Les pères ________________________.

(oo) (lay)(mehtr)
Où les mettre
Where to put them

Adjectives are usually placed after the nouns they modify except when they are short, common, and express **Beauty, Age, Goodness and Size (BAGS)**: **beau, joli, jeune** (young), **vieux** (old), **nouveau** (new), **bon** (good), **petit, grand** (big)

le garçon intelligent
les femmes importantes

but

le petit garçon
les jolies femmes

ANSWERS

4. prêt, **5.** lourds, **6.** intelligentes, **7.** généraux **8.** surpris

11

(vwa-yahzh) (a-vyohn)

Voyages en avion

Plane trips

(kew-ryoh-zee-tay)

Visites des curiosités

Sightseeing

A plane trip within a country is often an easy and enjoyable way to travel. Note that in France, (la-ay-ro-por) (sharl) (gohl) **l'Aéroport Charles de Gaulle** is for international flights; Le Bourget (boor-zheh) is mostly for domestic flights; Orly (or-lee) is for medium-length domestic and international flights. Study the following vocabulary and then follow the tourist as he goes to one of France's most popular resorts, Cannes.

Pouvez-vous trouver . . .

(kohn-pa-nyee) (a-ay-ryehn)
la compagnie aérienne
airline

(kohn-twar) (bee-yay)
le comptoir des billets
ticket counter

(or-lozh)
l'horloge
clock

(ehs-ka-lyay) (roo-lahn)
l'escalier roulant
escalator

(tro-twar)
le trottoir roulant
moving sidewalk

(dwah-nyeh) (dwah-nyehr)
le douanier, la douanière
customs officer

(kohn-trohl) (pas-por)
le contrôle des passeports

(ans-pehk-tūhr)
l'inspecteur
inspector

(sor-tee)
la sortie
gate, exit

(ba-gahzh)
les bagages
luggage

(pee-lot) (koh-pee-lot)
le pilote, le co-pilote

(oh-tehs) (ehr)
l'hôtesse de l'air
stewardess

(toor)
la tour de contrôle
control tower

(ka-myohn)
le camion
truck

L'HÔTESSE **Votre carte d'embarquement,** *(ahn-bar-kuh-mahn)* **s'il vous plaît.**	Your boarding pass, please.
LE TOURISTE **Oui . . . Je l'ai . . . Mais où est-elle?**	Yes . . . I have it . . . but where is it?
L'HÔTESSE **Dépêchez-vous, s'il vous plaît.** *(day-pay-shay)*	Hurry up, please.
Il y a une longue queue derrière vous. *(lohng) (kūh)*	There is a long line behind you.
LE TOURISTE (Il fouille dans toutes ses poches.) *(foo-y)*	(He searches through all his pockets.)
L'HÔTESSE **Monsieur, l'avion part dans quelques minutes.** *(mee-newt)*	Sir, the plane is leaving in a few minutes.
LE TOURISTE **Ça y est! La voilà enfin!**	There we are! Here it is at last!

L'AVION

The Plane

(ew-bloh) **le hublot** porthole

(ewr-zhahns) **la sortie d'urgence** emergency exit

(sehk-syohn) (few-muhr) **la section fumeurs** smoking section

(nohn) (few-mūhr) **la section non-fumeurs** non-smoking section

(ay-kee-pahzh) **l'équipage** crew

(day-ko-lazh) **le décollage** takeoff

(ka-been) **la cabine** cabin

(pla-toh) **le plateau** tray

(fewz-lahzh) **le fuselage**

(peest) **la piste** runway

(a-teh-ree-sahzh) **l'atterrissage** landing

(san-tewr) (say-kew-ree-tay) **la ceinture de sécurité** safety-belt

(pa-sa-zhay) (pa-sa-zhehr) **le passager, la passagère**

(syehzh) **le siège** seat

LE PILOTE	**Nous allons décoller** *(day-ko-lay)* **dans quelques minutes. Veuillez** *(vuh-yay)* **attacher vos ceintures de sécurité et ne pas fumer.**	We are going to take off in a few minutes. Please fasten your seat belts and refrain from smoking.

(Later)

LE PILOTE	**Nous allons atterrir à Cannes à quatorze heures trente. Nous volons à une altitude** *(al-tee-tewd)* **de dix mille mètres. Le temps à Cannes est nuageux et pluvieux** *(plew-vyūh)* **et la température est trente-et-un degrés Centigrade** *(sahn-tee-grad)*.	We are going to land in Cannes at 2:30 P.M. We are flying at an altitude of 10,000 meters. The weather in Cannes is cloudy and rainy. And the temperature is 31 degrees Celsius.
PREMIER PASSAGER	**Mademoiselle, est-ce que vous servez un déjeuner** *(day-zhūh-nay)* (lunch)**?**	Miss, do you serve lunch?
L'HOTESSE	**Je vous l'apporte** *(a-port)* **dans un instant.**	I'll bring it to you in a moment.
DEUXIÈME PASSAGER	**Chic!** *(sheek)* **J'adore manger en avion. Ça fait passer** *(pah-say)* **le temps.**	Good! I love eating on the plane. It makes the time pass quickly.
PREMIER PASSAGER	**Mademoiselle! Je voudrais une boisson** *(bwa-sohn)*, **s'il vous plaît.**	Miss! I would like a drink, please.
L'HÔTESSE	**Tout** *(toot)* **de suite** *(sweet)*.	Right away.

(Later)

PREMIER PASSAGER **J'ai sommeil.**	I'm sleepy.
Mademoiselle, pourriez-vous me	Miss, can you give me
(koo-vehr-tewr) (sew-play-mahn-tehr) **donner une couverture supplémentaire?**	an extra blanket?
(day-rahnzh) (ay-tan) (lew-myehr) **Ça vous dérange si j'éteins la lumière?**	Does it bother you if I turn off the light?
(rohnfl) DEUXIÈME PASSAGER **Mon Dieu! Il ronfle**	My God! He is already snoring!
déjà! Et moi qui ne peux jamais	And I can never
dormir en avion!	sleep on planes!

Can you give the French equivalent for these expressions?

1. Your boarding pass, please.
2. I have it.
3. Hurry up.
4. Right away.
5. I'm sleepy.

Encore des verbes

More verbs

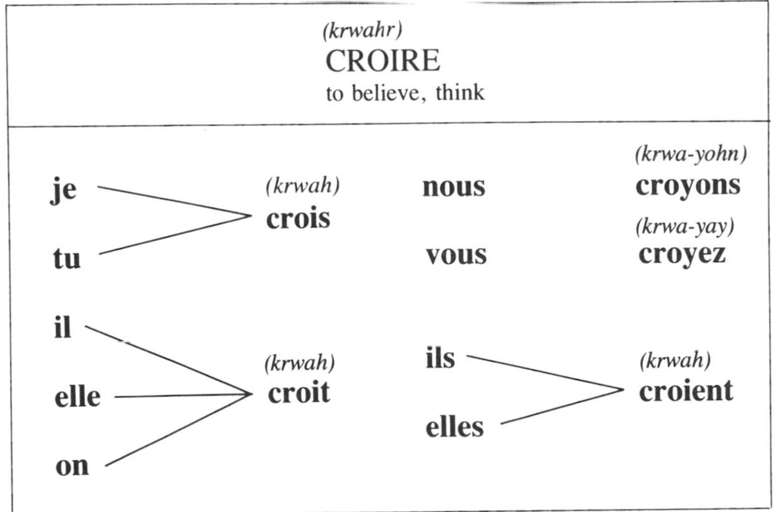

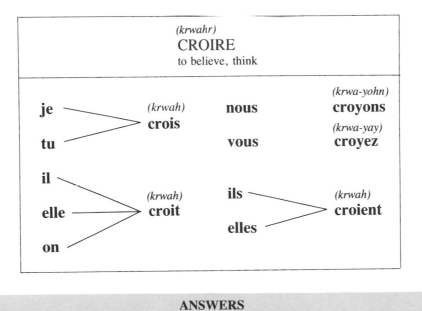

(krwahr)
CROIRE
to believe, think

je, **tu**	*(krwah)* **crois**	**nous**	*(krwa-yohn)* **croyons**
		vous	*(krwa-yay)* **croyez**
il, **elle**, **on**	*(krwah)* **croit**	**ils**, **elles**	*(krwah)* **croient**

ANSWERS

Equivalents **1.** Votre carte d'embarquement, s'il vous plaît. **2.** Je l'ai. **3.** Dépêchez-vous. **4.** Tout de suite. **5.** J'ai sommeil.

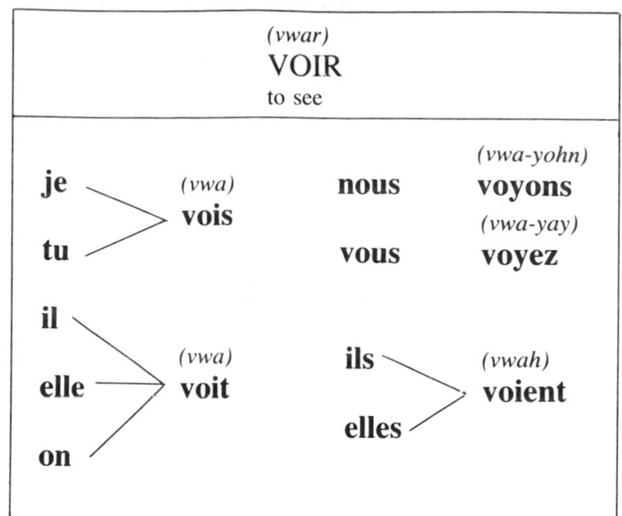

(vwar)
VOIR
to see

je, tu	*(vwa)* **vois**	**nous**	*(vwa-yohn)* **voyons**
		vous	*(vwa-yay)* **voyez**
il, elle, on	*(vwa)* **voit**	**ils, elles**	*(vwah)* **voient**

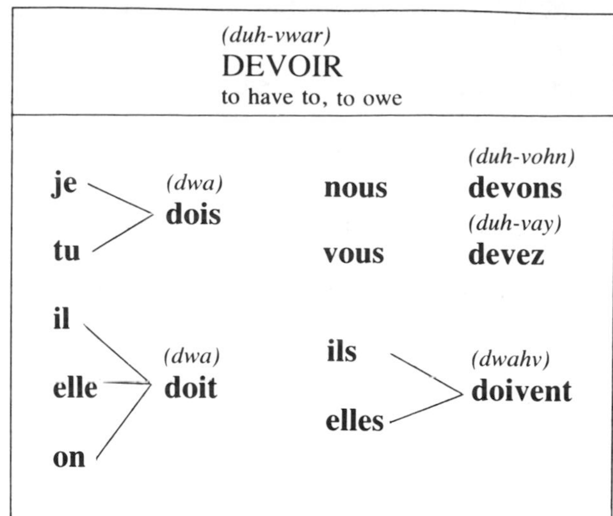

(duh-vwar)
DEVOIR
to have to, to owe

je, tu	*(dwa)* **dois**	**nous**	*(duh-vohn)* **devons**
		vous	*(duh-vay)* **devez**
il, elle, on	*(dwa)* **doit**	**ils, elles**	*(dwahv)* **doivent**

How about practicing these verbs in sentences:

1. Je ______________________ qu'il va faire beau temps demain.
   believe

2. ______________________-vous ce beau lever du soleil?
   see

3. Nous ______________________ le garçon.
   believe

4. Marc ______________________ qu'il y a un terrain de camping près d'ici.
   believes

5. En France, on ______________________ la Tour Eiffel.
   sees

(gra-mehr)
Un peu de grammaire
Some grammar

The direct object pronouns are:

***me, m'**	me	**nous**	us
te, t' (before a vowel)	you (fam.)	**vous**	you (polite, plural)
le, l' (before a vowel)	it, him	**les**	them
la, l' (before a vowel)	it, her		

*__Me__ becomes **moi** in affirmative commands.

ANSWERS

Verbs (fill ins)
1. crois **2.** Voyez **3.** croyons **4.** croit **5.** voit

They are placed before the verb:

Paul me voit.	Paul sees me.
Paul m'aime.	Paul loves me.
Paul te voit.	Paul sees you.
Paul t'aime.	Paul loves you.
Paul le (la) voit.	Paul sees him (her).

Direct object pronouns replace direct object nouns:

Je regarde [le] film.	I watch the film.
Je [le] regarde.	I watch it.
Il cherche [Anne].	He looks for Anne.
Il [la] cherche.	He looks for her.

Direct object pronouns are placed before the verb except in an affirmative command:

Vous [me] regardez.	You look at me.
Vous [le] prenez.	You take it.
Regardez-[moi].	Look at me.
Prenez-[le].	Take it.

In negative sentences, the word order is:

Je ne [le] regarde pas.	I don't watch it.
Il ne [la] cherche pas.	He does not look for it.

In negative commands, the word order is:

Ne [me] regardez pas.	Don't look at me.
Ne [le] prenez pas.	Don't take it.

Replace the noun by a pronoun as in the example which follows:

Je prends le livre.	**Je le prends.**
Nous regardons la télévision.	1. **Nous** ______________ **regardons.**
J'aime les films.	2. **Je** ______________ **aime.**

ANSWERS

Pronouns **1.** la **2.** les

J'apporte le dîner. — 3. **Je** ____________ **apporte.**

Tu connais François Mitterand? — 4. **Tu** ____________**?**

Il n'aime pas ce film. — 5. **Il ne** ____________ **aime pas.**

Je ne comprends pas les exercices. — 6. **Je ne** ____________ **comprends pas.**

Regardez les garçons! — 7. **Regardez-**____________**!**

(foh-toh)
Prenez la photo! — 8. **Prenez-**____________**!**

(ad-mee-ray) *(mohn-ta-nyuh)*
Admirez les montagnes! — 9. **Admirez-**____________**!**

(veel)
En ville
In the city

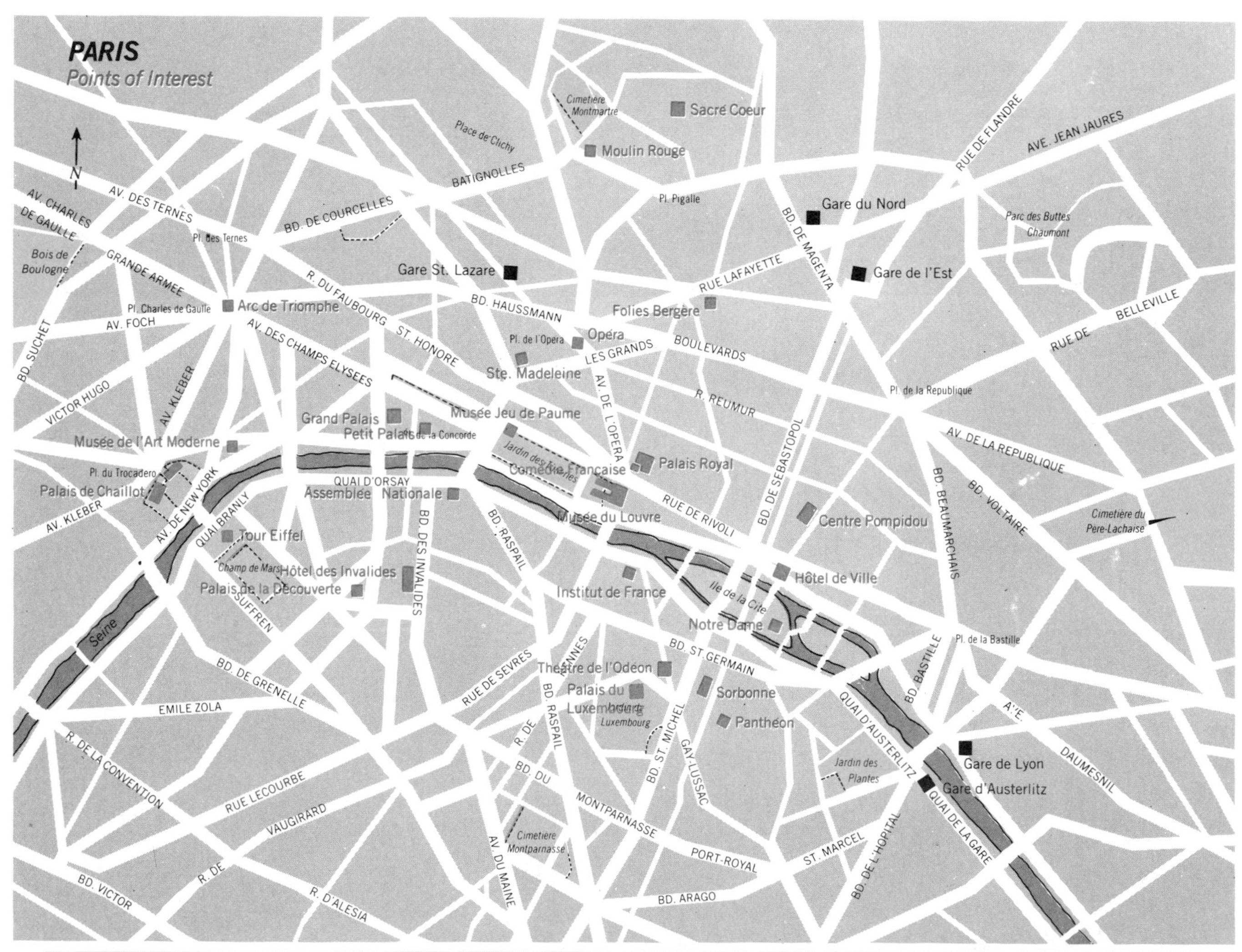

ANSWERS

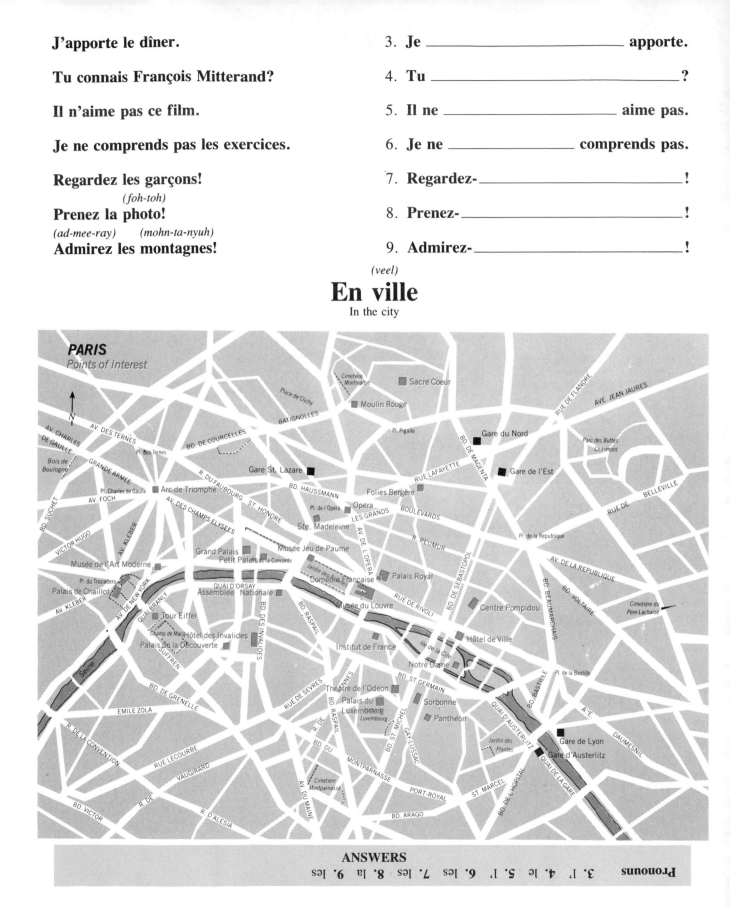

Pronouns **3.** l' **4.** le **5.** l' **6.** les **7.** les **8.** la **9.** les

Back in Paris, our tourist decides to do some sightseeing.

LE TOURISTE **Pardon, Monsieur.**	Excuse me, Sir.
Pouvez-vous me dire où se trouve le (is found)	Can you tell me where the
(zhew) (pom) **"Jus de Pomme"?**	"Apple Juice" is?
(pa-ree-zyan) (kwa) LE PARISIEN **Le quoi?**	The what?
(say-lehbr) LE TOURISTE **Mais oui! Le célèbre**	But yes! The famous
(mew-zay) (ta-bloh) **musée qui a tous les tableaux**	museum which has all
(an-preh-syo-neest) **impressionnistes.**	the Impressionist paintings.
(zhūh) LE PARISIEN **Vous voulez dire le Jeu**	You mean the Jeu
(pohm) (zhews-tuh-mahn) **de Paume? Je vais justement dans cette**	de Paume? I happen to be going in that
(dee-rehk-syohn) (mohn-tray) **direction. Je vais vous montrer.**	direction. I'll show you.
(eh-mahbl) LE TOURISTE **Vous êtes très aimable.**	You are very kind.
(dohtr) LE PARISIEN **Avez-vous visité d'autres**	Have you visited other
(mo-new-mahn) **monuments?**	monuments?
LE TOURISTE **Oui. La magnifique**	Yes. The magnificent
Cathédrale de Notre-Dame et la Sainte	Notre Dame and Sainte
Chapelle. Demain matin je vais faire	Chapelle. Tomorrow morning I'll tour
(oh-toh-kar) **le tour de la ville en autocar et**	the city by bus and
demain après-midi je vais prendre un	tomorrow afternoon I'll take a
(ba-toh) (moosh) (sehn) **bateau-mouche sur la Seine. Je**	bateau-mouche on the Seine. I sightseeing barge
(kohnt) **compte aussi aller au Louvre,**	also intend to go to the Louvre,
naturellement.	of course.
LE PARISIEN **Avez-vous vu des**	Have you seen any
(plahzh) **plages et des montagnes?**	beaches and mountains?

LE TOURISTE **Je suis allé à Cannes et à Nice.**	I have been to Cannes and Nice.
(ruh-vuh-neer) **J'espère revenir une autre fois pour**	I hope to come back another time to
voyager dans les Alpes. Je voudrais	travel in the Alps. I would like
(tay-lay-fay-reek) **prendre le téléphérique de**	to take the Aiguille du Midi cable car.
(ay-gwee-y) (mee-dee) **l'Aiguille du Midi.**	
LE PARISIEN **Voilà le Jeu de Paume.**	Here is the Jeu de Paume!
(say-zhoor) **Au revoir et bon séjour!**	Good-bye, have a pleasant stay!
LE TOURISTE (à lui-même) **Que les**	How friendly the
Parisiens sont aimables!	Parisians are!

Can you match the questions in the left column with the answers in the right column?

1. Avez-vous visité d'autres monuments?
2. Avez-vous vu des plages?
3. Comment aller au Jeu de Paumes?
4. Qu-est-ce que vous allez faire demain matin?
5. Quel musée a des tableaux impressionistes?

A. Je suis allé à Cannes et à Nice.
B. Le Jeu de Paume a des tableaux impressionistes.
C. Oui, la Cathédrale de Notre-Dame et la Sainte Chapelle.
D. Demain matin je vais faire le tour de la ville en autocar.
E. Je vais justement dans cette direction.

ANSWERS

Matching 1. C 2. A 3. E 4. D 5. B

ENTERTAINMENT

(dees-trak-syohn)
Les Distractions

12 | (tay-ahtr) **Le théâtre** theater | (see-nay-ma) **le cinéma** movies | (feht) **les jours de fête** holidays

Jack and Suzanne are a middle-aged couple from Portland, Maine, who for the first time take a trip to France. They like the theater. It is their second day in Paris. Being of French descent, they both speak French quite well. "Not one word of English during our vacation," they decide.

LE THÉÂTRE

Theater

À L'HÔTEL

JACQUES	**Qu'est-ce que tu as envie** (ahn-vee) **de faire ce soir?**	What do you feel like doing tonight?
SUZANNE	**On pourrait aller au théâtre? Il paraît qu'il y a plus de 55 salles à Paris.**	We could go to the theater. It seems there are more than 55 theaters in Paris.
JACQUES	**On donne *Phèdre*** (fehdr) **de Racine** (ra-seen) **à la Comédie** (ko-may-dee) **Française. Mais c'est samedi et il ne reste probablement que des places** (plas) **au poulailler** (poo-la-yay).	They are giving *Phèdre* by Racine is playing at the Comédie-Française. But it's Saturday and the only seats left are probably in the chicken coop.

SUZANNE	**Qu'est-ce que c'est que ça?**	What's that?
JACQUES	*(bal-kohn) (ahn) (oh)* **Le quatrième balcon, tout en haut.**	The 4th balcony, way up.
	(fo-lee) **Est-ce que tu veux aller aux Folies-** *(ber-zhehr)* **Bergère?**	Do you want to go to the Folies- Bergère?
SUZANNE	**Ah non! C'est pour les touristes.**	No no! That's for tourists.
	(shahn-so-nyay) **On pourrait aller voir un chansonnier** **à Pigalle?**	We could go and see a stand-up comic at Pigalle.
JACQUES	*(shoo)* **Mais, mon chou, ces gens-là parlent** *(vee-tehs)* **à toute vitesse!**	But, my darling, those people speak horribly fast!
SUZANNE	**Dans ce cas, peut-être un bon** *(feelm)* **film français. . . .**	In that case, maybe a good French film. . . .
JACQUES	*(ee-day)* **Bonne idée!**	Good idea!
	(prom-nohn) **Promenons-nous sur les Champs-Elysées.**	Let's walk on the Champs-Elysees.
	Et s'il n'y a pas de bon film, *(san-pluh-mahn)* **nous allons simplement** *(vehr)* **prendre un verre dans un café.**	And if there is no good film, we'll simply have a drink in a cafe.

Answer these questions based on the dialogue:

1. Qu'est-ce que Marie a envie de faire ce soir? ______
2. Qu'est-ce qu'on donne? ______
3. Qu'est-ce que c'est que "le poulailler"? ______
4. Pourquoi Marc, n'a-t-il pas envie d'aller voir un chansonnier? ______
5. Quelle est la bonne idée de Marie? ______

ANSWERS

Dialogue **1.** Marie a envie d'aller au théâtre. **2.** On donne Phèdre de Racine. **3.** C'est le quatrième balcon, tout en haut. **4.** Ces gens-là parlent à toute vitesse. **5.** La bonne idée est de voir un bon film.

See how similar these words are:

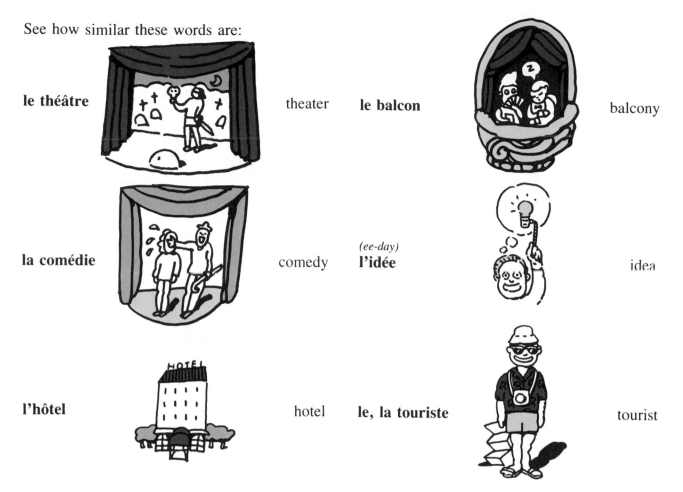

le théâtre  theater

le balcon  balcony

la comédie  comedy

(ee-day)
l'idée  idea

l'hôtel 

hotel

le, la touriste  tourist

If you go to the theater or the movies in France (and other European countries), be prepared to give a small *(poor-bwar)* **pourboire** to the *(oo-vrūhz)* **ouvreuse** (woman usher) after she has led you to your seat. At the movies, there is usually an *(ahn) (trakt)* **entr'acte** (intermission) during which advertisements are projected on the screen.

(pūh) (tew) (muh) (do-nay) (uhn) (pūh) (dahr-zhan)

Peux-tu me donner un peu d'argent?

Can you give a little money . . . to me?

Indirect Object Pronouns			
* **me, m'**	to me	**nous**	to us
te, t'	to you (fam.)	**vous**	to you (polite, plur.)
lui	to him, to her	**leur**	to them
se	to himself, to herself	**se**	to themselves

*__Me__ becomes **moi** in an affirmative command.

The chart below will show you how the direct and indirect pronouns are placed in sentences:

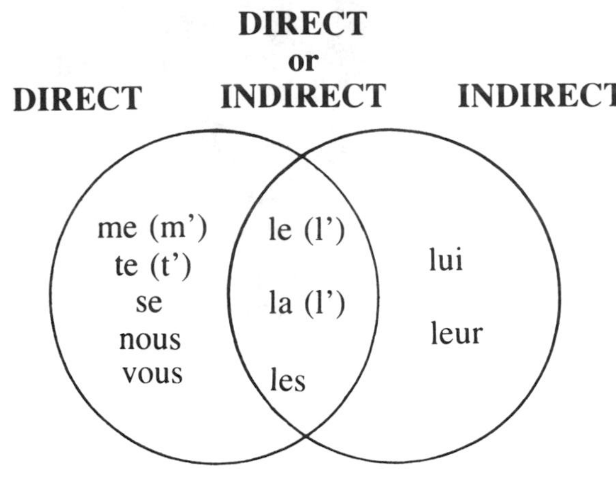

Indirect object nouns are preceded by a form of à (TO): (à, à la, à l', au, aux). Indirect object pronouns may replace indirect object nouns:

Je parle [à Anne].
I speak to Anne.

Je [lui] parle.
I speak to her.

Il parle [au garçon].
He speaks to the boy.

Il [lui] parle.
He speaks to him.

Vous parlez [aux hommes].
You speak to the men.

Vous [leur] parlez.
You speak to them.

Indirect object pronouns are placed before the verb except in an affirmative command:

Vous [lui] parlez.
You speak to him.

Vous ne [lui] parlez pas.
You don't speak to him.

Ne [lui] parlez pas!
Don't speak to him!

Vous [me] parlez.
You speak to me.

Vous ne [me] parlez pas.
You don't speak to me.

Ne [me] parlez pas!
Don't speak to me!

BUT

Parlez-[lui]!
Speak to him!

Parlez-[moi]!
Speak to me!

Replace the indirect object noun with the correct pronoun and then write the sentence.

1. Je parle *à Georges*. ____________________

2. Il n' écrit pas *au garçon*. ____________________
   writes

3. Ne lisez pas *aux enfants*. ____________________
   reads

4. Elle parle *à Henri et à Michel*. ____________________

5. Parlez *au docteur*. ____________________

Since ME, TE, NOUS, VOUS may be direct object pronouns, indirect object pronouns or reflexive pronouns, their use is relatively easy. For the other pronouns just remember:

le—him, it	lui—to him, to her	se—(to) himself
la—her, it	leur—to them	herself
les—them		itself
		themselves

LES JOURS DE FÊTE
Holidays

JACQUES **C'est intéressant** *(an-tay-reh-sahn)* **de comparer** *(kohn-pa-ray)* **les fêtes françaises avec les fêtes américaines. Six jours après le Nouvel** *(noo-vehl)* **An** *(ahn)*, **les Français célèbrent l'Épiphanie** *(ay-pee-fa-nee)*, **la fête des rois** *(rwah)* **mages** *(mahzh)*.

It's interesting to compare the French holidays with the American ones. Six days after New Year's Day, the French celebrate the Epiphany, the feast of the three kings.

SUZANNE **Peut-être qu'ils ont besoin d'un jour de congé** *(kohn-zhay)* **quelques jours après le réveillon** *(ray-veh-yohn)* **. . .**

Maybe they need a holiday a few days after the holiday meal . . .

ANSWERS

Indirect Object Pronouns **1.** Je lui parle. **2.** Il ne lui écrit pas. **3.** Ne leur lisez pas. **4.** Elle leur parle. **5.** Parlez-lui.

	(pahk)	
JACQUES	**Et à Pâques, ils ont congé le Jeudi**	And at Easter time, they have days off on Good
	Saint, le Vendredi Saint et le Lundi de	Thursday, Good Friday and Easter Monday.
	(pohn)	
	Pâques. Ils font le pont et ont presque	They take a long weekend and have almost
	une semaine de vacances! Ensuite il y	a week's vacation! Then there is
	(a-sahn-syohn) *(pahnt-koht)*	
	a l'Ascension puis la Pentecôte . . .	Ascension Day, then Pentecost Day . . .
	(prehsk)	
SUZANNE	**. . . et c'est presque l'été et les**	. . . and it's almost summer and the
	grandes vacances.	big vacation.
JACQUES	**Exactement. Au mois d'août.**	Exactly. In August.
SUZANNE	**Est-ce qu'on célèbre la Journée du**	Do they celebrate Labor Day?
	(tra-vah-y)	
	Travail?	
JACQUES	**Oui, le premier mai.**	Yes, on May 1st.
SUZANNE	**Et en automne?**	And in the fall?
	(ahr-mees-tees)	
JACQUES	**Il y a la fête de l'Armistice le 11**	There is Armistice Day on November 11 and All
	(too-san)	
	novembre et la Toussaint le premier	Saints Day on November 1.
	(pro-poh)	
	novembre. À propos, sais-tu pourquoi	By the way, do you know why
	nous ne devons pas apporter de	we mustn't bring
	(kry-zahn-tehm)	
	chrysanthèmes à ta tante Sophie	mums to your Aunt Sophie
	demain?	tomorrow?
SUZANNE	**Pourquoi?**	Why?
JACQUES	**Parce que la Toussaint est une**	Because All Saints Day is a
	(so-la-nehl) *(mor)*	
	journée solennelle pour les morts et	solemn day for the dead and
	les gens apportent des chrysanthèmes	people bring mums
	(seem-tyehr)	
	au cimetière.	to the cemetery.
	(vreh-mahn)	
SUZANNE	**Vraiment?**	Really?
	(toot) *(ma-nyehr)*	
JACQUES	**De toute manière, peu après la**	Anyway, shortly after All Saints Day
	(no-ehl)	
	Toussaint, il y a Noël, et un autre réveillon!	there is Christmas, and another big feast!

Fill in the correct French word:

1. À Paris, il y a plus de ______________ théâtres.
   55

2. C'est ______________ de comparer les fêtes françaises avec les fêtes américaines.
   interesting

3. Jacques et Suzanne vont voir un film ______________.
   French

4. Qui est-ce que Jacques et Suzanne vont voir demain?

   Ils vont voir ______________.
   Aunt Sophie

5. Si vous êtes invités à dîner chez *(shay)* une famille française, il ne faut pas apporter de ______________.
   chez: at the home of
   Chrysanthemums

6. La fête de l'Armistice est ______________.
   November 11

7. La Toussaint est une ______________ solennelle.
   day

8. Les Français ont beaucoup de jours de ______________.
   off

9. Jacques et Suzanne ______________ le théâtre.
   like

10. Noël ______________.
    is December 25

ANSWERS

Fill in blanks **1.** cinquante-cinq **2.** intéressant **3.** français **4.** Tante Sophie **5.** chrysanthèmes **6.** le onze novembre **7.** journée **8.** congé **9.** aiment **10.** est le vingt-cinq décembre.

13 Les sports

(spor)

Sports

LA MARCHE ET LE JOGGING

(marsh) (zho-geen)

Hiking and Jogging

(ruh-por-tehr) (luh-for) UN REPORTER **Monsieur Lefort?**	Mr. Lefort?
LEFORT **Oui, c'est moi.**	Yes, that's me.
(sharl) (la-plewm) LE REPORTER **Je suis Charles Laplume.**	I am Charles Laplume.
(ay-kree) (zhoor-nal) **J'écris pour le journal *France-Amérique*.**	I write for the paper *France-Amerique*.
(ahn-shahn-tay) LEFORT **Enchanté!**	Delighted!
(mwa) (mehm) LE REPORTER **Moi de même.**	Me too.
(an-tehr-vyoo) LEFORT **Vous voulez une interview?**	You want an interview?
LE REPORTER **Exactement.**	Exactly.
(sew-zheh) LEFORT **À quel sujet?**	About what?
(pray-zee-dahn) LE REPORTER **Comme président de la**	As president of the
(leeg) (a-ma-tūhr) **Ligue Française des amateurs de**	French Amateur Sport League,
(sehr-teh n-mahn) **sport, vous êtes certainement très**	you are certainly very

(koo-rahn) (kohn-sehrn)	
au courant de tout ce qui concerne le	well informed about everything concerning
(see-kleesm)	
jogging, la marche, le cyclisme et la	jogging, hiking, cycling and
(na-ta-syohn)	
natation.	swimming.
(fla-tay)	
LEFORT **Vous me flattez.**	You flatter me.
LE REPORTER **Je voudrais écrire un article**	I would like to write an article
(lad-sew)	
là-dessus.	about that.
(a-lay) (zee) (swee-vay)	
LEFORT **Allez-y! Et suivez-moi!**	Go ahead! And follow me!
LE REPORTER **D'abord, le jogging.**	First, jogging.
(po-pew-lehr)	
LEFORT **Oui, c'est très populaire ici.**	Yes, it's very popular here.
Comme beaucoup d'autres choses, ça	Like many other things, it
vient naturellement d'Amérique et	comes from America, and
(mant-nahn)	
maintenant les Européens en sont	now the Europeans are
(foo)	
fous.	crazy about it.
(an-por-tohn) (moh)	
Nous importons même le mot. On ne	We even import the word.
(koor)	
court plus, on fait du jogging.	One doesn't run any more, one jogs.
LE REPORTER **Vous aussi, Monsieur?**	You too, Sir?
LEFORT **Et comment! Le jogging est un**	And how! Jogging is a
(san) (mar-shay) (sūhl)	
sport sain et bon marché. Les seuls	healthy and inexpensive sport. The only
(an-vehs-tees-mahn) (sweht-shūhrt)	
investissements sont une sweatshirt	investments are a sweat shirt
et une paire de	and a pair of
(shoh-sewr)	
chaussures de	comfortable jogging shoes.
jogging	
confortables.	
LE REPORTER **Et que pensez-vous de la**	And what do you think about
marche?	hiking?

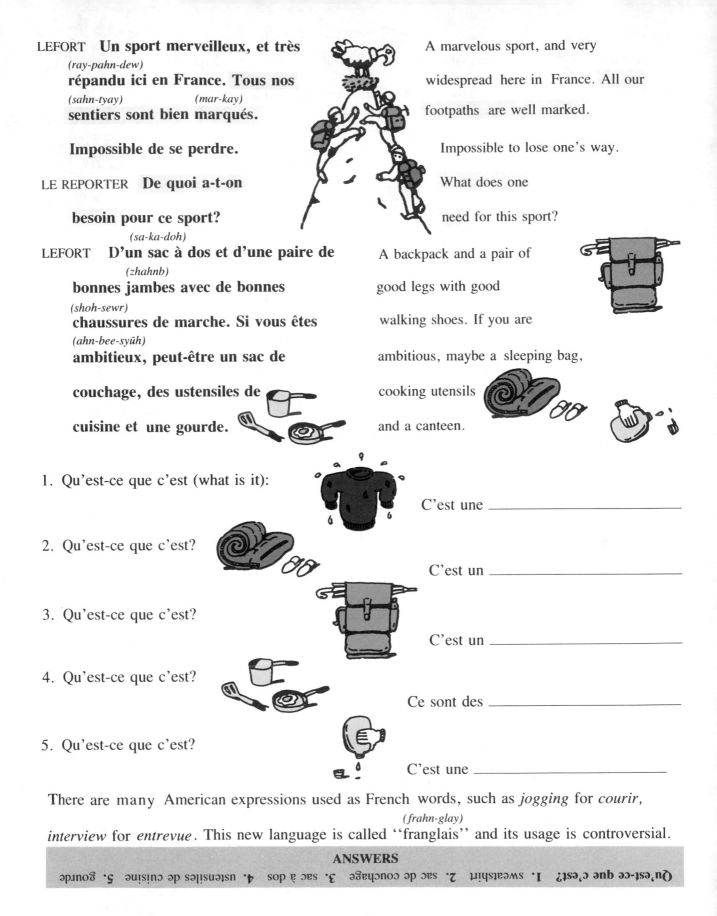

LEFORT **Un sport merveilleux, et très**
(ray-pahn-dew)
répandu ici en France. Tous nos
(sahn-tyay) *(mar-kay)*
sentiers sont bien marqués.

Impossible de se perdre.

A marvelous sport, and very widespread here in France. All our footpaths are well marked.

Impossible to lose one's way.

LE REPORTER **De quoi a-t-on besoin pour ce sport?**

What does one need for this sport?

(sa-ka-doh)
LEFORT **D'un sac à dos et d'une paire de**
(zhahnb)
bonnes jambes avec de bonnes
(shoh-sewr)
chaussures de marche. Si vous êtes
(ahn-bee-syūh)
ambitieux, peut-être un sac de couchage, des ustensiles de cuisine et une gourde.

A backpack and a pair of good legs with good walking shoes. If you are ambitious, maybe a sleeping bag, cooking utensils and a canteen.

1. Qu'est-ce que c'est (what is it):

   C'est une ____________________

2. Qu'est-ce que c'est?

   C'est un ____________________

3. Qu'est-ce que c'est?

   C'est un ____________________

4. Qu'est-ce que c'est?

   Ce sont des ____________________

5. Qu'est-ce que c'est?

   C'est une ____________________

There are many American expressions used as French words, such as *jogging* for *courir*, *interview* for *entrevue*. This new language is called *(frahn-glay)* "franglais" and its usage is controversial.

ANSWERS

Qu'est-ce que c'est? 1. sweatshirt **2.** sac de couchage **3.** sac à dos **4.** ustensiles de cuisine **5.** gourde

Retenez
Remember

Que pensez-vous de la marche? | **QUE, QU' (before a vowel)** What | What do you think about hiking?

refers to a thing, but is not preceded by a preposition.

De quoi a-t-on besoin? | **QUOI** What | What does one need? (*lit:* of what does one have need?)

refers to a thing and is preceded by a preposition (de, à, avec, sur).

Encore des verbes
More verbs

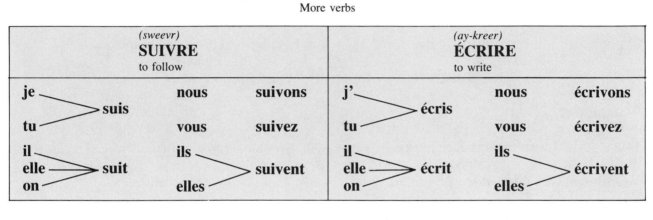

(sweevr) **SUIVRE** to follow		*(ay-kreer)* **ÉCRIRE** to write	
je, tu suis	**nous suivons**	**j', tu écris**	**nous écrivons**
	vous suivez		**vous écrivez**
il, elle, on suit	**ils, elles suivent**	**il, elle, on écrit**	**ils, elles écrivent**

Fill in the blanks with the appropriate form of the verb:

1. Le lundi, j' ________________ toujours à ma mère.
   (write)
2. ________________-moi, je vais vous montrer le Jeu de Paume.
   (follow)
3. Vous ________________ bien en français.
   (write)
4. Charles Laplume ________________ pour France-Amérique.
   (writes)
5. Est-ce que tu vas ________________ à ton frère?
   (write)
6. Nous ________________ des cartes postales. *(kart) (pos-tahl)*
   (write)

ANSWERS

Fill in blanks **1.** écris **2.** Suivez **3.** écrivez **4.** écrit **5.** écrire **6.** écrivons

(see-kleesm) *(na-ta-syohn)*

LE CYCLISME ET LA NATATION

Bicycling and Swimming

LE REPORTER **Que pensez-vous du cyclisme, Monsieur?**

What do you think of bicycle riding, Sir?

(stew-peed) (mwa-yan) (trahns-por) (an-sa-tees-fuh-zahn) (sahn) (zan-tay-reh) (ma-shan) (reh-gluh-mahn) (tehl-mahn) (streekt) (far)

LEFORT **Un sport stupide, un moyen de transport insatisfaisant. C'est sans intérêt. Pas de vitesse, rien. Et à la montée, il faut pousser le machin. Et les règlements sont tellement stricts! Est-ce qu'en Amérique vous devez avoir des phares devant et derrière?**

A stupid sport, unsatisfactory means of transportation. It's without interest. No speed, nothing. And up hill you have to push the thing. And the rules are so strict! In America, do you have to have lights in front and in the rear?

LE REPORTER **Non. Que pensez-vous de la natation?**

No. What do you think of swimming?

(ahn-too-zyast) (dok-tūhr) (dee) (ma-yoh) (ban)

LEFORT **Ah! La natation! Là, je suis enthousiaste. Mon docteur me dit que c'est le meilleur et le plus sain des sports. Et c'est un autre sport bon marché: un maillot de bain, c'est tout ce qu'il faut.**

Ah! Swimming! There, I am enthusiastic. My doctor tells me it's the best and the healthiest of sports. And it's another inexpensive sport: a bathing suit, that's all you need.

(ay-vahn-tew-ehl-mahn) (bee-kee-nee)

LE REPORTER **Éventuellement un bikini.**

Perhaps a bikini.

(lew-neht) (plohn-zhay)

LEFORT **C'est tout . . . Peut-être des lunettes de plongée.**

That's all . . . Maybe diving goggles.

(day-bew-tahn)

LE REPORTER **Comment un débutant commence-t-il ici?**

How does a beginner start here?

(bras)

LEFORT **Avec la brasse. Ensuite viennent**

With the breast stroke. Then come

le crawl et la nage sur le dos. — the crawl and the backstroke.

(ay-prūhv)
LE REPORTER **Vous avez des épreuves** — Do you have tests
(ray-gew-lyehr-mahn)
régulièrement? — regularly?

LEFORT **Absolument. Si on passe l'épreuve** — Absolutely. If someone passes the free-swimming
(fyehr-mahn)
de nage libre, on peut fièrement — test, one can proudly
(por-tay) *(an-seen-y)*
porter un petit insigne sur son maillot — wear a little badge on one's bathing suit.
de bain.

LE REPORTER **Monsieur, je vous remercie** — Sir, I thank you
pour l'interview. — for the interview.

Now let's see if you can remember the adjectives that describe M. Lefort's opinion about these sports:

Selon M. Lefort, le cyclisme est: 1. ______________________
according to
2. ______________________
3. ______________________
4. ______________________

Selon M. Lefort, la natation est: 5. ______________________
6. ______________________

Retenez
Remember

Éventuellement. Watch this word, and how you use it. In French it means *possibly* or *perhaps*. **Actuellement** is another traitor: it means *now*, *at the present time*, not *in fact* or *actually*.

ANSWERS

Opinion **1.** un sport stupide. **2.** un moyen de transport insatisfaisant. **3.** sans intérêt. **4.** sans vitesse. **5.** le meilleur et le plus sain des sports. **6.** un autre sport bon marché.

Il faut, an expression you have encountered a few times before, is very common and very useful. It means: *It is necessary*, *one must*, *you have to*, *one needs to*, and may be followed by an infinitive:

C'est tout ce qu'il faut.	That's all that's required.
Il faut pousser le machin.	It's necessary to push the thing.

In the negative, put NE and PAS around FAUT:

Il ne faut pas partir.	It's not necessary to leave. You don't need to leave.

Encore des verbes

More verbs

(koo-reer) COURIR to run		*(deer)* DIRE to say	
je / tu *(koor)* **cours**	**nous** *(koo-rohn)* **courons**	**je / tu** *(dee)* **dis**	**nous** *(dee-zohn)* **disons**
	vous *(koo-ray)* **courez**		**vous** *(deet)* **dites**
il / elle / on *(koor)* **court**	**ils / elles** *(koor)* **courent**	**il / elle / on** *(dee)* **dit**	**ils / elles** *(deez)* **disent**

Give the correct form of the verb.

COURIR

1. Nous ______________ à l'école.
2. Il ______________ vite.
3. ______________-tu au cinéma?
4. Vous ne ______________ pas au marché.

DIRE

1. Que ______________-vous?
2. Je ______________ la vérité.
3. Elles ______________ "Non".
4. Paul ne ______________ pas "Bonjour".

ANSWERS

Verbs **COURIR: 1.** courons **2.** court **3.** Cours **4.** courez
DIRE: 1. dites **2.** dis **3.** disent **4.** dit

ORDERING FOOD

(shah-zee-sahn) *(ruh-pah)*
Choisissant des Repas

14 Les repas / la nourriture

(noo-ree-tewr)
Meals / Food

J'aime manger

I like to eat

You're going to want to taste some French specialties on your trip, whether it's **Pâté de foie gras,** or **coq au vin de Bourgogne,** or **framboises**. So be sure to learn how to request what you'd like. Note below, that you can request some items by saying you'd like *the* or *some* of it, just like in English.

THE		SOME
(sohs) **J'aime** | **la** | **sauce.**		**Je mange** | **de la** | **sauce.**
(loh) (vee-shee) **J'aime** | **l'** | **eau de Vichy.** Vichy water		**Après le déjeuner, je vais boire** | **de l'** | **eau de Vichy.**

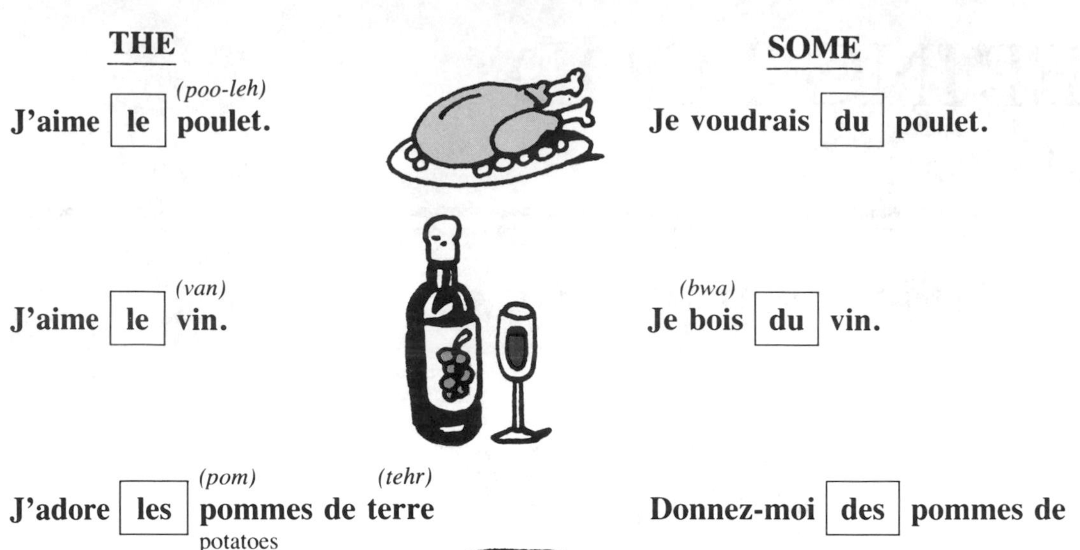

THE	SOME
J'aime **le** *(poo-leh)* poulet.	Je voudrais **du** poulet.
J'aime **le** *(van)* vin.	*(bwa)* Je bois **du** vin.
J'adore **les** *(pom)* pommes de *(tehr)* terre (potatoes) *(freet)* frites (fried).	Donnez-moi **des** pommes de terre frites, s'il vous plaît.

SOME, ANY

Sometimes you just can't eat the whole thing, but you can eat a part of it. Refer to the following chart to choose the form of "SOME" or "ANY" that you use before the noun.

	Singular	Plural
masculine noun (starting with a consonant)	DU	DES
feminine noun (starting with a consonant)	DE LA	DES
masculine or feminine noun (starting with a vowel)	DE L'	DES

Je mange le gâteau.

Je mange du gâteau.

When talking of something you like or dislike in general, use LE, LA, L' or LES.

J'aime la glace.
I like ice cream.

When talking of something you would like a part of, use DE LA, DU or DE L', DES.

Je mange | **de la** | **glace.**

I eat some ice cream.

When the item is countable (potatoes, string beans, strawberries, and so forth—in English, you use the plural), use LES or DES, and UN or UNE if you want one item.

Je n'aime pas | **les** | **légumes.**

I don't like vegetables.

In the negative, simply use DE or D', and no article. (DE means any in a negative sentence.)

Je ne veux pas | **de** | **légumes.**

I don't want any vegetables.

> Try to remember that whenever SOME or ANY is implied, you must use DE LA, DU, DE L' in affirmative sentences, and DE (D') in negative sentences and after expressions of quantity.

Try this:

1. Je fais ______________________ sport.
2. J'adore ______________________ musique (fem.) *(mew-zeek)*
3. Je déteste ______________________ épinards. *(ay-pee-nar)* spinach
4. Les chiens sont ______________________ animaux. *(a-nee-moh)* animals

A little practice? See the pictures of food items and the French words for them. Then decide whether to use LE, LA, L', DU, DE LA, DES, or DE (D' before a vowel).

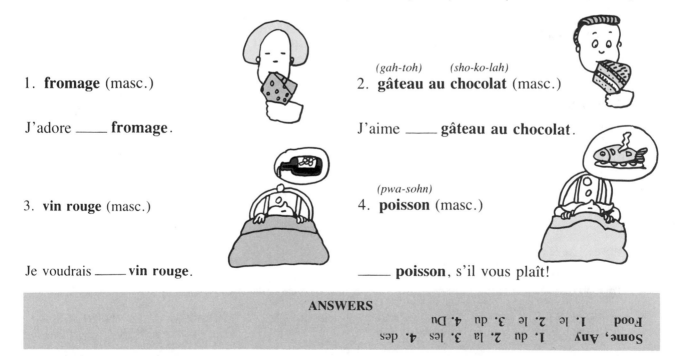

1. **fromage** (masc.)

J'adore ____ **fromage**.

2. *(gah-toh)* *(sho-ko-lah)* **gâteau au chocolat** (masc.)

J'aime ____ **gâteau au chocolat**.

3. **vin rouge** (masc.)

Je voudrais ____ **vin rouge**.

4. *(pwa-sohn)* **poisson** (masc.)

____ **poisson**, s'il vous plaît!

ANSWERS

Some, Any **1.** du **2.** la **3.** les **4.** des

Food **1.** le **2.** le **3.** du **4.** Du

(sa-lad)
5. **salade** (fem.)

6. **eau** (fem.)

J'aimerais ____ **salade**.

J'ai soif! Donnez-moi ____ **eau**, s'il vous plaît.

(lay) (zad-vehrb) (kahn-tee-tay)

Les adverbes de quantité

Adverbs of quantity

Je bois beaucoup de vin.
a lot of

(troh)
Il boit trop de whisky.
too much

(fro-mahzh)
J'ai assez de fromage.
enough — cheese

(soh-see-sohn)
Je voudrais un peu de saucisson.
a little — salami

(em-reh) (an) (toop) (tee) (pūh)
J'aimerais un tout petit peu d' eau.
would like — a tiny little bit

After expressions of quantity, use DE or D' (before a vowel).
Fill in the blanks:

1. Je mange ______________ poulet.
   (a lot of)
2. Il boit ______________ vin.
   (enough)
3. Je voudrais ______________ eau.
   (a little)
4. Elle a ______________ gâteau.
   (too much)
5. Aimerais-tu ______________ sauce?
   (a tiny little bit of)

ANSWERS

Fill in the blanks **1.** beaucoup de **2.** assez de **3.** un peu d' **4.** trop de **5.** un tout petit peu de

Food **5.** de la **6.** de l'

Un nouveau verbe

A new verb

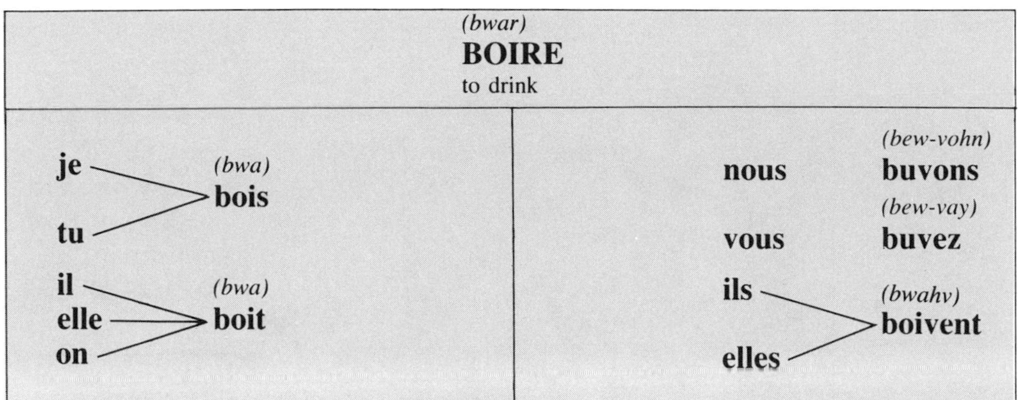

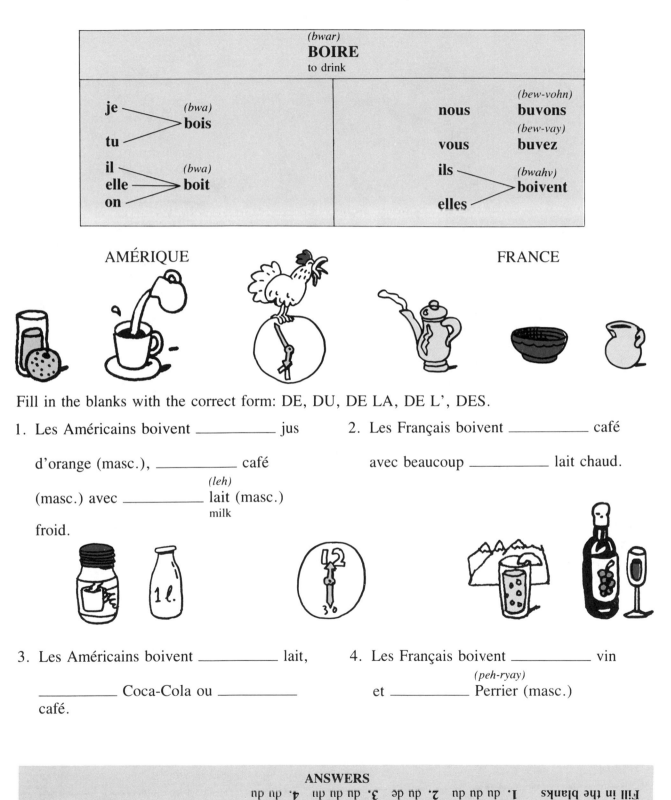

(bwar) **BOIRE** to drink			
je, **tu**	*(bwa)* **bois**	**nous**	*(bew-vohn)* **buvons**
il, **elle**, **on**	*(bwa)* **boit**	**vous**	*(bew-vay)* **buvez**
		ils, **elles**	*(bwahv)* **boivent**

Fill in the blanks with the correct form: DE, DU, DE LA, DE L', DES.

1. Les Américains boivent __________ jus d'orange (masc.), __________ café (masc.) avec __________ *(leh)* lait (masc.) milk froid.

2. Les Français boivent __________ café avec beaucoup __________ lait chaud.

3. Les Américains boivent __________ lait, __________ Coca-Cola ou __________ café.

4. Les Français boivent __________ vin et __________ *(peh-ryay)* Perrier (masc.)

ANSWERS

Fill in the blanks **1.** du du du **2.** du de **3.** du du du **4.** du du

Verbes avec des changements orthographiques
(shahnzh-mahn) (or-to-gra-feek)

Verbs with spelling changes

To keep the ZH sound in verbs that end in -GER (MANGER, CHANGER), it is necessary to add **E** between A, O, or U that follows it.

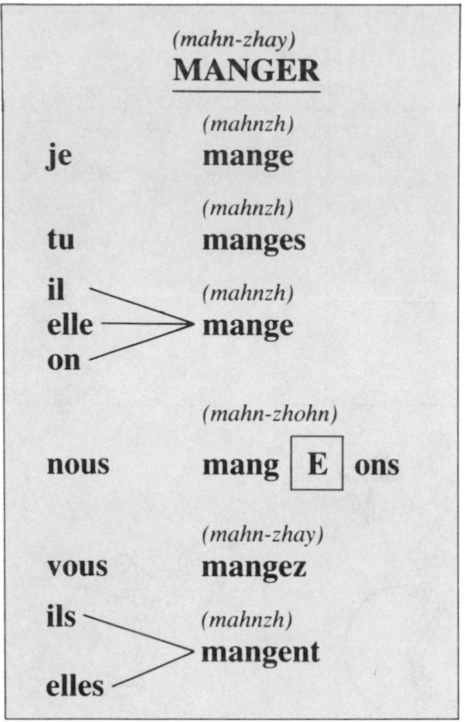

(mahn-zhay)
MANGER

je	*(mahnzh)* **mange**
tu	*(mahnzh)* **manges**
il / elle / on	*(mahnzh)* **mange**
nous	*(mahn-zhohn)* **mang E ons**
vous	*(mahn-zhay)* **mangez**
ils / elles	*(mahnzh)* **mangent**

Something happens also with verbs ending in É or E + consonant + ER, such as PRÉFÉRER:

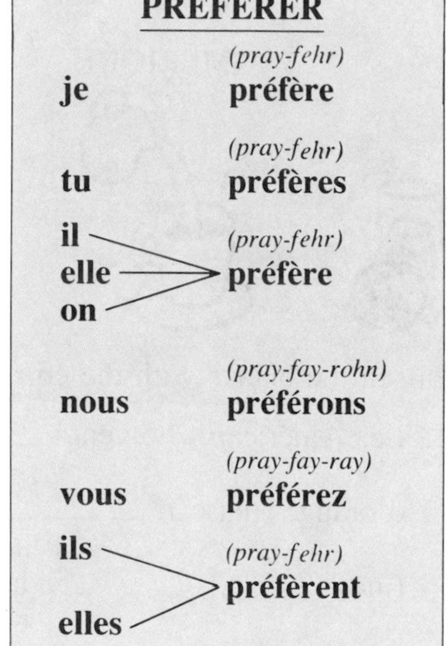

(pray-fay-ray)
PRÉFÉRER

je	*(pray-fehr)* **préfère**
tu	*(pray-fehr)* **préfères**
il / elle / on	*(pray-fehr)* **préfère**
nous	*(pray-fay-rohn)* **préférons**
vous	*(pray-fay-ray)* **préférez**
ils / elles	*(pray-fehr)* **préfèrent**

To keep the S sound in verbs that end in -CER (COMMENCER), it is necessary to add a **Ç** before A, O, or U:

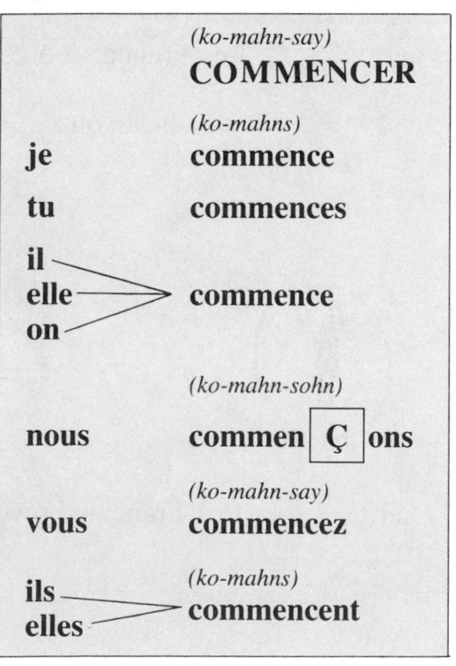

(ko-mahn-say)
COMMENCER

je	*(ko-mahns)* **commence**
tu	**commences**
il / elle / on	**commence**
nous	*(ko-mahn-sohn)* **commen Ç ons**
vous	*(ko-mahn-say)* **commencez**
ils / elles	*(ko-mahns)* **commencent**

Note: ´ is called **accent aigu** *(ak-sahn) (tay-gew)*; ` is called **accent grave** *(grahv)*. Now, let's practice some of the phrases you're going to use as you dine.

1. Les Américains ______________ (eat) de la viande (vyahnd) (meat).

2. Les Français ______________ (prefer) des omelettes.

In France **le déjeuner** (day-zhŭh-nay) (lunch) is still the most important meal in most places. In large cities, however, many people **mangent sur le pouce** (poos) (literally, on the thumb) that is, lightly and quickly, at a McDonald's or other fast food place. Breakfast **(le petit déjeuner)** (puh-tee) (small) consists simply of bread, croissants, or rolls, butter and jam and **café au lait**, and supper **(le dîner)** (dee-nay) is more like lunch in the U.S. But there are many exceptions to the rule.

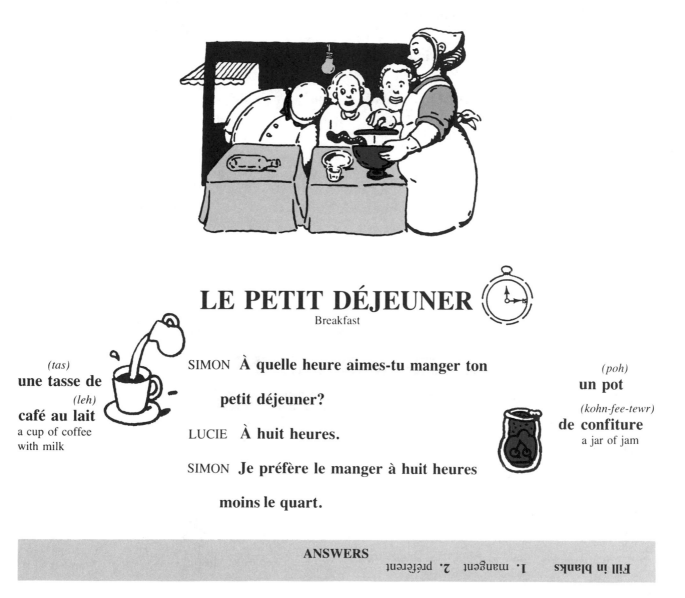

LE PETIT DÉJEUNER

Breakfast

(tas) **une tasse de** (leh) **café au lait**
a cup of coffee with milk

SIMON **À quelle heure aimes-tu manger ton petit déjeuner?**

LUCIE **À huit heures.**

SIMON **Je préfère le manger à huit heures moins le quart.**

(poh) **un pot** (kohn-fee-tewr) **de confiture**
a jar of jam

ANSWERS

Fill in blanks **1.** mangent **2.** préfèrent

(sa-sheh) **un sachet** *(tay)* **de thé**
a tea bag

(tas) **une tasse** **de thé**
a cup of tea

(bŭhr) **le beurre**
butter

LUCIE **Est-ce que tu prends du café au lait ou du café noir?**
black

SIMON **Je n'aime pas le café. Je préfère le** *(tay)* **thé. Ma mère sert toujours du thé.**
tea serves always

LUCIE **Est-ce que tu aimes le pain grillé avec du beurre et de la confiture?**

SIMON **Quelle idée! Dans ma famille, nous mangeons des croissants.**
What an idea

LUCIE **Aimes-tu le jus d'orange?**

SIMON **Oui, mais je ne bois** *(zha-meh)* **jamais de jus de fruit le matin.**
never

LUCIE **Mon Dieu! Comment allons-nous voyager ensemble?**
together

(pan) **du pain** *(gree-yay)* **grillé**
toast

(bree-yuhsh) **les brioches**
breakfast rolls

(vehr) **un verre** **de** *(zhew)* **jus** *(o-rahnzh)* **d'orange**
a glass of orange juice

(toh-maht) **le jus de tomate**
tomato juice

Imagining that you are in France, how would you answer these questions from the dialogue?

1. À quelle heure aimez-vous manger le petit déjeuner?
2. Est-ce que vous prenez du café au lait ou du café noir?
3. Est-ce que vous aimez le pain grillé avec du beurre et de la confiture?
4. Aimez-vous le jus d'orange?

ANSWERS

Dialogue 1. J'aime manger le petit déjeuner à huit heures. **2.** Je n'aime pas le café. Je prends du thé. **3.** J'aime le pain grillé avec du beurre. **4.** Je n'aime pas le jus d'orange.

(tah-bl)

LA TABLE

The Table

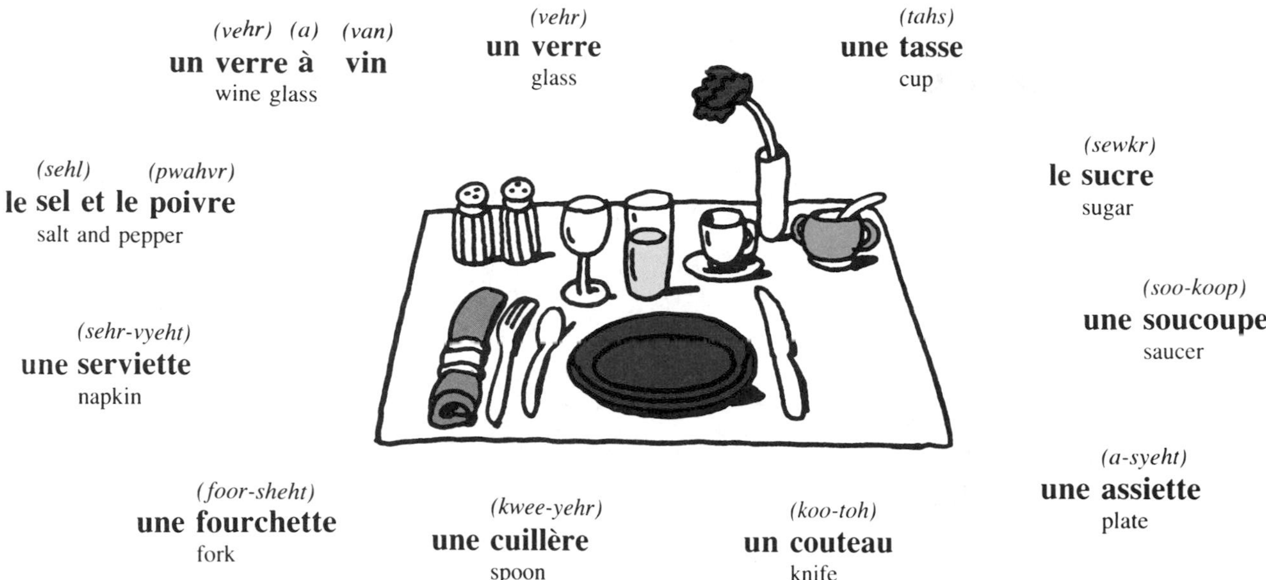

(vo-ka-bew-lehr)

Encore du vocabulaire

More vocabulary

(bwa-sohn)
une boisson — a beverage

(see-trohn) (preh-say)
un citron pressé — a lemonade

(byehr)
une bière — a beer

(ka-raf) (frehsh)
une carafe d'eau fraîche — a carafe of water

(soop)
une soupe — a soup

(day) (or) (dūhvr)
des hors-d'oeuvre — appetizers

(ar-tee-shoh)
des artichauts — artichokes

(as-pehrzh)
des asperges — asparagus

(shahn-pee-nyohn)
des champignons — mushrooms

(ehs-kar-goh)
des escargots — snails

(pah-tay)
du pâté — pate

(ra-dee)
des radis (masc.) — radishes

(soh-see-sohn)
du saucisson — sausage

de la viande — meat

(zhahn-bohn)
du jambon — ham

(la-pan)
du lapin — rabbit

(pwa-sohn) **du poisson**	fish
(poo-leh) **du poulet**	chicken
(ros-beef) **du rosbif**	roast beef
(voh) **du veau**	veal
des légumes	vegetables
(ka-rot) **des carottes**	carrots
(shoo) (flūhr) **du chou-fleur**	cauliflower
(kohn-kohnbr) **du concombre**	cucumber
des épinards	spinach
(day) (a-ree-koh) (vehr) **des haricots verts**	string beans
(o-nyohn) **des oignons**	onions
(ptee) (pwah) **des petits pois**	peas
(ree) **du riz**	rice
(to-mat) **des tomates**	tomatoes
(a-bree-koh) **des abricots**	apricots
(ba-nan) **des bananes**	bananas
(suh-reez) **des cerises**	cherries
(frehz) **des fraises**	strawberries
(frahn-bwahz) **des framboises**	raspberries
(muh-lohn) **du melon**	melon
(o-rahnzh) **des oranges**	oranges
(pahn-pluh-moos) **des pamplemousses**	grapefruit
(pehsh) **des pêches**	peaches
(pwar) **des poires**	pears
(pom) **des pommes**	apples
(reh-zan) **des raisins**	grapes
(sek) **des raisins secs** (secs = dry)	raisins
(dee-zhes-teef) **un digestif**	an after-dinner drink
(lee-kūhr) **une liqueur**	a sweet after-dinner drink (Grand Marnier, etc.)
(ehks-prehs) **un express**	an espresso
(sho-ko-la) **du chocolat**	hot chocolate
(say-ray-ahl) **des céréales**	cereal
(ya-oort) **du yaourt**	yogurt

(ruh-pah) (pran-see-pal)

LE REPAS PRINCIPAL (LE DÉJEUNER)

The Main Meal

Note that cheese is not served as an appetizer and green salad is not served as a first course.

UN REPAS FRANÇAIS

A French Meal

1. **les hors-d'oeuvre**
2. **la soupe**
   (ahn-tray)
3. **l'entrée (viande ou poisson avec légumes)**
4. **la salade**
5. **le fromage**
   (deh-sehr)
6. **le dessert**
   (lee-kūhr)
7. **le café et la liqueur ou le digestif.**

Following are pictures of the courses of a French meal, but they are out of order, and the patron doesn't know where to start. Help him by writing numbers above each to show the right order. Of course, he can start the wine when he likes.

Now can you say the courses aloud, in order and from memory?

ANSWERS

Courses 1. hors-d'oeuvre 2. soupe 3. viande/poisson/légumes 4. salade 5. fromage 6. dessert 7. café

Les restaurants Les pourboires

(rehs-toh-rahn) (poor-bwar)

Tipping

"A LA CUISSE DE GRENOUILLE"

42 RUE DES GOURMETS
Paris 6e

CUISINE RAFFINÉE
P. Lebon, Propriétaire

MENU TOURISTIQUE—145 F

CARTE

HORS-D'OEUVRE

Menu touristique

(va-ryay)
Hors-d'oeuvre variés
assorted

(ko-kee-y) (frwee) (mehr)
Coquille de fruits de mer
shell fruit sea

(teh-reen) (shehf)
Terrine du Chef

(kwees) (gruh-noo-y)
Cuisses de grenouille
legs frog

Soupe du jour

Carte

Hors-d'oeuvre variés 22 F

(shar-kew-tree)
Assiette de charcuterie 28 F
cold cuts

(ko-kee-y) (san) (zhahk)
Coquille St. Jacques 30 F

Terrine Maison 34 F

(grah) (trew-fay)
Pâté de foie gras truffé 75 F
goose liver with truffles

(cok-tehl) (kruh-veht)
Cocktail de crevettes 40 F
shrimps

Soupe du jour 16 F

PLATS DU JOUR

Menu touristique

Steak, frites
French fried potatoes

(ro-nyohn) (voh) (ma-dehr) (ree)
Rognons de veau, sauce madère, riz
kidneys veal madeira

(kok) (rees-leen) (va-pūhr)
Coq au Riesling, pommes vapeur
capon potatoes steamed

Carte

(boor-gon-y)
Coq au vin de Bourgogne 65 F
Burgundy

Coq au Riesling 65 F

(foh) (fee-leh)
Faux-filet pommes rissolées 85 F
Sirloin potatoes

(toor-nuh-doh) (bay-ar-nehz)
Tournedos sauce béarnaise 110 F

(ro-tee) *(ree-so-lay)*
Poulet rôti, pommes rissolées
roasted sauteed

Salade verte

(fee-leh) (sol) (mūh-nyehr)
Filet de sole meunière **65 F**

(vehrt)
Salade verte **17 F**
green

DESSERTS

Au choix:
choice of

(pla-toh)
Plateau de fromages
tray cheese

(krehm) (ka-ra-mehl)
Crème caramel
flan

(tart) (ta-tan)
Tarte Tatin maison
tart

(trahnsh) (na-po-lee-tehn)
Tranche napolitaine
slice

(pla-toh)
Plateau de fromages **25 F**

(pro-fee-trol)
Profiterolles **30 F**

(par-feh) (mees-tehr)
Parfait-Mystère **25 F**

(soo-flay) (grahn) (mar-nyay)
Soufflé au Grand Marnier (2 pers.) **80 F**

(oh) (mee-nay-rahl) (ay-vyahn)
BOISSONS—Eaux minérales (Vichy, Évian)

(roh-zay) (blahn)
Vins (rouge, rosé, blanc):

(mews-ka-deh) (lee)
Muscadet sur lie **55 F**
lees

(boh-zho-leh)
Beaujolais **50 F**

(ka-ra-fohn)
carafon (4 dl) **25 F**

(ka-raf)
carafe (8 dl) **48 F**

(bor-doh) (blahn)
Bordeaux blanc **55 F**

(shah-toh-nūhf) (pap)
Châteauneuf du Pape **105 F**
pope

Service 15% en sus—Boissons non comprises

Note: **SERVICE COMPRIS** on the menu means that the service is included. If service is **EN SUS**, pay a **pourboire** of 15%.

François et Pierre go to a fine restaurant in Paris, one rated with three forks and two stars. (Five forks indicate extremely expensive and posh places, three stars indicate the highest possible quality according to the *Guide Michelin*). The waiter arrives and brings them the menu. They order the dishes they are going to have.

(or) (dūhvr)
les hors-d'oeuvre
appetizers

(soop)
la soupe
soup

(gar-sohn) (meh-syūh) (kart)
LE GARÇON **Messieurs, voici la carte.**
menu

(spay-sya-lee-tay)
Nos spécialités sont les cuisses de
legs
grenouille et le coq au Riesling.
frog capon

FRANÇOIS **Apportez-nous des hors-d'oeuvre et une assiette de charcuterie.**

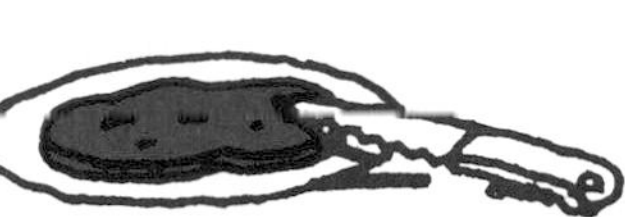

(shar-kew-tree)
la charcuterie
cold cuts

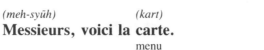

PIERRE **Ensuite je vais prendre un coq au Riesling avec des pommes rissolées.**

(sa-lad)
la salade
salad

(poo-leh)
le poulet
chicken

(fee-leh) (sol)
FRANÇOIS **Pour moi, du poisson: un filet de sole**
(mūh-nyehr)
meunière.

(pom) (freet)
les pommes frites
french fried potatoes

LE GARÇON **De la salade?**

PIERRE **Oui, deux salades vertes. Ensuite, apportez-**
Then bring
nous le plateau de fromages.

(sehl) (pwahvr)
le sel et le poivre
salt and pepper

(pan)
le pain
bread

LE GARÇON **Et comme boisson?**

(meh-zohn)
FRANÇOIS **Du vin de la maison—un carafon de blanc, un de rouge.**

(pwa-sohn)
le poisson
fish

(prahn-dray)
LE GARÇON **Vous prendrez un dessert?**
will take

(reh-zan)
les raisins
grapes

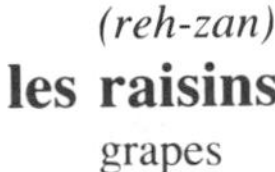

PIERRE **Un soufflé au Grand Marnier pour deux**
(pehr-son)
personnes. Et ensuite deux express et deux
(ko-nyak) (a-dee-syohn)
cognacs. Et l'addition, s'il vous plaît.
check

(fro-mahzh)
le fromage
cheese

(ka-fay)
le café
coffee

(poor-bwar)
FRANÇOIS **(À Pierre) N'oublions pas le pourboire!**
Let's not forget tip

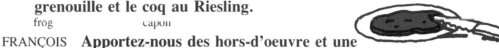

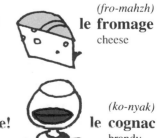

(ko-nyak)
le cognac
brandy

Using the menu, the pictures and the conversation, try filling in the blanks:

(klee-yahn)
1. __________ (The waiter) apporte le menu aux clients.
customers

2. La __________ (specialty) de la maison est

les __________ ____ __________ (frog's legs).

3. François demande des __________ (appetizers).

4. Le garçon __________ (brings) des haricots verts.

(ko-mahnd)
5. Pierre commande ______ ____ __________ (some salad).
orders

(boo-teh-y)
6. Ils vont boire une bouteille de __________ (red wine).
bottle

ANSWERS

Menu **1.** Le garçon **2.** spécialité, cuisses de grenouilles **3.** hors-d'oeuvre **4.** apporte **5.** de la salade **6.** vin rouge

HOW'RE WE DOING?

(ko-mahn) *(sa)* *(va)*
Comment ça va?

This section is designed to help you see where you are at this point. We have covered a lot of ground so far. The following activities and games may help you define your strengths and weaknesses.

Can you match the questions on the left with the answers on the right?

1. Comment vous appelez-vous?
2. Quelle heure est-il?
3. Pouvez-vous nous donner une chambre pour une semaine?
4. Combien coûte un billet aller et retour?
5. À quelle heure aimes-tu prendre ton petit déjeuner?
   (at what)
6. Qu'est-ce que vous allez prendre?
7. Quel temps fait-il?
8. Qu'est-ce qui se passe?
9. Comment allez-vous?
10. Pouvez-vous nous dire où se trouve le musée?

A. Je vais très bien merci, et vous?
B. Il fait un temps superbe.
C. Continuez tout droit jusqu'à la rue Molière.
D. Je m'appelle Mark Smith.
E. Il est midi.
F. Impossible, il n'y a plus de chambres.
G. Cinquante-cinq francs.
H. Je vais prendre un coq au Riesling.
I. À huit heures.
J. Cet idiot a tamponné ma voiture.

Would you use **TU** or **VOUS** when speaking to the following people?

1. votre mari ____________________
2. votre soeur ____________________
3. un agent de police ____________________
4. vos parents ____________________
5. un pompiste ____________________

ANSWERS

TU or VOUS 1. tu 2. tu 3. vous 4. vous 5. vous

Match questions-answers 1. D 2. E 3. F 4. G 5. I 6. H 7. B 8. J 9. A 10. C

Can you fill in the correct French word below?

1. ______________ mère
   His
2. ______________ parents
   Her
3. ______________ automobile
   My
4. ______________ hôtel
   Their
5. ______________ dîner
   Your (polite)

Can you make five questions from the five following statements using EST-CE QUE? Two examples:

Il aime les épinards. Est-ce qu'il aime les épinards ?

Vous aimez manger (quand). Quand est-ce que vous aimez manger ?

1. François et Pierre vont manger (quand). ______________ ?
2. Vous allez en France (pourquoi?). ______________ ?
3. Il y a un terrain de camping près d'ici (où). ______________ ?
4. Tu aimes manger ton petit déjeuner (à quelle heure?). ______________ ?
5. Ils voyagent à Paris (comment). ______________ ?

Magnifique! See how it's all making sense? Now form questions using inversion, for instance:

Vous parlez français (quand?). Quand parlez-vous français ?

Vous allez à Paris (pourquoi?). Pourquoi allez-vous à Paris ?

1. Vous aimez voyager (quand?). ______________ ?
2. Vous allez (comment?). ______________ ?

ANSWERS

Fill in **1.** sa **2.** ses **3.** mon **4.** leur **5.** votre

Make five questions **1.** Quand est-ce que François et Pierre vont manger? **2.** Pourquoi est-ce que vous allez en France? **3.** Où est-ce qu'il y a un terrain de camping près d'ici? **4.** À quelle heure est-ce que tu aimes manger ton petit déjeuner? **5.** Comment est-ce qu'ils voyagent à Paris?

Inverted questions **1.** Quand aimez-vous voyager? **2.** Comment allez-vous?

Amusez-vous as you continue your review.

(Moh) *(krwah-zay)*

Mots croisés

Crossword puzzle

1					2					3		4
					5							
6												
							7					
		8										
					9							10
	11								12			
					13							
									14			
				15								

ACROSS

1. Boy, waiter
5. Plate
6. Ticket
8. To see
9. Spinach
11. Museum
13. Mountain
14. Too much
15. To be

DOWN

2. Naturally
3. Summer
4. The (pl.)
7. Eight
8. Car
10. Salt
12. Pie

ANSWERS

Crossword puzzle ACROSS **1.** garçon **5.** assiette **6.** billet **8.** voir **9.** épinards **11.** musée **13.** montagne **14.** trop **15.** être

DOWN **2.** naturellement **3.** été **4.** les **7.** huit **8.** voiture **10.** sel **12.** tarte

Can you make the following sentences negative?

Example: Je prends du poisson. Je ne prends pas de poisson.

1. Je suis très fatigué. ____________________
2. Vous avez soif. ____________________
3. Je me sens très bien. ____________________
4. J'aime les haricots verts. ____________________
5. La banque est loin d'ici. ____________________

Describe the pictures in simple sentences.
Example:

Le chat est sous la table.

1. Le garçon ____________________

2. M. Smith ____________________

3. Le chien ____________________

4. La souris ____________________

ANSWERS

Negative sentences **1.** Je ne suis pas très fatigué. **2.** Vous n'avez pas soif. **3.** Je ne me sens pas très bien. **4.** Je n'aime pas les haricots verts. **5.** La banque n'est pas loin d'ici.
Describe pictures **1.** Le garçon est à côté de la porte. **2.** M. Smith est dans la cuisine. **3.** Le chien est devant le garage. **4.** La souris est derrière la porte.

Can you order your **déjeuner** at the TROIS CANARDS?

(ka-nar)
AUX TROIS CANARDS
ducks

Plat du Jour:
Menu à 110 francs

Lapin au vin blanc
ou
Steak/pommes frites

Salade verte

Plat du Jour:
Menu à 150 F

(ehs-ka-lop)
Escalopes de veau au madère
ou
(kan-tohn)
Caneton rôti

Salade verte

Desserts—
Crème caramel
(moos)
Mousse au chocolat
Parfait
(sa-ba-yohn)
Sabayon (15 F supplément)

Boissons—eaux minérales (Évian, Vichy)
vins de la maison (rouge, blanc, rosé)
café, thé
(Boissons non comprises)

4 RUE LECOQ
MONBOUDIN

JEAN LAPOULE,
PROPRIÉTAIRE

You don't know what **caneton** and **sabayon** mean, so you ask the waiter.

1. ____?

You find this meal delicious, so you tell the waiter:

2. ____!

At the end of the meal, you ask if the service is included.

3. ____?

Check please!

4. ____!

ANSWERS

Conversation with waiter (sample answers)
1. Qu'est-ce que c'est que ça? **2.** C'est délicieux! **3.** Est-ce que le service est compris? **4.** L'addition, s'il vous plaît!

AT THE STORE

(ma-ga-zan)
Au Magasin

16 Les magasins de confection

(ma-ga-zan) *(kohn-fek-syohn)*

Clothing stores

Tailles et mesures/Couleurs principales

(ta-y) *(muh-zewr)* *(koo-lūhr)* *(pran-see-pal)*

Sizes and measurements / Basic colors

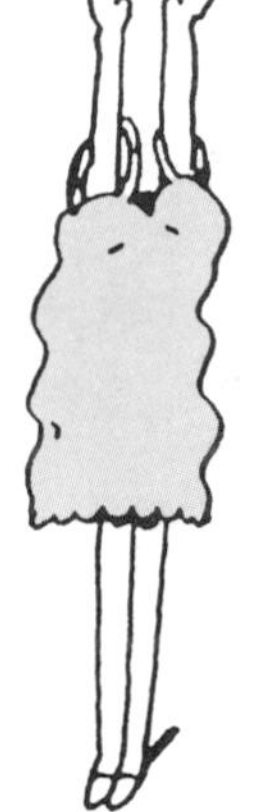

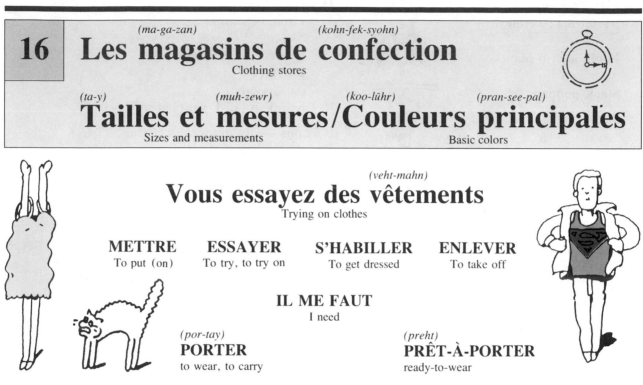

Vous essayez des vêtements

(veht-mahn)

Trying on clothes

METTRE To put (on)

ESSAYER To try, to try on

S'HABILLER To get dressed

ENLEVER To take off

IL ME FAUT I need

(por-tay) **PORTER** to wear, to carry

(preht) **PRÊT-À-PORTER** ready-to-wear

Here are some verbs that will come in very handy if you want to purchase any of the lovely French fashions.

(ahnl-vay) ENLEVER				*(ash-tay)* ACHETER to buy			
j'	*(ahn-lehv)* **enlève**	**nous**	*(ahnl-vohn)* **enlevons**	**j'**	*(a-sheht)* **achète**	**nous**	*(ash-tohn)* **achetons**
tu	*(ahn-lehv)* **enlèves**	**vous**	*(ahnl-vay)* **enlevez**	**tu**	*(a-sheht)* **achètes**	**vous**	*(ash-tay)* **achetez**
il / elle / on	*(ahn-lehv)* **enlève**	**ils / elles**	*(ahn-lehv)* **enlèvent**	**il / elle / on**	*(a-sheht)* **achète**	**ils / elles**	*(a-sheht)* **achètent**

NOTE: **Enlever** and **Acheter** (to buy) undergo spelling changes, like **Préférer**.

The verbs **enlever** and **acheter** (as well as other French verbs whose infinitives end in E + CONSONANT + ER) take an accent grave over the E that precedes a silent E in the **je, tu, il, elle, on, ils, elles** forms.

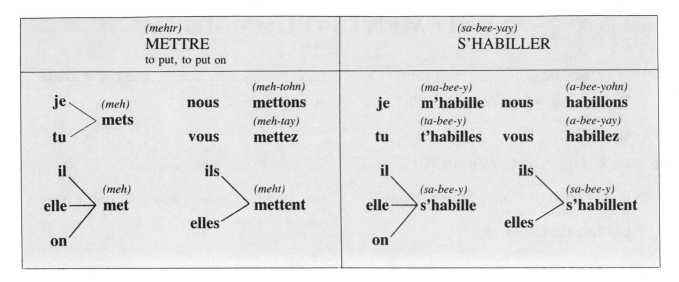

(mehtr) **METTRE** to put, to put on			
je, tu	*(meh)* **mets**	nous	*(meh-tohn)* **mettons**
		vous	*(meh-tay)* **mettez**
il, elle, on	*(meh)* **met**	ils, elles	*(meht)* **mettent**

(sa-bee-yay) **S'HABILLER**			
je	*(ma-bee-y)* **m'habille**	nous	*(a-bee-yohn)* **habillons**
tu	*(ta-bee-y)* **t'habilles**	vous	*(a-bee-yay)* **habillez**
il, elle, on	*(sa-bee-y)* **s'habille**	ils, elles	*(sa-bee-y)* **s'habillent**

S'HABILLER is a reflexive verb (remember SE LAVER and S'AMUSER in Chapter 6):

Give the correct form of the verb for the persons listed.

	JE, J'	NOUS	ILS
1. **enlever**			
2. **acheter**			
3. **mettre**			
4. **s'habiller**			

Il me faut is another idiomatic way of saying I need (you have encountered **J'ai besoin de**). It means, literally, it is necessary to me (to you, to him, etc.). You use the personal pronoun-indirect object and place it between **il** and **faut**:

Il me faut	I need
Il te faut	You (fam.) need
Il lui faut	He/she needs
Il nous faut	We need
Il vous faut	You (pol., plur.) need
Il leur faut	They need

When **aller** is preceded by these indirect object pronouns, its meaning changes to **fit**:

Cette chemise vous va bien! This shirt fits you well (or looks nice on you).

ANSWERS

Verbs **1.** enlève, enlevons, enlèvent **2.** achète, achetons, achètent **3.** mets, mettons, mettent **4.** m'habille, nous habillons, s'habillent

VÊTEMENTS D'HOMME

Men's Clothes

(pahn-ta-lohn) CLIENT **Ces pantalons sont trop petits. Pouvez-vous me montrer la taille** *(oh) (duh-sew)* **au-dessus?**	These trousers are too small. Can you show me the next larger size?
VENDEUR **(apportant des pantalons** *(zhohn) (see-trohn)* **jaunes citron): Voilà. Nous n'avons** (lemon) *(blūh)* **pas votre taille en bleu.**	(Bringing bright yellow trousers): Here you are. We don't have your size in blue.
(oh-rūhr) CLIENT **Quelle horreur!**	How horrible!
VENDEUR **C'est la grande mode en France. Essayez-les! Ils vous vont** *(sew-pehr)* **bien! Super chic!**	It's the fashion in France. Try them on! They look nice on you! Very chic!
CLIENT **Non, vraiment, je ne peux pas** *(por-tay)* **porter ça.**	No, really, I can't wear that.
(ruh-vyan) VENDEUR **(revient avec des pantalons bleus beaucoup trop grands):**	(comes back with blue trousers that are much too big):
(pehr) **Excusez-moi! Essayez cette paire de** *(ehg-zak-tuh-mahn)* **pantalons bleus exactement de votre taille.**	Excuse me! Try this pair of blue trousers which are exactly your size.
(ehr) CLIENT **(l'air épuisé):** (the air)	(looking exhausted):
Ça y est. Qu'est-ce que vous pensez?	There . . . what do you think?
(par-feht-mahn) VENDEUR **Ils vous vont parfaitement!** *(gahn)* **Comme un gant . . .**	They fit you perfectly! Like a glove . . .

Match the French phrases with their English equivalents.

1. Ces pantalons sont trop petits.
2. Pouvez-vous me montrer la taille au-dessus?
3. Nous n'avons pas votre taille.
4. C'est la grande mode en France.
5. Ils vous vont bien.

a. Can you show me the next size?
b. It's the fashion in France.
c. These trousers are too small.
d. They look nice on you.
e. We don't have your size.

(shoh-seht)
des chaussettes
socks

Un villageois va à un magasin de confection pour hommes dans la grande ville.
(villageois: villager)

LE VENDEUR **Vous désirez?**

LE VILLAGEOIS **Je me marie** *(ma-ree)* **ce week-end et il me faut des vêtements neufs** *(nūhf)*. **Il me faut des sous-vêtements** *(soo) (veht-mahn)* **et aussi une chemise** *(shuh-meez)* **blanche** *(blahnsh)* **et une cravate** *(kra-vat)* **noire** *(nwar)*.
(Je me marie: I'm getting married; neufs: new; sous-vêtements: underwear)

LE VENDEUR **Est-ce qu'il vous faut un complet** *(kohn-pleh)*?
(complet: suit)

LE VILLAGEOIS **Oui. Pourriez-vous me montrer un complet noir? Je porte du quarante-quatre.**

LE VENDEUR **Nous n'avons rien dans cette taille. Puis-je vous montrer un veston** *(vehs-tohn)* **et pantalon de sport?**
(rien: nothing; veston: sport jacket)

LE VILLAGEOIS **D'accord. Puis-je les essayer? (Il les essaie.)**
(Puis-je: Can I)

(shuh-meez)
une chemise
shirt

(kra-vat)
une cravate
tie

(pahn-ta-lohn)
des pantalons
trousers

(pew-lo-vehr)
un pullover
sweater

(sha-poh)
un chapeau
hat

(par-duh-sew)
un pardessus
coat

(po-sheht)
une pochette
(moo-shwar)
un mouchoir
handkerchief

(kal-sohn)
un caleçon
undershorts

(ma-yoh) (kor)
un maillot de corps
undershirt

(kas-ket)
une casquette
cap

ANSWERS

Matching 1. c 2. a 3. e 4. b 5. d

(pa-ra-plwee)
un parapluie
umbrella

(an-per-may-ahbl)
un imperméable
raincoat

(kohn-ple)
un complet
suit

(ves-tohn) (spor)
un veston de sport
sport jacket

(san-tewr)
une ceinture
belt

LE VENDEUR **Ils vous vont à merveille.** *(mer-ve-y)* marvelously **Maintenant je crois qu'il vous faut une nouvelle ceinture!** *(san-tewr)* **Voilà la facture.** *(fak-tewr)* bill **Vous payez à la caisse,** *(kes)* cash register **s'il vous plaît.**

(gahn)
des gants
gloves

(bot)
des bottes
boots

FACTURE	
(eh-gwee-y) **3, rue de l'Aiguille du Midi** needle	
Chamonix, Haute Savoie	
VESTON	**552 F 50**
PANTALON	**290 F 90**
CHEMISE	**150 F**
CRAVATE	**85 F 90**
CEINTURE	**127 F 90**
SOUS-VÊTEMENTS	**72 F 50**
TOTAL	**1.288 F 80**

LE VILLAGEOIS **Monsieur, Il y a une erreur** *(e-ruhr)* **dans votre facture.**

LE VENDEUR **Ah! Vous avez raison.** *(reh-zohn)* You are right **Mille deux cent soixante dix-neuf** *(dee)* **francs soixante-dix.**

Au revoir Monsieur.
good bye

Le client a raison. The customer is right.

Le vendeur a tort. The clerk is wrong.

Can you tell me if the following statements are correct? Write **vous avez raison** (you are right) or **vous avez tort** (you are wrong):

1. Le villageois a besoin de vêtements neufs. ______________________________
2. Il ne lui faut pas de sous-vêtements. ______________________________
3. Le villageois porte du 54. ______________________________
4. Il essaie les pantalons. ______________________________
5. Les pantalons sont trop petits pour lui. ______________________________

Tailles

Sizes

VÊTEMENTS D'HOMME

Men's Clothes

CHEMISES (SHIRTS)								
Taille Américaine	14	14½	15	15½	16	16½	17	17½
Taille Européenne	36	37	38	39	40	41	42	43
AUTRES VÊTEMENTS (OTHER CLOTHING)								
Taille Américaine	34	36	38	40	42	44	46	48
Taille Européenne	44	46	48	50	52	54	56	58

If you are a man, what size shirt do you wear? (Je porte du ____________.) What size pants, suit and jacket do you wear? (Je porte du ____________.)

If you are a female, look for the sizes of a male friend or relative: (Il porte du ____________ pour les chemises et du ____________ pour les pantalons, les vestons et les complets).

ANSWERS

True or False **1.** vous avez raison **2.** vous avez tort **3.** vous avez tort **4.** vous avez raison **5.** vous avez tort

Fill in the blanks with the words depicted:

1. Quand il fait froid, je porte un ______________

2. Quand il fait frais, j'enlève mon pardessus et je mets un ______________

3. Quand il neige, je mets mes __________

4. Quand il pleut, j'enlève mon pardessus et je mets mon __________

5. Quand il pleut, je porte aussi mon __________

(fam)

VÊTEMENTS DE FEMME

Women's Clothes

(koo-lūhr) (pran-see-pal)

Les couleurs principales

Basic Colors

(blooz) (vehrt) (shuh-mee-zyay)
la blouse verte chemisier
green blouse

(zhew-pohn) (blahn)
le jupon blanc
white slip

(zhewp) (roozh)
la jupe rouge
red skirt

(sak) (mahn)
le sac à main noir
black purse

(sleep) (zhohn)
le slip jaune
yellow panties

(soo-tyahn) (gorzh) (zhohn)
le soutien-gorge jaune
yellow bra

(rob) (blūh)
la robe bleue
blue dress

(foo-lar) (zhohn)
le foulard jaune et noir
yellow and black scarf

ANSWERS

Fill in blanks **1.** un pardessus **2.** pullover **3.** bottes **4.** imperméable **5.** parapluie

Remembering the rules about adjective agreement—final letter E for feminine, ES for feminine plural; no change with an adjective like **rose** and **rouge** in the feminine because the masculine form ends with E; irregular feminine of **blanc: blanche**—can you answer these questions about the pictures? Example: De quelle couleur est la jupe? La jupe est rouge.

1. De quelle couleur est le foulard? ____________________

2. De quelle couleur est la blouse? ____________________

Can you continue asking yourself questions and answering them about the remaining pictures above?

Tailles

Sizes

VÊTEMENTS DE FEMME

Women's Clothing

LES BLOUSES OU CHEMISIERS (BLOUSES)

Taille Américaine	32	34	36	38	40	42	44
Taille Européenne	40	42	44	46	48	50	52

AUTRES VÊTEMENTS (OTHER CLOTHING)

Taille Américaine	8	10	12	14	16	18
Taille Européenne	36	38	40	42	44	46

Et moi, je porte du 48.
And I wear size 48.

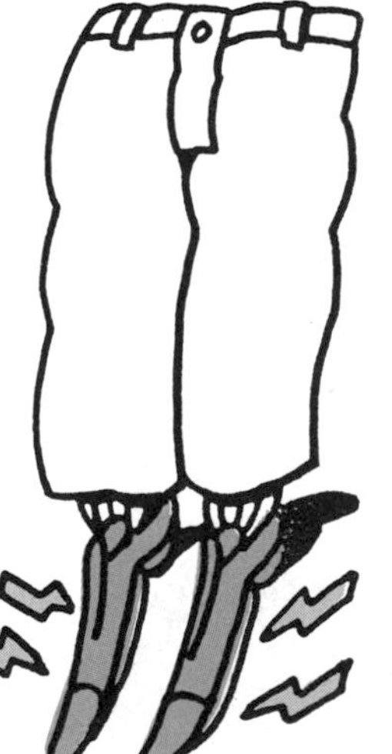

(shoh-sewr)

CHAUSSURES POUR HOMMES ET FEMMES

Shoes for Men and Women

Elles sont trop
(ay-trwat)
étroites pour moi.
(sehr)
Elles me serrent.
They are too narrow for me. They pinch me.

Elles sont trop
(larzh)
larges pour moi.
They are too wide for me.

ANSWERS

De quelle couleur . . . . (sample answers)

1. Le foulard est jaune et noir.

2. La blouse est verte.

Tailles

Sizes

What size shoes do you wear? (Consult the two charts below.)

(shohs)
Je chausse du ________________.

(veel) *(sahn-dahl)* **CHAUSSURES POUR HOMMES (CHAUSSURES DE VILLE, BOTTES, SANDALES)** Men's Shoes (city shoes, boots, sandals)										
TAILLE AMÉRICAINE	7	7½	8	8½	9	9½	10	10½	11	11½
TAILLE EUROPÉENNE	39	40	41	42	43	43	44	44	45	45
CHAUSSURES POUR FEMMES Women's Shoes										
TAILLE AMÉRICAINE	5	5½	6	6½	7	7½	8	8½	9	
TAILLE EUROPÉENNE	35	35	36	37	38	38	38	39	40	

We don't suppose you are the least bit fussy. But if you were very particular, here are some words and expressions just made to impress the clerk:

(kel-kuh) *(shohz)*
Je voudrais quelque chose en:
something

nylon ________ *(nee-lohn)* **nylon**

leather ________ *(kweer)* **cuir**

suede ________ *(dan)* **daim**

cotton ________ *(ko-tohn)* **coton**

denim ________ *(twahl)* *(dzheen)* **toile à jean**

silk ________ *(swah)* **soie**

Pourriez-vous prendre mes mesures? — Could you take my measurements?

(meh-yūhr) *(ka-lee-tay)*
Je voudrais quelque chose de meilleure qualité. — I would like something of better quality.

(a) (la) (man)
Est-ce fait à la main? — Is it handmade?

(sahnbl) *(lohn)* *(koor)*
Ça me semble un peu long (grand, court, petit). — It looks a little long (big, short, small) on me.

(ruh-toosh)
Pouvez-vous faire une retouche? — Can you do alterations?

Je n'aime pas cette couleur; je préfère le bleu. — I don't like this color; I prefer blue.

Note that, when used as nouns, colors are masculine.

17 Les magasins d'alimentation

(a-lee-mahn-ta-syohn)

Food stores

Poids et mesures

(pwah)

Weights and measures

(leh-tree) (krehn-ree) **la laiterie-crémerie** dairy

(boosh-ree) **la boucherie** butcher shop

(ay-pees-ree) **l'épicerie** (fem.) grocery

(boo-lahnzh-ree) **la boulangerie** bakery

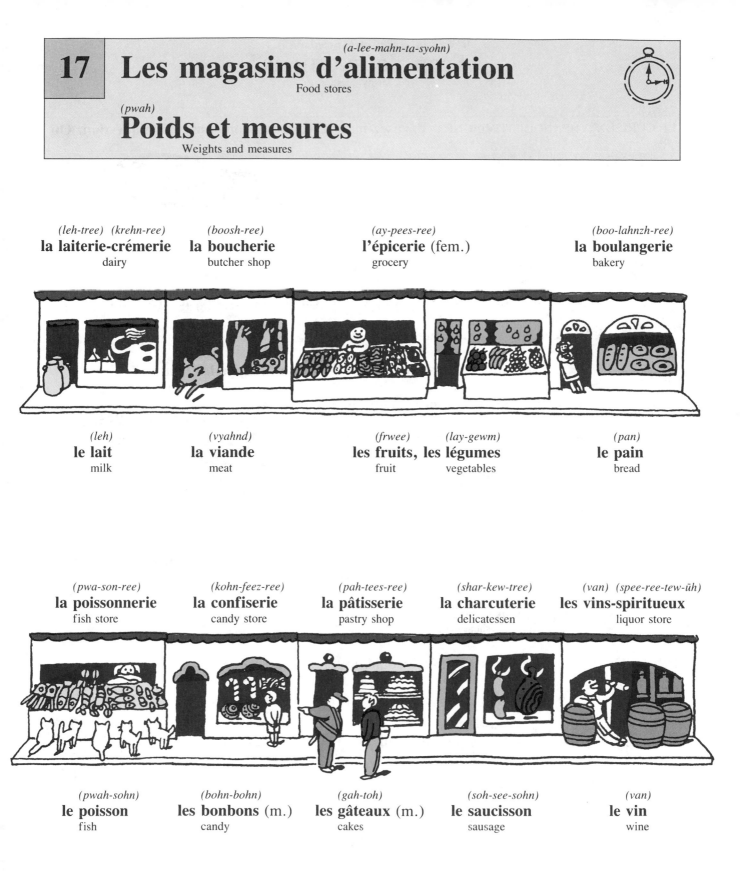

(leh) **le lait** milk

(vyahnd) **la viande** meat

(frwee) (lay-gewm) **les fruits, les légumes** fruit, vegetables

(pan) **le pain** bread

(pwa-son-ree) **la poissonnerie** fish store

(kohn-feez-ree) **la confiserie** candy store

(pah-tees-ree) **la pâtisserie** pastry shop

(shar-kew-tree) **la charcuterie** delicatessen

(van) (spee-ree-tew-ŭh) **les vins-spiritueux** liquor store

(pwah-sohn) **le poisson** fish

(bohn-bohn) **les bonbons** (m.) candy

(gah-toh) **les gâteaux** (m.) cakes

(soh-see-sohn) **le saucisson** sausage

(van) **le vin** wine

(troh) (duh) (kehs-tyohn)

Trop de questions?

Too many questions?

(kew-ryūh)

LE CURIEUX (THE INQUISITIVE ONE) **Excusez-moi, je voudrais vous poser une question. Où puis-je acheter du lait?**

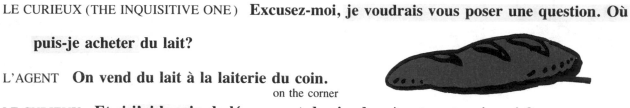

L'AGENT **On vend du lait à la laiterie du coin.**
on the corner

LE CURIEUX **Et si j'ai besoin de légumes et de viande, où est-ce que je vais?**

L'AGENT **À l'épicerie et à la boucherie, bien sûr.**
of course

LE CURIEUX **Et si je veux des fruits et du pain, où est-ce que je peux les acheter?**

L'AGENT **À l'épicerie et à la boulangerie.**

LE CURIEUX **Et s'il me faut du poisson et des bonbons, où puis-je les trouver?**

L'AGENT **Vous pouvez aller à la poissonnerie et à la confiserie.**

LE CURIEUX **Et si je veux des gâteaux?**

L'AGENT **Vous allez à la pâtisserie.**

(glas)

LE CURIEUX **Et pour la glace et le vin?**
ice cream

(shay) (ehg-zas-pay-ray)

L'AGENT **Allez à la pâtisserie et chez le négociant en vin. (exaspéré) Et si vous me posez encore**
wine merchant exasperated

(kree-yay)

une question, je vais crier.
shout

Draw a line through the items which you could *not* find in each store:

(rohs-beef)

1. crémerie—beurre, fromage, vin rosé
2. boucherie—rosbif, oranges, veau

(sew-kray) (leh-tew)

3. épicerie—petits pains sucrés, raisins, laitue
   sweet rolls lettuce
4. charcuterie—raisins, pain, salami
5. boulangerie—jambon, crevettes, croissants

ANSWERS

Items that you could not find

1. vin rosé **2.** oranges **3.** petits pains sucrés **4.** raisins, pain **5.** jambon, crevettes

6. poissonnerie—bonbons, sole, eau minérale

7. confiserie—confiture, asperges, truite *(trweet)* (trout)

8. pâtisserie—riz *(ree)* (rice), lait, petits fours *(foor)* (small cakes)

9. marchand de vin—poulet, bouteilles, épinards

Notice that many of the store names are formed by adding -ERIE to the end of the product they sell. To name the person who sells the product, we often start the name of his/her store and substitute the ending -ER/-ÈRE Example:

lait—laiterie—laitier—laitière
milk dairy milkman milkwoman

And if we want to say "I am going to the butcher's" instead of "I am going to the butcher shop," we use the preposition CHEZ *(shay)*:

Je vais à la boucherie.	I am going to the butcher shop.
Je vais chez le boucher.	I am going to the butcher's.
Je vais chez la bouchère.	I am going to the butcher's (fem.).

POIDS ET MESURES
(pwah) *(muh-zewr)*

Weights and Measures

(puh-zay)
PESER
To Weigh

____

LE POIDS
The Weight

____

ANSWERS

Items that you could not find

6. bonbons, eau minérale **7.** asperges, truite **8.** riz, lait **9.** poulet, épinards

Although it has not yet caught on in the U.S., the metric system is the standard means for measuring in many other countries. Here are some common weights and measures:

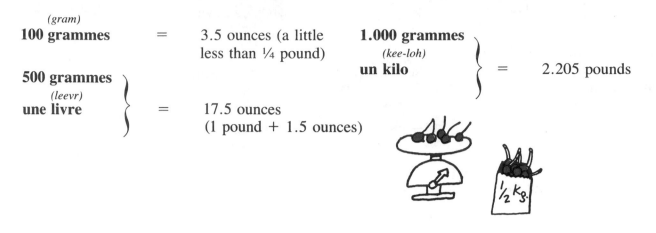

(gram) **100 grammes**	=	3.5 ounces (a little less than ¼ pound)
500 grammes / *(leevr)* **une livre**	=	17.5 ounces (1 pound + 1.5 ounces)
1.000 grammes / *(kee-loh)* **un kilo**	=	2.205 pounds

Note that "one thousand" is 1.000, not 1,000, and that "three point five" is 3,5, not 3.5. *Just the opposite of the American system.*

(mee-lee-leetr) **1 millilitre**	=	0.034 liquid ounces
(sahn-tee-leetr) **1 centilitre**	=	0.33 liquid ounces
(day-see-leetr) **1 décilitre**	=	3.3 liquid ounces
(duh-mee) **1 demi-litre** ½	=	0.53 quarts
1 litre	=	1.06 quarts

Here are some useful expressions to use when buying food. Try writing them out:

(doo-zen) **une douzaine de (d')**	a dozen of ________________
une demi-douzaine de (d')	a half dozen of ________________
un kilo de (d')	a kilo of ________________
une livre de (d')	a half kilo of ________________
deux cent cinquante grammes de (d')	a quarter kilo of ________________
un litre de (d')	a liter of ________________
Ça pèse combien?	How much does it weigh? ________________
C'est trop.	It's too much. ________________
C'est combien la douzaine?	How much are they per dozen? ________________
C'est combien?	How much does it cost? ________________
Ils/elles sont à combien?	How much do they cost? ________________
C'est trop cher.	It's too expensive. ________________

A L'ÉPICERIE

(roo-loh) *(pa-pyay)*
un rouleau de papier
(ee-zhyay-neek)
hygiénique
a roll of toilet paper

(boh-kal)
un bocal de café
(ans-tahn-ta-nay)
instantané
a jar of instant coffee

Ask the clerk for the items in the pictures. Use the names of the containers they come in or the measurement. Try asking some questions like HOW MUCH DOES IT (DO THEY) COST? HOW MUCH ARE THEY PER DOZEN, PER BOX, and so forth?

(suh-reez)
des cerises pesées
cherries being weighed
(ba-lahns)
sur une balance
on a scale

(leevr)
une livre de cerises
a pound of cherries

(bwaht) *(bees-kwee)*
une boîte de biscuits
box of cookies

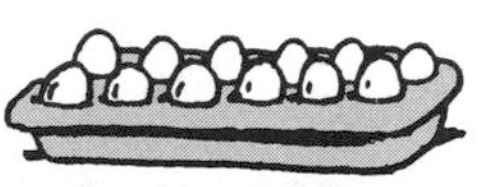

(doo-zehn) *(dūh)*
une douzaine d'oeufs
a dozen eggs

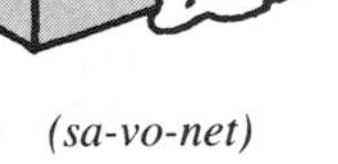

(sa-vo-net)
une savonnette
cake of soap

(kee-loh) *(sewkr)*
un kilo de sucre
1 kilo of sugar

1. Je voudrais ______________________.

   Combien coûte ______________________?

(leetr) *(leh)*
un litre de lait
a liter of milk

2. J'ai besoin d'______________________.

   Combien coûte ______________________?

(duh-mee) *(doo-zehn)* *(see-trohn)*
une demi-douzaine de citrons
½ dozen lemons

3. Je voudrais ______________________.

   Combien coûte ______________________?

(lay-gewm) *(kohn-sehrv)*
une boîte de légumes en conserve
can of vegetables

ANSWERS

Fill in blanks (À l'épicerie) **1.** un litre de lait **2.** une demi-douzaine de citrons **3.** une boîte de légumes en conserve

Nowadays, it is not always necessary to go to different stores to buy groceries. Many countries have North American style supermarkets where we can buy them in one place: bakery items, meat, eggs, a box of cookies, a roll of toilet paper, a liter of milk, a half-dozen oranges, a kilo of sugar, a package of candy. Of course, it is still interesting to go to the

(mar-shay) (ahn) (pleh) (nehr) *(vo-la-y)*
open-air markets **(les marchés en plein air)** to see the great variety of **volaille,** (poultry) **fruits,**

(fehr-myay)
légumes, and other products which the **fermiers** (farmers) sell each day. It is a good way to observe the foods typical of the country or the region.

Indicate the correctness of the statements by writing **vous avez raison** or **vous avez tort**.

1. De nos jours (Nowadays), il est nécessaire d'aller dans beaucoup de magasins différents *(dee-fay-rahn)* pour acheter des produits alimentaires *(a-lee-mahn-tehr)* (food). ____________________
2. Il n'y a pas de supermarchés *(sew-per-mar-shay)* dans les autres pays.

   ____
3. On ne peut pas acheter de papier hygiénique dans les supermarchés français.

   ____
4. Dans les marchés en plein air, on peut acheter beaucoup de produits différents.

   ____
5. Pour trouver les produits typiques de la région, il faut aller dans les supermarchés.

   ____

ANSWERS

True or false
1. Vous avez tort. **2.** Vous avez tort. **3.** Vous avez tort. **4.** Vous avez raison. **5.** Vous avez tort.

18 Droguerie Pharmacie

(dro-gree) **Droguerie** — Drugstore

(far-ma-see) **Pharmacie** — Pharmacy

The **pharmacies** and the **drogueries** are often combined **(Pharmacie-Droguerie)**. Otherwise, one buys prescriptions, drugs, things like tissues, sanitary napkins and some cosmetics in the **pharmacie**. Drugstores sell no prescriptions. But they carry over-the-counter drugs, all kinds of cosmetics and beauty products and also teas and some health foods, as well as cleaning products for the house. What you do not find in either place are ice cream, coffee or sandwiches. Lunch counters are nonexistent in drugstores and pharmacies, unless you go to the now famous *Le Drugstore des Champs-Élysées*, a big and fancy imitation of an American drugstore.

À LA DROGUERIE

At the Drugstore

(ay-pangl) **les épingles à** *(shuh-vūh)* **cheveux**
bobby pins

la crème *(day-ma-kee-yahnt)* **démaquillante**
cleansing cream

(dee-sol-vahn) **le dissolvant**
nail polish remover

(vehr-nee) **le vernis à** *(ohngl)* **ongles**
nail polish

(fahr) **le fard**
rouge

(mee-rwar) **un miroir**
mirror

(paht) **la pâte** *(dahn-tee-frees)* **dentifrice**
toothpaste

(peh-ny) **un peigne**
comb

(mas-ka-ra) **le mascara**
mascara

(lak) **la laque**
hairspray

(bros) **la brosse** *(dahn)* **à dents**
toothbrush

(roo-zh) **le rouge** *(lehvr)* **à lèvres**
lipstick

(moo-shwar) **les mouchoirs** *(pa-pyay)* **en papier**
tissues

Monique and Pascale enter the drugstore and go to the cosmetics section. Monique looks at herself in the mirror.

(poh)
MONIQUE **Je dois acheter des épingles à cheveux, un pot de crème démaquillante**
jar

et des mouchoirs en papier.

(ew-tee-leez)
PASCALE **Je n'utilise jamais de crème démaquillante; c'est trop cher. Tu achètes**
(ma-kee-yahzh) *(reesh)*
toujours ton maquillage ici? C'est un magasin pour les riches, pas pour les
(pohvr)
pauvres comme nous.
poor like

MONIQUE **Tu as raison, mais je ne peux jamais trouver de bons**
(kar-tyay)
produits dans mon quartier.
neighborhood

PASCALE **Je vais te dire quelque chose. Je ne vais rien acheter ici. C'est trop cher.**
something

(may-dam)
LA VENDEUSE **Bonjour Mesdames. Vous désirez?**

(fla-kohn)
MONIQUE **J'ai besoin d'un peigne, d'une brosse à cheveux et d'un flacon de laque.**
bottle

Il me faut aussi une brosse à dents et de la pâte dentifrice. Ça coûte combien?

LA VENDEUSE **La brosse à dents coûte 10 francs 50 et la pâte dentifrice 7 francs 90.**

(day-pahn-say)
PASCALE **Tu vois? Tu vas dépenser beaucoup d'argent!**
to spend

MONIQUE **Maintenant je voudrais voir vos produits de maquillage—le fard,**
make-up

le rouge à lèvres, le mascara, s'il vous plaît. Ah! et

aussi le vernis à ongles et le dissolvant.

PASCALE **Mais tu dépenses trop.**

MONIQUE **Ça ne fait rien. Ce n'est pas**
it doesn't matter

pour moi, c'est pour mon mari.

(ay-to-nay)
PASCALE **(l'air étonné): Qu'est-ce que tu**
astonished

dis?

True or false?

1. Je peux acheter des mouchoirs en papier à la droguerie. T F
2. On trouve des produits de maquillage **au** *(ray-ohn)* **rayon** des cosmétiques. T F
   department
3. Les *(pree)* prix sont chers à la droguerie. T F
   prices
4. Pascale ne veut rien dépenser à la droguerie. T F

Ce qu'il faut dire quand vous *devez* faire quelque chose

What you must say when you *have* to do something

DEVOIR + INFINITIVE
must, to have to do something

Je dois acheter quelque chose.
I have to buy something.

IL FAUT + INFINITIVE
it is necessary to do something

Il faut aller à la laiterie pour acheter du lait.
It is necessary to go to the dairy to buy milk.

(duh-vwar)
DEVOIR
must, to have to, to owe

je, **tu**	*(dwa)* **dois**	**nous**	*(duh-vohn)* **devons**
		vous	*(duh-vay)* **devez**
il, **elle**, **on**	*(dwa)* **doit**	**ils**, **elles**	*(dwahv)* **doivent**

Il faut is a generalization (It is necessary, one must . . .). To make it more specific, you can use the construction **il me faut** (+ infinitive), **il te faut**, and so on, which you learned in lesson 16.

Let's practice **devoir** + infinitive first. Try starting each sentence with the subjects suggested in parentheses. Say the sentences aloud:

1. **Je dois acheter quelque chose.** (Nous, Tu, Ils, Elle, Vous, Il)
2. **Il ne doit rien manger.** (Je, Nous, Tu, Vous, Ils, Elle)
3. **Elle ne doit pas trop dépenser.** (Vous, Nous, Ils, Je, Elles, Tu)

Can you answer these questions with il faut + INFINITIVE?

1. Est-ce qu'il faut manger pour vivre? ______________________
2. Où faut-il aller pour acheter de la viande? ______________________
3. Qu'est-ce qu'il faut utiliser pour enlever le vernis à ongles?
   ____
4. Où faut-il aller pour acheter du maquillage? ______________________

ANSWERS

True or false **1.** T **2.** T **3.** T **4.** T

Answer questions **1.** Oui, il faut manger pour vivre. **2.** Il faut aller à la boucherie pour acheter la viande. **3.** Il faut utiliser du dissolvant. **4.** Il faut aller à la droguerie.

Let's hope you will never have the problems that this unfortunate traveler has.

HENRI **Est-ce que vous avez des bonbons?**

VENDEUR **Non, nous n'avons pas de bonbons. Pour acheter des bonbons, il faut aller à la confiserie.**

HENRI **Et où trouve-t-on des cigarettes et des briquets?**

VENDEUR **Pour acheter des cigarettes, vous devez aller au bureau de tabac.**
(bew-roh) (ta-ba)

HENRI **Merci. Je voudrais un flacon de déodorant,** *(day-o-do-rahn)* **un rasoir et des lames de rasoir.** *(lahm)* **Mon rasoir électrique ne marche pas dans ce pays.** *(marsh)* function

VENDEUR **Il vous faut aller dans un autre magasin pour acheter un transformateur.** *(trahns-for-ma-tūhr)* voltage converter

HENRI **Mon Dieu! Que de problèmes!** What

VENDEUR **J'ai la solution.** *(so-lew-syohn)* **Laissez-vous pousser la barbe et la moustache comme moi. Les femmes m'adorent.**
Let grow beard

1. Name two things you find at the tobacco shop:

_______________, _______________

2. What things does a man use to shave with?

_______________, _______________

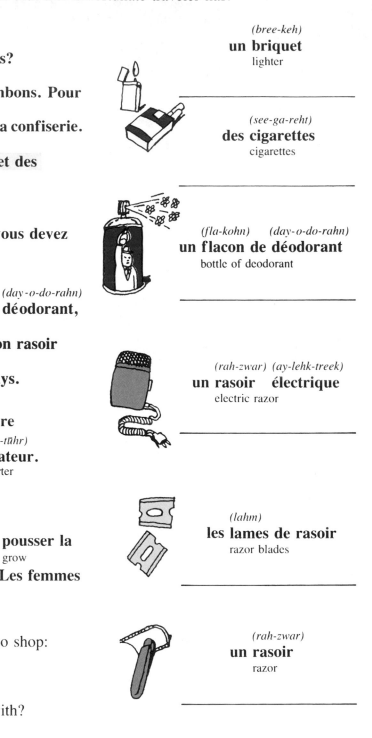

(bree-keh)
un briquet
lighter

____

(see-ga-reht)
des cigarettes
cigarettes

____

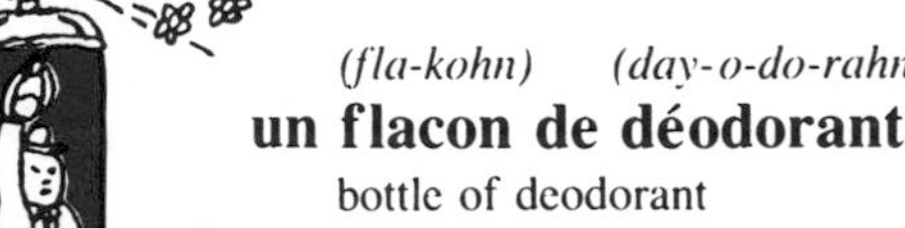

(fla-kohn) (day-o-do-rahn)
un flacon de déodorant
bottle of deodorant

____

(rah-zwar) (ay-lehk-treek)
un rasoir électrique
electric razor

____

(lahm)
les lames de rasoir
razor blades

____

(rah-zwar)
un rasoir
razor

____

ANSWERS

Tobacco shop (sample answers) **1.** un briquet, des cigarettes **2.** un rasoir, des lames de rasoir

À LA PHARMACIE

At the Pharmacy

You can identify the pharmacy by the green cross displayed outside its door. Pharmacies will not only fill a prescription *(or-do-nahns)* **(une ordonnance)**, some will also treat *minor* emergencies.

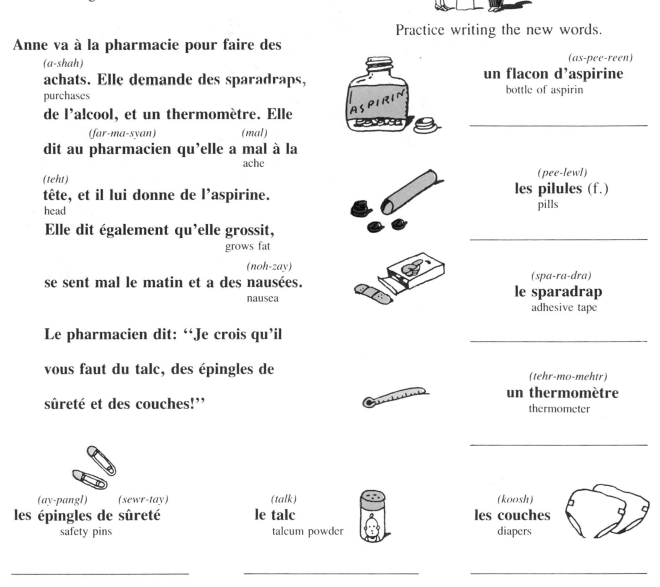

Anne va à la pharmacie pour faire des *(a-shah)* **achats** (purchases)**. Elle demande des sparadraps, de l'alcool, et un thermomètre. Elle dit au pharmacien** *(far-ma-syan)* **qu'elle a mal** *(mal)* (ache) **à la tête** *(teht)* (head)**, et il lui donne de l'aspirine. Elle dit également qu'elle grossit** (grows fat)**, se sent mal le matin et a des nausées** *(noh-zay)* (nausea)**.**

Le pharmacien dit: "Je crois qu'il vous faut du talc, des épingles de sûreté et des couches!"

Practice writing the new words.

(as-pee-reen)
un flacon d'aspirine
bottle of aspirin

____

(pee-lewl)
les pilules (f.)
pills

____

(spa-ra-dra)
le sparadrap
adhesive tape

____

(tehr-mo-mehtr)
un thermomètre
thermometer

____

(ay-pangl) (sewr-tay)
les épingles de sûreté
safety pins

____

(talk)
le talc
talcum powder

____

(koosh)
les couches
diapers

____

Here are some useful phrases for your *minor* complaints and hygienic needs:

Il me faut quelque chose pour l'indigestion *(an-dee-zhehs-tyohn)***, le rhume** *(rewm)* (cold)**, la constipation** *(kohns-tee-pa-syohn)***, le mal de gorge** *(gorzh)* (sore throat)**.**

(dya-ray)
J'ai . . . la diarrhée

(mee-grehn)
une migraine
migraine

(fyehvr)
de la fièvre

(krahnp)
des crampes
cramps

(greep)
la grippe
flu

(dahn)
un mal aux dents
a toothache

(koo) (so-leh-y)
un coup de soleil
sunburn

(toos)
Je tousse
I cough

(koo-pay)
Je me suis coupé (e)
I cut myself

(a-see-dee-tay)
Je voudrais . . . un produit contre l'acidité
acidity

(day-zan-fehk-tahn)
un désinfectant
antiseptic

(yod)
de l'iode
iodine

(pahns-mahn)
des pansements
bandages

(ko-tohn) (wat)
du coton (de l'ouate)
absorbent cotton

(see-zoh)
des ciseaux
scissors

(lak-sa-teef)
Je dois acheter . . . un laxatif
laxative

(sehr-vyeht) (ee-zhyay-neek)
des serviettes hygiéniques
sanitary napkins

(see-roh) (too)
du sirop pour la toux
cough syrup

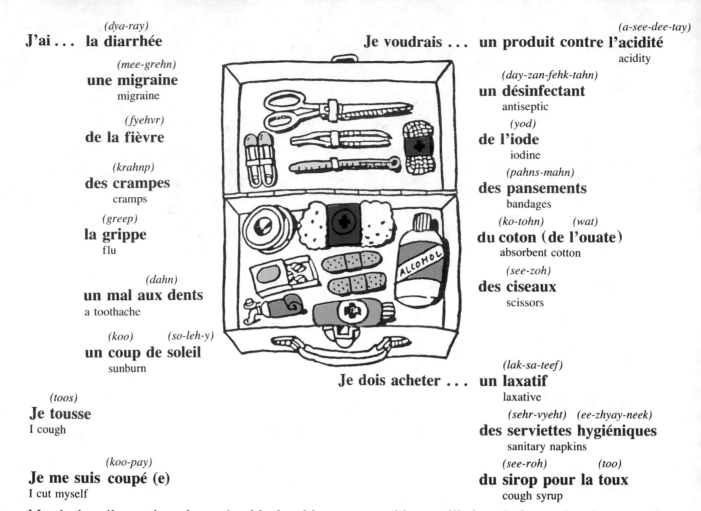

Match the ailment in column 1 with the thing you would most likely ask for at the pharmacy in column 2. Sometimes more than one answer may be possible.

	Column 1	Column 2
______	1. constipation	A. des sparadraps
______	2. une coupure	B. de l' insuline
		C. un laxatif
______	3. de la fièvre	D. un produit contre l'acidité
______	4. une migraine	E. de l'aspirine
______	5. des crampes	F. un désinfectant
______	6. diabète *(dya-beht)*	G. des couches
		H. un thermomètre
______	7. la toux	I. du sirop pour la toux
______	8. mal à l'estomac *(es-to-ma)*	J. des pansements

ANSWERS

Match 1. (C) **2.** (A)(F)(J) **3.** (H) **4.** (E) **5.** (E) **6.** (B) **7.** (I) **8.** (D)

19 La blanchisserie La teinturerie

(blahn-shees-ree) **La blanchisserie** — Laundry
(tan-tew-ruh-ree) **La teinturerie** — Dry cleaning

Laundromats are not as common in France as in the United States. Laundries are very good but fairly slow (3–4 days) and many are closed Saturdays and Monday morning. For your dry cleaning needs, you can find 24-hour service in most cities. August is vacation month, and many shops are closed at that time. In general, the easiest method is to ask your hotel to take care of your dry cleaning and laundry. Even easier—and cheaper—is to take as many permanent press clothes with you as possible.

Avoir l'air

To seem, to look

This is another very common and idiomatic construction with **avoir** (remember **avoir chaud**, **avoir froid**, **avoir envie**, **avoir besoin**, and so forth). It means, literally: to have the air. . . . **Vous avez l'air fatigué aujourd'hui**. You look tired today. **L'agent de police a l'air exaspéré**. The policeman looks exasperated. **Pascale a l'air étonné**. Pascale looks (seems) astonished. **Ça n'a pas l'air suffisant**. It doesn't look sufficient. **Il a l'air de mauvaise humeur** *(ew-mūhr)*. He seems to be in a bad mood. **Il a l'air de bonne humeur**. He seems to be in a good mood.

LA LAVERIE AUTOMATIQUE

(la-vree) *(oh-to-ma-teek)*

The Laundromat

Susan, a foreign exchange student, goes to wash her clothes for the first time at the laundromat. Fortunately for her, a woman who has several children with her is also doing her wash.

(pa-keh) **le paquet** *(le-seev)* **de lessive**
box of soap powder

SUSAN **S'il vous plaît, pouvez-vous m'aider? Combien de lessive** (soap powder) **est-ce que je dois mettre dans la machine** *(ma-sheen)* **à laver** *(la-vay)* **pour laver mon linge** *(lanzh)* (laundry)**?**

(plahnsh) **la planche** *(ruh-pah-say)* **à repasser**
ironing board

(say-shwar)
le séchoir
dryer

(kord)
la corde à linge
clothesline

LA DAME **Jamais plus d'une demi-tasse** *(duh-mee)(tas)* ½ cup **pour si peu de vêtements.**

SUSAN **(à elle-même) Ça n'a pas l'air suffisant.** *(sew-fee-zahn)* sufficient **(Elle met deux tasses de lessive dans la machine qui commence à déborder.)** *(day-bor-day)* overflow

LA DAME **Jamais plus d'une tasse.**

Probablement moins . . .

(fehr)
le fer à repasser
iron

(pans)
les pinces à linge (fem.)
clothespins

(kor-beh-y) *(lanzh)*
la corbeille à linge
laundry basket

Susan is ready to dry her clothes. Another young woman, a student, is nearby.

SUSAN **Pouvez-vous me dire combien de pièces de monnaie il faut mettre dans la fente du séchoir? Et, à propos, où est la fente? (Le séchoir ne marche pas.)**
(pyehs) pieces — *(mo-neh)* change — *(fahnt)* slot — *(a) (proh-poh)* on the subject

L'ÉTUDIANTE **Il faut appuyer sur ce bouton. Comme ça, la machine marche et sèche vos habits.**
(a-pwee-yay) press — *(boo-tohn)* button — *(kom) (sa)* This way — *(a-bee)* clothes

SUSAN **C'est la première fois que je lave mes habits depuis que je suis étudiante ici.**
(duh-pwee) since

L'ÉTUDIANTE **Tu es une nouvelle étudiante? C'est ma troisième année.**

SUSAN **Tu es étudiante aussi? J'aimerais bien te revoir. J'ai tant de questions à te poser!**
(ehm-reh) would like — *(ruh-vwar)* see again — *(tahn)* so many

1. If you are going to the laundromat, what should you take along?

____________________, ____________________

ANSWERS

Going to the laundromat **1.** un paquet de lessive, une corbeille à linge

2. In the laundromat, with what machines do you have to deal?

____________________, ____________________

(blahn-shee-sahzh)

SERVICES DE BLANCHISSAGE ET DE

(neh-twa-yahzh) *(a)* *(sehk)*

NETTOYAGE À SEC DANS LES HÔTELS

Hotel Laundry Services and Dry Cleaning

If you decide to use the laundry services of the hotel where you are staying, these expressions might get you by:

Est-ce que vous avez un service de blanchissage?	Do you have a laundry service?
J'ai du linge à faire laver.	I have some clothes to be washed.
Pouvez-vous coudre un bouton sur ma chemise?	Can you sew a button on my shirt?
(ruh-koodr) (mahnsh) **Pouvez-vous recoudre la manche de cette blouse?**	Can you mend the sleeve of this blouse?
(na-mee-do-nay) **N'amidonnez pas mes caleçons.**	Don't use starch on my undershorts.
Pourriez-vous repasser cette chemise encore une fois?	Could you iron this shirt again?
(neh-twa-yay) **Pourriez-vous faire nettoyer à sec ce complet?**	Could you have this suit dry cleaned?
(tash) **Pouvez-vous enlever cette tache?**	Can you take out this spot?

Try filling in the blanks with the key words from the sentences above. Then read the sentences aloud:

1. Pouvez-vous enlever cette __________?
2. Pouvez-vous __________ un bouton sur ma chemise?
3. Est-ce que vous avez un service de __________?

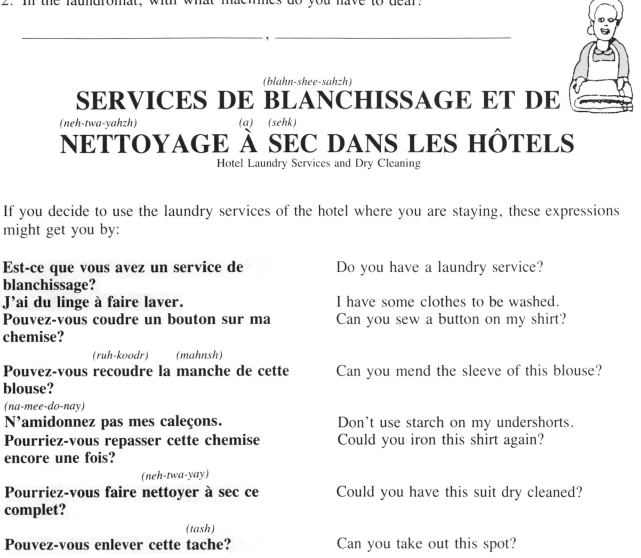

ANSWERS

Going to the laundromat **2.** une machine à laver, un séchoir

Fill in blanks **1.** tache? **2.** coudre **3.** blanchissage?

4. Pouvez-vous faire ____________ ce complet?

5. Pouvez-vous ____________ la ____________ de cette blouse?

(ahn-vwah)
Jean envoie toujours son linge à la blanchisserie de l'hotel. Mais cette fois, il y a des
sends ... time

(par-tee) ... (ra-port) (a-par-tyehn) (kel-kuhn)
problèmes. Une grande partie des vêtements qu'on lui rapporte appartiennent à quelqu'un
part ... brings back belong ... somebody else

(dohtr) (plandr) (zhay-rahn) ... (soo-tyan) (gorzh)
d'autre. Il va se plaindre au gérant. D'abord, il ne porte jamais de soutien-gorge ou de
complain manager First of all ... never bra or

(ko-lahn) ... (a-mee-do-nay) ... (fee-shew) (brew-lay)
collants. Ensuite, ses chemises sont trop amidonnées et une d'elles est fichue; elle est brûlée.
pantyhose Next ... starched ... ruined ... scorched

(ahn) (plews) (mahnk) ... (ruh-swah)
En plus, il lui manque deux chaussettes, une rouge et une verte. Le complet qu'il reçoit
In addition he's missing ... receives

(tash)
de la teinturerie a une tache sur la manche. Il a raison de se plaindre, vous ne trouvez pas?
spot ... complain

How would you complain about such things? You might want to use some of the following phrases:

I have to complain.	**Je dois me plaindre.**
There is a mistake.	**Il y a une erreur.**
These clothes are somebody else's.	**Ce linge est à quelqu'un d'autre.**
This shirt has too much starch.	**Cette chemise est trop amidonnée.**
My clothes are ruined.	**Mes habits sont fichus.**
This shirt is scorched.	**Cette chemise est brûlée.**
There's a button missing.	**Il manque un bouton.**
There's a spot on these trousers.	**Il y a une tache sur ces pantalons.**
I'm missing a pair of socks.	**Il me manque une paire de chaussettes.**

ANSWERS

Fill in blanks **4.** nettoyer à sec **5.** recoudre manche

20 Le salon de beauté Le coiffeur pour dames Le coiffeur pour hommes

(sa-lohn) (boh-tay) (kwah-fuhr) (dam) (om)

The beauty shop — The hairdresser — The barber shop

AU SALON DE BEAUTÉ

At the Beauty Shop

Henriette goes to the beauty shop for her weekly visit.

(shuh-vüh)
on lave les cheveux de la jeune femme
young woman's hair being washed

(shahn-pwan)
le shampooing
shampoo

(per-ma-nahnt)
la permanente
permanent

LA COIFFEUSE **Qu'est-ce que vous désirez cette semaine, Madame?**

HENRIETTE **Un shampooing– mise (mee) en (zahn) plis (plee) (set), s'il vous plaît. Et une retouche (ruh-toosh) (touch up). Pouvez-vous aussi me faire un massage facial et une manucure?**

LA COIFFEUSE **Vous êtes brunette (brew-neht) maintenant. Vous voulez un rinçage (ran-sahzh) (rinse) de quelle teinte (tant) (color)? De la même couleur ou plus foncé (fohn-say) (darker)?**

HENRIETTE **Un peu plus clair (kler) (lighter), s'il vous plaît. Je voudrais aussi des boucles (bookl) (curls) sur le côté et**

(bee-goo-dee)
les bigoudis
curlers

(ma-new-kewr)
la manucure
manicure

(ma-sahzh) (fa-syal)
le massage facial
facial massage

(bro-say)
brosser
to brush

(ohn-dew-la-syohn) **des ondulations** (waves) **sur la tête. Pourriez-vous** *(ra-koor-seer)* **raccourcir** (shorten) **un peu mes cheveux sur** *(newk)* **la nuque?** (back of neck) **Je n'aime pas avoir les cheveux** *(lohn)* **longs,** (long) **je préfère les avoir** *(koor)* **courts.** (short)

(Une heure plus tard, la coiffeuse brosse les cheveux d'Henriette, et Henriette se regarde dans le miroir.)

HENRIETTE **Je suis** *(blohnd)* **blonde!** (blond)

une brosse à cheveux
hairbrush

(say-shwar)
le séchoir
hair dryer

se regarder *(meer-wahr)* **dans le miroir**
to look at oneself in the mirror

FOR WOMEN ONLY: You are going to the "salon de beauté." What would you say to the "coiffeuse"?

Je désire 1. ______________________

2. ______________________

3. ______________________

Here are some useful expressions a woman might want to know before she goes to the beauty shop. Try writing them out:

I'd like to make an appointment for tomorrow.	*(rahn-day) (voo)* **Je voudrais prendre rendez-vous pour demain.**

____

Could you give me a rinse?	*(ran-sahzh)* **Pourriez-vous me faire un rinçage?**

____

Could you cut my hair?	*(koo-pay)* **Pourriez-vous me couper les cheveux?**

____

ANSWERS

FOR WOMEN ONLY 1. un shampooing–mise en plis. **2.** une retouche. **3.** une manucure.

Don't use any hairspray.	**Ne mettez pas de laque.**
I would like my hair cut in bangs.	*(frahnzh)* **Je voudrais une frange.**

CHEZ LE COIFFEUR

At the Hairdresser

Unisex hairdressers are just beginning to appear but are not widespread. Here are a few more useful expressions you may need at **LE COIFFEUR POUR DAMES, LE COIFFEUR POUR HOMMES** (or **MESSIEURS**) or **LE COIFFEUR UNISEXE** *(ew-nee-sehks)*.

Could you blow dry my hair?	*(bra-sheeng)* **Pourriez-vous me donner un brushing?**
I would like a light trim.	*(ay-ga-lee-zay)* **Je voudrais me faire égaliser les cheveux.**
Can you give me a light tint?	*(tan-tay) (lay-zhehr-mahn)* **Pouvez-vous me teinter légèrement les cheveux?**
I would like an Afro.	*(kwah-fewr)(a-froh)* **Je voudrais une coiffure afro.** hairdo
I would like my hair frosted.	*(day-ko-lo-ra-syohn)* **Je voudrais une légère décoloration des** *(mehsh)* **mèches.** locks
Can you tease my hair just a little?	*(kreh-pay)* **Pouvez-vous me crêper les cheveux un tout petit peu?**

After practicing these expressions aloud, try to fill in the blanks in the sentence below, using the words which follow.

1. Pourriez-vous me donner un ______________?
2. Je voudrais me faire ______________ les cheveux.
3. Je voudrais une ______________ afro.

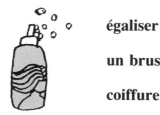

égaliser

un brushing

coiffure

ANSWERS

Fill in blanks **1.** un brushing **2.** égaliser **3.** coiffure

4. Pouvez-vous me _____________ les cheveux un tout petit peu?

5. Je voudrais une légère _____________.

décoloration des mèches

crêper

CHEZ LE COIFFEUR POUR HOMMES

At the Barber Shop

Mon Dieu! Je suis chauve!

(rah-zay)
raser
to shave

(moos-tash)
une moustache
(barb)
une barbe
beard

(peh-nyay)
peigner
to comb

se raser
to shave oneself

(pat)
des pattes
sideburns

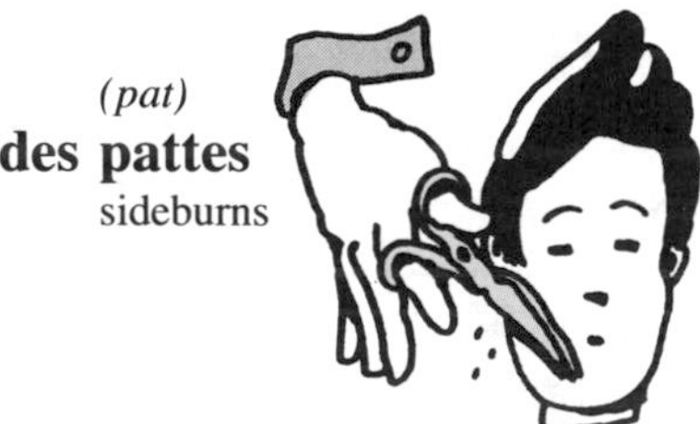

se peigner
to comb one's hair

(ay-bar-buhr)
un ébarbeur—
(tohn-dūhz)
(une tondeuse)
clippers

la crème à raser
shaving cream

le rasoir

(koop)
une coupe de cheveux
haircut

(shohv)
un homme chauve
bald

(see-zoh)
les ciseaux

ANSWERS

Fill in blanks **4.** crêper **5.** décoloration des mèches

Philippe va chez le coiffeur parce qu'il a besoin d'une coupe de cheveux. D'abord, le coiffeur le rase et lui rafraîchit *(ra-freh-shee)* trims **la barbe. Puis** then **il lui fait un shampooing et lui coupe les cheveux. Comme Philippe aime avoir les cheveux très courts, le coiffeur coupe beaucoup sur la tête et sur la nuque. Philippe est très fatigué, et il s'endort** *(sahn-dor)* falls asleep **dans son fauteuil** *(foh-tūh-y)* armchair**. Le coiffeur coupe de plus** *(plew)* more **en** *(zahn)* and **plus** *(plew)* more**. Finalement il déclare: "Voilà, Monsieur." Philippe se regarde dans le miroir et voit qu'il est chauve. "Combien est-ce que je vous dois?" demande-t-il. Le coiffeur répond: "Vous pouvez me payer pour six mois. Je ne crois pas que vous allez bientôt** *(byan-toh)* soon **revenir** *(ruhv-neer)* come back**.**

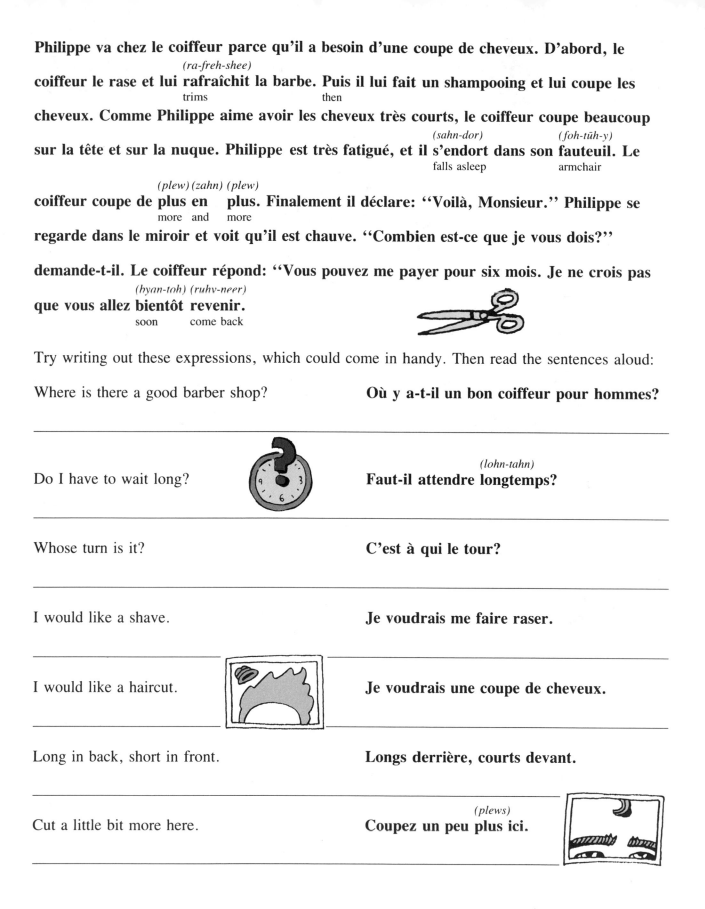

Try writing out these expressions, which could come in handy. Then read the sentences aloud:

Where is there a good barber shop? — **Où y a-t-il un bon coiffeur pour hommes?**

____

Do I have to wait long? — **Faut-il attendre longtemps** *(lohn-tahn)***?**

____

Whose turn is it? — **C'est à qui le tour?**

____

I would like a shave. — **Je voudrais me faire raser.**

____

I would like a haircut. — **Je voudrais une coupe de cheveux.**

____

Long in back, short in front. — **Longs derrière, courts devant.**

____

Cut a little bit more here. — **Coupez un peu plus** *(plews)* **ici.**

____

21 Le kiosque La papeterie

(kyosk) **Le kiosque** — Newsstand

(pa-pe-tree) **La papeterie** — Stationery store

AU KIOSQUE

(ma-ga-zeen)
le magazine
magazine

(zhoor-nal)
le journal
newspaper

(kart) (pos-tahl)
les cartes postales
postcards

(tanbr)
les timbres (avion)
postage stamps (air mail)

(see-ga-reht)
les cigarettes

LE JEUNE HOMME **Pardon. Avez-vous des** *(zhoor-noh)* **journaux en anglais?**	Excuse me. Do you have newspapers in English?
(pro-pry-ay-tehr) LE PROPRIÉTAIRE DU KIOSQUE (owner) **Oui, nous avons un bon** *(shwah)* **choix** (selection) **de journaux anglais et américains.**	Yes, we have a good selection of English and American newspapers.
LE JEUNE HOMME **Je voudrais aussi des cartes postales de Paris.**	I would also like some postcards of Paris.

LE PROPRIÉTAIRE **Voilà des vues** *(vew)* **intéressantes de la capitale.** *(ka-pee-tahl)*

Here are some interesting views of the capital.

LE JEUNE HOMME **Avez-vous des timbres-poste?**

Do you have postage stamps?

LE PROPRIÉTAIRE **Non, mais vous pouvez en trouver au bureau de tabac.**

No, but you can find some at the tobacco shop.

LE JEUNE HOMME **Et du tabac?** *(ta-ba)* **Je voudrais un paquet de cigarettes américaines.**

And tobacco? I would like a package of American cigarettes.

LE PROPRIÉTAIRE **Vous voyez l'enseigne** *(ahn-sehn-y)* **devant le bureau de tabac là-bas? Ça veut dire qu'on vend des cigarettes.**

You see the sign with a plug of tobacco on it in front of the tobacco shop down there? That means they sell cigarettes.

LE JEUNE HOMME **Merci. Et est-ce que vous avez des magazines avec des photos?** *(foh-toh)* **<u>Oui</u> par exemple? Ce n'est pas pour moi, c'est pour mon grand-père.**

Thank you. And do you have picture magazines? *Oui*, for example? It's not for me; it's for my grandfather.

LE PROPRIÉTAIRE **(il fronce** *(frohns)* frowns **les sourcils** *(soor-see)* eyebrows**): Oui, naturellement.**

Yes, of course.

LE JEUNE HOMME **Bon. Je prends le journal, les cartes postales et le magazine. Je vous dois combien?**

Good. I'll take the newspaper, the postcards, and the magazine. How much do I owe you?

NOTE: Au bureau de tabac, on peut aussi acheter des bonbons, du chocolat, des allumettes, *(a-lew-met)* **du papier à lettres,** *(letr)* stationery **quelquefois** *(kehl-kuh-fwa)* sometimes **de la glace. Les bureaux de tabac sont souvent** *(soo-vahn)* often **ouverts** *(oo-vehr)* open **le dimanche matin.**

Try reading aloud several times the conversation between the youth and the owner of the kiosk. When you feel confident of its meaning, see if you can match the phrases on the next page.

Match these French words or phrases from the dialogue with their English equivalents:

1. les journaux
2. les cartes postales
3. les timbres-poste
4. le bureau de tabac
5. le paquet de cigarettes

a. postcards
b. tobacco store
c. newspapers
d. package of cigarettes
e. postage stamps

À LA PAPETERIE

At the Stationery Store

(stee-loh) (bee-y)
un stylo à bille
ballpoint pen

____

(ka-yay)
un cahier
notebook

____

(ahnv-lop)
une enveloppe
envelope

____

(blok)
un bloc
writing pad

____

(kreh-yohn)
un crayon
pencil

____

(skotsh)
du scotch
transparent tape

____

(fee-sehl)
de la ficelle
string

____

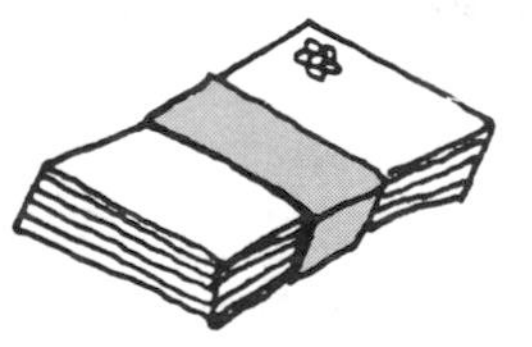

(lehtr)
du papier à lettres
stationery

____

Si j'ai besoin d'un stylo à bille ou d'un crayon, je vais à la papeterie. Si je veux écrire une lettre, j'utilise du papier à lettre, et je mets la lettre dans une enveloppe. On vend aussi des cahiers à la papeterie. Je peux écrire des notes dans un cahier ou dans un bloc. Si je veux envelopper (*ahnv-lo-pay*, wrap) **un paquet, il me faut du scotch, de la ficelle, et du papier d'emballage** (*ahn-ba-lahzh*, wrapping paper)**.**

Pour demander quelque chose, je dis: ***Je voudrais . . .***

ANSWERS

Matching 1. c 2. a 3. e 4. b 5. d

Now, let's take a trial run.

1. What two objects can you write with? ______________, ______________.

2. If you write a letter, what do you write it on? ______________.

3. What two things do you use to wrap a package? ______________, ______________.

4. What two things can you write notes on? ______________, ______________.

5. Where can you buy des timbres avion (a-vyohn) [airmail stamps]? ______________.

6. Can you find the following words below? Circle them as in the example. (You should be able to find six more): envelope, pencil, newspaper, cigarettes, stamp, paper

E	M	I	G	U	J	O	N	(B	L	O	C)
N	E	X	C	E	O	T	R	O	S	U	A
V	I	C	E	S	U	S	D	U	R	E	T
E	C	I	G	A	R	E	T	T	E	S	I
L	S	R	E	C	N	L	E	E	E	H	M
O	A	M	A	L	A	P	A	I	E	R	B
P	U	T	I	Y	L	P	A	P	I	E	R
P	T	E	D	E	O	R	E	L	A	T	E
E	B	L	I	M	S	N	E	E	A	Q	U

ANSWERS

Fill in the blanks

1. un stylo, un crayon **2.** du papier à lettres **3.** de la ficelle, du scotch. **4.** un bloc, un cahier **5.** au kiosque **6.** enveloppe, crayon, journal, cigarettes, timbre, papier

22 La bijouterie L'horlogerie (fem.)

(bee-zhoo-tree) **La bijouterie** — Jewelry store

(or-lozh-ree) **L'horlogerie** (fem.) — Watchmaker's shop

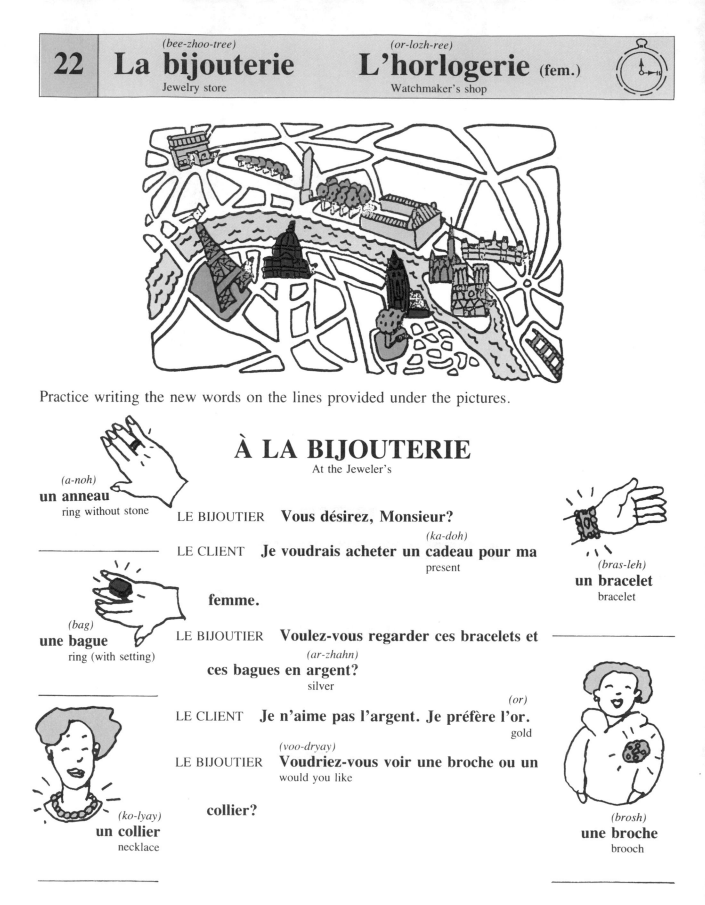

Practice writing the new words on the lines provided under the pictures.

À LA BIJOUTERIE

At the Jeweler's

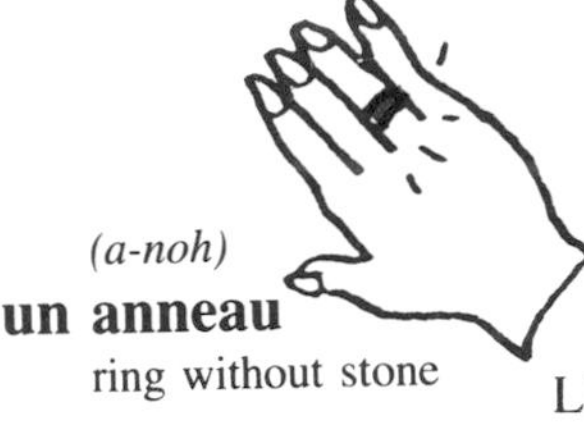

(a-noh)
un anneau
ring without stone

____

LE BIJOUTIER **Vous désirez, Monsieur?**

LE CLIENT **Je voudrais acheter un cadeau (ka-doh) pour ma femme.**
cadeau = present

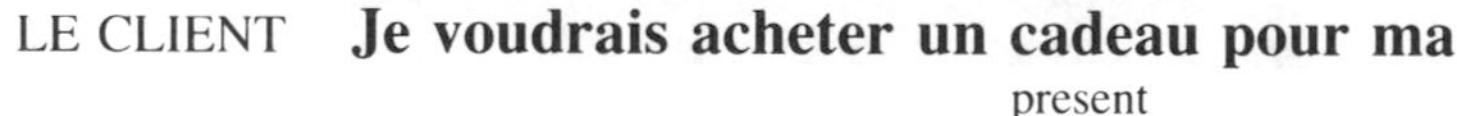

(bras-leh)
un bracelet
bracelet

____

LE BIJOUTIER **Voulez-vous regarder ces bracelets et ces bagues en argent (ar-zhahn)?**
argent = silver

(bag)
une bague
ring (with setting)

____

LE CLIENT **Je n'aime pas l'argent. Je préfère l'or (or).**
or = gold

LE BIJOUTIER **Voudriez-vous (voo-dryay) voir une broche ou un collier?**
voudriez-vous = would you like

(ko-lyay)
un collier
necklace

____

(brosh)
une broche
brooch

____

LE CLIENT **Oui. Montrez-moi un bracelet, un anneau en or, ou peut-être une paire de boucles d'oreille, s'il vous plaît.**
(pūh-tehtr) peut-être = maybe

LE BIJOUTIER **À pendentif?**

LE CLIENT **Oui. Et une bague avec une monture de pierres précieuses, et une chaînette en or.**
(mohn-tewr) monture = setting; *(pyer)* pierres = stones; *(pray-syūhz)* précieuses = precious

LE BIJOUTIER **Que pensez-vous de cette émeraude? Elle est superbe, n'est-ce pas?**
(em-rohd) émeraude; *(nes-pah)* n'est-ce pas = isn't it true?

LE CLIENT **Combien font les boucles d'oreille, la bague et la chaînette en or en tout?**
(fohn) font = make; *(ahn) (too)* en tout = altogether

LE BIJOUTIER **55.000 francs.**

LE CLIENT **La Place Vendôme est aussi chère que la Cinquième Avenue à New York! (Mettant sa main dans sa poche) haut les mains, s'il vous plaît!**
(oh-see) aussi = as . .; que = as . .; *(me-tahn)* Mettant = putting; *(man)* main = hand; poche = pocket; haut les mains = hands up

(bookl) **les boucles (fem.)** *(o-reh-y)* **d'oreille**
earrings

____

____

(sheh-neht) **une chaînette**
chain

____

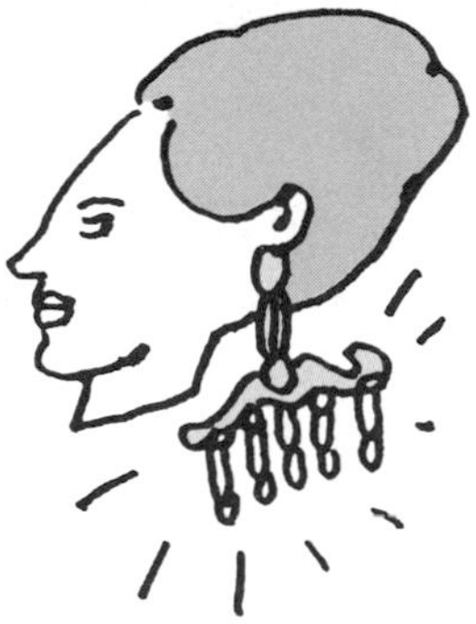

les boucles d'oreille *(pahn-dahn-teef)* **à pendentif**
pendant earrings

____

____

1. Name two items of jewelry you might wear on your fingers.

______________, ______________

2. What two sorts of jewelry do women wear on their ears?

______________, ______________

ANSWERS

Jewelry **1.** une bague, un anneau **2.** des boucles d'oreille, des boucles d'oreille à pendentif

3. What two types of jewelry are worn around the neck?

______________________, ______________________

4. What is worn on the wrist? ______________________

5. What might a woman pin on her dress? ______________________

If you're a big spender and well-heeled, you might want to know the names of some valuable **pierres précieuses**. Try writing them out even if your wallet is not too thick.

(dya-mahn)
un diamant
diamond

(pehrl)
des perles
pearls

(sa-feer)
un sapphir
sapphire

(aym-rohd)
une émeraude
emerald

(rew-bee)
un rubis
ruby

(to-pahz)
une topaze
topaze

(pla-teen)
le platine
platinum

(ar-zhahn)
l'argent
silver

(or)
l'or
gold

ANSWERS

3. un collier, une chaînette **4.** un bracelet **5.** une broche

L'HORLOGERIE

The Watchmaker's Shop

(mohntr)
une montre-bracelet
wristwatch

(ray-veh-y) (ma-tan)
un réveille-matin
alarm clock

(or-lozh-ree)
l'horlogerie
watchmaker's shop

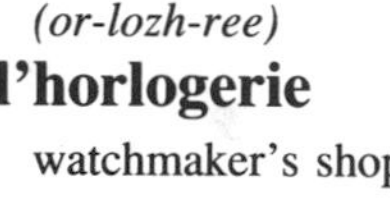

(or-lo-zhay)
l'horloger
watchmaker

Practice writing the new words by filling in the blanks under the pictures. Once you have done this, read aloud the sentences below which may help you when you visit the watchmaker's. After you have practiced them aloud, try writing them out in the spaces provided:

(ray-pa-ray) **Pouvez-vous réparer cette montre?**	Can you fix this watch?
Pouvez-vous nettoyer ma montre?	Can you clean my watch?
(a-vahns) **Ma montre avance.**	My watch is fast.
Mon réveille-matin retarde.	My alarm clock is slow.
(a-reh-tay) **Ma montre s'est arrêtée.**	My watch has stopped.
Elle ne marche pas bien.	It doesn't run well.

Notice: In France, watches, clocks (as well as cars, washing machines and other machines) don't run; they're more leisurely; they walk (the verb *marcher* literally means to walk).

(ruh-mohn-tay) **Je ne peux pas la remonter.**	I can't wind it.
(krees-tal) **Il me faut un cristal.**	I need a crystal.
Quand est-ce qu'elle va être prête?	When will it be ready?
(ruh-sew) **Pouvez-vous me donner un reçu?**	Can you give me a receipt?

Try reading this paragraph to see if you can understand it. You may need to refer to the previous sentences.

Ma montre ne marche pas bien. Un jour elle avance; un autre jour elle retarde. Aujourd'hui elle s'est arrêtée et je ne peux pas la remonter. Je vais l'apporter chez l'horloger et l'horloger va la réparer. Il va aussi la nettoyer. Si je dois laisser *(leh-say)* leave **ma montre à l'horlogerie, l'horloger va me donner un reçu.**

1. If you are always arriving late, what could be wrong with your watch?

   Ma montre ne ____________________ bien. Elle ____________________.

2. When you always seem to be early for appointments, what might be the matter?

   Ma montre ____________________.

ANSWERS

Fill in blanks
1. marche pas retarde. **2.** avance.

23 Le magasin de souvenirs

(soov-neer)

Gift Shop

Le magasin de musique

(mew-seek)

Music Store

Le magasin de photographie

(fo-to-gra-fee)

Photography Shop

(ka-doh)
un cadeau
present

(foo-lar)
un foulard
scarf

(ruh-pro-dewk-syohn)
une reproduction
reproduction

(par-fuhn)
du parfum
perfume

(por-tuh-fuh-y)
un portefeuille
wallet

(por-tuh) (klay)
un porte-clés
key ring

(port) (bo-nūhr)
un porte-bonheur
charm

(bee-zhoo)
un bijou
jewel

(port) (mo-neh)
un porte-monnaie
change purse

(sa) (ka) (man)
un sac à main
handbag

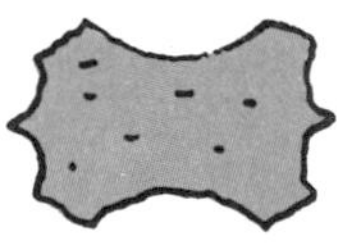

(kweer)
du cuir
leather

(ar-zhahn-tree)
de l'argenterie
silverware

(boo-teek)
UNE BOUTIQUE
boutique

Here are a few adjectives which may be useful when shopping for gifts and souvenirs:

(boh) (bel) **beau, belle**	beautiful	*(tee-peek)* **typique**	typical
(zho-lee) **joli, jolie**	pretty	*(fohn-say)* **foncé, foncée**	dark
(ra-vee-sahn) (ra-vee-sahnt) **ravissant, ravissante**	lovely	*(klehr)* **clair, claire**	light
cher, chère	expensive	*(bohn) (mar-shay)* **bon marché**	inexpensive

AU MAGASIN DE SOUVENIRS

At the gift shop

LA VENDEUSE **Vous désirez?**
Can I help you?

LE TOURISTE **Je voudrais un cadeau typiquement français.**
I would like a typically French present.

LA VENDEUSE **Pour un monsieur ou pour une dame?**
For a man or for a woman?

LE TOURISTE **Pour une dame.**
For a woman.

LA VENDEUSE **Un foulard en soie peut-être? Un sac en cuir, du parfum? Nous avons aussi ces belles reproductions des tableaux du Louvre et du Jeu de Paume.**
A silk scarf perhaps? A leather bag, some perfume? We also have these beautiful reproductions of paintings from the Louvre and from the Jeu de Paume.

LE TOURISTE **Combien coûte ce foulard?**
How much does the scarf cost?

LA VENDEUSE **Deux cent quinze francs. C'est un beau souvenir. Regardez: c'est une carte de la France avec tous les monuments.** *(mo-new-mahn)*
Two hundred fifteen francs. It is a beautiful souvenir. Look: it is a map of France with all the monuments.

LE TOURISTE **Je le prends. Pouvez-vous faire un joli paquet?**
I'll take it. Can you gift-wrap it?

(While the clerk gift-wraps the package, the tourist takes out his wallet.)

LE TOURISTE **Zut! Je n'ai pas assez d'argent. (À ce moment, sa femme entre dans le magasin.)**

Darn it! I don't have enough money. (At this moment, his wife enters the store.)

LA TOURISTE **Mais qu'est-ce que tu fais ici?**

But what are you doing here?

LE TOURISTE **Euh . . . . j'achète un cadeau pour toi . . . . Chérie, peux tu me prêter cent cinquante francs?**

(shay-ree) Chérie = darling; *(pre-tay)* prêter = lend

Uh . . . . I bought you a present . . . . Darling, can you lend me 150 francs?

Answer these questions based on the dialogue in French.

1. Qu'est-ce que le touriste voudrait acheter?
2. Pour qui?
3. Qu'est-ce que la vendeuse suggère?
4. Combien coûte le foulard?
5. Quel est le problème du touriste?
6. Le touriste a besoin de combien de francs?

AU MAGASIN DE DISQUES

At the Record Store

NOTE: A **magasin de musique** sells records, cassettes, radios, musical scores and musical instruments. A **magasin de disques** sells records, cassettes and record players, as well as radios.

(tay-lay-vee-zyohn)
une télévision
television

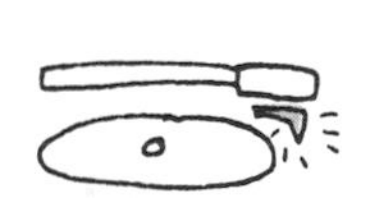

(dee-ah-mahn)
un diamant
needle

(trahnt) (trwah) (toor)
un 33 tours
33 rpm

(ka-rahnt) (san) (toor)
un 45 tours
45 rpm

(ra-dyoh)
une radio
radio

(toorn) (deesk)
un tourne-disque
record player

(ma-nyay-to-fon)
un magnétophone
tape recorder

ANSWERS

Dialogue 1. Le touriste voudrait acheter un cadeau typiquement français. **2.** Pour une dame. **3.** La vendeuse suggère un foulard en soie, un sac en cuir, du parfum, et des belles reproductions. **4.** Le foulard coûte deux cent quinze francs. **5.** Il n'a pas assez d'argent. **6.** Il a besoin de 150 francs.

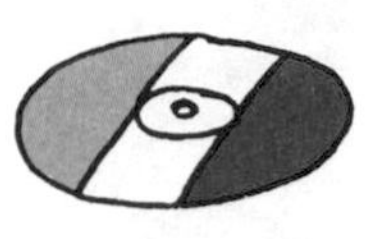

un disque
record

(ka-seht)
une cassette
cassette

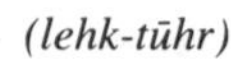

(lehk-tūhr)
un lecteur de cassette portatif
portable cassette player

(bahnd)
une bande
tape

La musique française

French music

La musique américaine

American music

(kla-seek)
La musique classique

Classical music

(fol-klo-reek)
La musique folklorique

Folk music

La musique pop (pop)

Pop music

(groh) (sewk-seh)
Un (gros) succès

A hit

Monsieur Laflûte adore la musique classique, mais il n'a pas beaucoup d'argent. Tous les samedis après-midi, il prend l'autobus ou le métro pour aller dans un magasin de disques, chaque fois dans un quartier *(kar-tyay)* section **différent** *(dee-fay-rahn)* different **de la ville. Il prend trois ou quatre disques, s'installe** *(sans-tal)* settles **dans une cabine et écoute ses compositeurs** *(kohn-poh-see-tūhr)* **préférés pendant** *(pahn-dahn)* for **deux heures au moins** *(mwan)* at least**. Puis il retourne chez lui** to his home**, heureux** *(ūh-rūh)* happy**, se réjouissant** *(suh) (ray-zhoo-ee-sahn)* looking forward **déjà du concert** *(kohn-sehr)* concert **de la semaine prochaine** *(pro-shehn)* next**.**

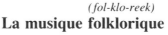

Can you answer the following questions?

1. Où va M. Laflûte le samedi? ____________________

2. Qu'est-ce que M. Laflûte aime? ____________________

3. Est-ce que M. Laflûte est riche? ____________________

4. Qu'est-ce que M. Laflûte écoute (ay-koot) [listens] tous les samedis après-midi?

____

5. Pourquoi M. Laflûte est-il heureux quand il retourne chez lui? Parce qu'il se réjouit du

____

AU MAGASIN DE MUSIQUE

At the Music Store

Madame Smith se promène, *(pro-mehn)* [walks around] **l'air un peu perdu,** *(pehr-dew)* [lost] **dans un magasin de disques. Après un long moment, le vendeur s'approche** *(sa-prosh)* [comes near] **d'elle.**

LE VENDEUR **Qu'est-ce que je peux faire pour vous?**

MARIE SMITH **Je cherche un disque pour un jeune Américain.**

LE VENDEUR **Est-ce qu'il aime la musique classique? La musique populaire? Les chansons?**

Les chansons populaires *(shan-sohn) (po-pew-lehr)*

Folk songs

MARIE SMITH **Je ne sais pas vraiment. C'est mon neveu,** *(nūh-vūh)* [nephew] **je ne le connais** [know] **pas très bien.**

LE VENDEUR **Peut-être les dernières** *(dehr-nyehr)* [latest] **chansons de Maxime Forestier** *(mak-seem) (fo-rehs-tyay)*?

MARIE SMITH **Maxime? Le restaurant?**

ANSWERS

Reading Paragraph 1. Il va au magasin de disques. **2.** Il aime la musique classique. **3.** Il n'a pas beaucoup d'argent. **4.** Il écoute des disques. **5.** concert de la semaine prochaine.

(nee) *(sew-pehr-trahnp)*
LE VENDEUR **N'y pensez plus. J'ai une idée: les Supertramps. Un gros succès ici.**
forget it

MARIE SMITH **C'est un groupe français?**

(sew-pehr-shoo-et)
LE VENDEUR **Mais oui! Superchouette!**
sensational!

MARIE SMITH **D'accord.**

(Un peu plus tard, à l'hôtel)

MARC **Alors, qu'est-ce que tu as trouvé pour Johnny?**
what did you find

MARIE **Les Supertramps. Ils sont superchouettes.**

(pohvr) *(shoo)*
MARC **Mais mon pauvre chou, les Supertramps sont américains. Tu vas retourner au**
poor darling
magasin demain, ça va être un bon exercice de français pour toi.

True or false?

1. Madame Smith voudrait acheter de la musique de Claude Debussy. T F
2. Il y a un restaurant à Paris qui s'appelle Chez Maxime. T F
3. Les Supertramps sont un groupe français. T F
4. Si Madame Smith retourne au magasin de disques demain, elle va faire un bon exercice de français. T F

AU MAGASIN DE PHOTOGRAPHIE

At the Photography Shop

une photo
print

(a-grahn-dees-mahn)
un agrandissement
enlargement

(ka-may-rah)
une caméra
movie camera

(dya-poh-zee-teev)
des diapositives (fem.)
slides

(a-pa-reh-y) (foh-toh-gra-feek)
un appareil photographique
camera

(roo-loh) *(feelm)*
un rouleau de film
roll of film

ANSWERS

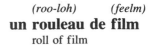

True or False **1.** F **2.** T **3.** F **4.** T

(dayv-lo-pay)
MARC **Je voudrais faire développer ce film.**

(dya-poh)
L'EMPLOYÉ **Vous voulez des diapos?**

MARC **Non. Des photos sur papier**

(mat)
mat, sept sur onze centimètres.
mat

(foh-toh)
L'EMPLOYÉ **Vos photos vont être prêtes dans trois**

jours. Voilà votre reçu.

(Three days later)

(shehr-shay)
MARC **Je viens chercher mes photos. Voilà mon reçu. Je voudrais aussi un rouleau de**
pick up

film en noir et blanc, trente-cinq millimètres, 20 photos.

(On the street, Mark opens the envelope.)

(groh) (bo-nom)
Mais qui est ce gros bonhomme?
fat fellow

(He goes back to the store.)

(fe) *(eh-rūhr)* *(vyan)*
L'EMPLOYÉ **Mon Dieu! J'ai fait une erreur. Le gros monsieur vient de partir avec vos**
I made mistake just left

(preh-say)
photos dans sa poche. Il a dit: "Je suis très pressé, je prends le train pour Marseille
he said in a big hurry

dans vingt minutes."

1. Quand Marc arrive au magasin de photos, il dit: "Je voudrais faire ______________ ce film."

2. L'employé demande: "Vous voulez des ______________?"

3. Marc répond: "Non. Des ______________________, sur papier ______________, sept sur ______________ centimètres."

4. L'employé dit que les photos vont être ____________ dans trois ______________.

ANSWERS

Questions 1. développer **2.** diapos **3.** photos mat onze **4.** prêtes jours

24 Les réparations:

(ray-pa-ra-syohn)

Repair services

Le cordonnier

(kor-do-nyay)

The shoemaker (cobbler)

L'opticien

(op-tee-syan)

The optometrist

Pour vraiment bien voir une ville ou un village, il faut marcher. Vous faites partie de la (are part) **foule** (fool) (crowd) **et la foule, vaquant** (va-kahn) (going about) **à ses occupations** (o-kew-pa-syohn) (chores)**, ne fait pas attention** (a-tahn-syohn) (pays no attention) **à vous. Vous pouvez observer** (ob-sehr-vay) **les visages** (vee-zahzh) (faces)**, entrer dans les magasins, examiner** (ehg-za-mee-nay) **les étalages** (ay-ta-lahzh) (displays) **des marchés en plein** (ahn) (plehn) **air** (ehr)**, marchander** (mar-shan-day) (bargain) **dans les marchés aux puces** (pews) (flea markets)**, flâner** (flah-nay) (stroll) **dans les jardins publics** (zhar-dan) (pew-bleek) (public gardens)**, lire les inscriptions** (ans-kreep-syohn) **sur les statues** (sta-tew)**. Pour tout cela** (suh-la) (that)**, il vous faut soit posséder** (swa) (po-seh-day) (either own) **de bonnes chaussures de marche, soit** (or) **connaître les mots et les expressions suivants** (swee-vahnt) (following)**:**

Pardon, pourriez-vous me dire s'il y a un cordonnier près d'ici?	Excuse me. Could you tell me if there is a shoemaker near here?

CHEZ LE CORDONNIER

At the Shoemaker

(shoh-sewr)
des chaussures
shoes

(la-seh)
des lacets
shoelaces

(sahn-dahl)
des sandales
sandals

le cordonnier
shoemaker

(ta-lohn) (kah-say) **Mon talon est cassé.** heel broken	My heel is broken.
(ray-pa-ray) **Est-il possible de réparer ma chaussure** *(pahn-dahn) (kuh) (zha-tahn)* **pendant que j'attends?**	Is it possible to fix my shoe while I wait?
Pour quand pouvez-vous la réparer? for when	When can you fix it?

Retenez . . .

Remember . . .

ouvert	open
jusqu'à	until
(suh-mel) **la semelle**	sole
(ew-zay) **usé**	worn
(ruh-suh-muh-lay) **ressemeler**	to resole
le plastique	plastic
temporaire	temporary
le talon	heel

CHEZ L'OPTICIEN

At the Optometrist's

l'opticien
optometrist

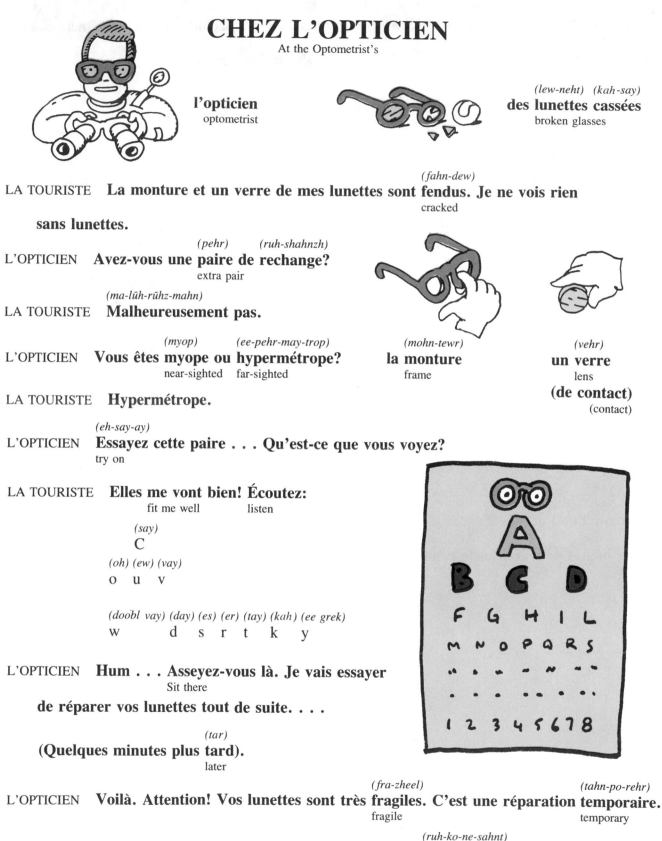

(lew-neht) (kah-say)
des lunettes cassées
broken glasses

(fahn-dew)
LA TOURISTE **La monture et un verre de mes lunettes sont fendus. Je ne vois rien**
cracked

sans lunettes.

(pehr) (ruh-shahnzh)
L'OPTICIEN **Avez-vous une paire de rechange?**
extra pair

(ma-lūh-rūhz-mahn)
LA TOURISTE **Malheureusement pas.**

(myop) (ee-pehr-may-trop)
L'OPTICIEN **Vous êtes myope ou hypermétrope?**
near-sighted far-sighted

(mohn-tewr)
la monture
frame

(vehr)
un verre
lens
(de contact)
(contact)

LA TOURISTE **Hypermétrope.**

(eh-say-ay)
L'OPTICIEN **Essayez cette paire . . . Qu'est-ce que vous voyez?**
try on

LA TOURISTE **Elles me vont bien! Écoutez:**
fit me well listen

(say)
C

(oh) (ew) (vay)
o u v

(doobl vay) (day) (es) (er) (tay) (kah) (ee grek)
w d s r t k y

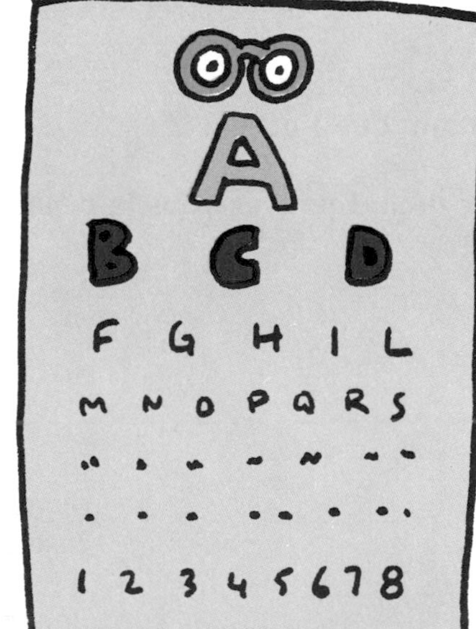

L'OPTICIEN **Hum . . . Asseyez-vous là. Je vais essayer**
Sit there

de réparer vos lunettes tout de suite. . . .

(tar)
(Quelques minutes plus tard).
later

(fra-zheel) (tahn-po-rehr)
L'OPTICIEN **Voilà. Attention! Vos lunettes sont très fragiles. C'est une réparation temporaire.**
fragile temporary

(ruh-ko-ne-sahnt)
LA TOURISTE **Merci mille fois, Monsieur. Je vous suis très reconnaissante.**
grateful

Retenez . . .
Remember . . .

réparer	to fix
(se-ray) **serrer**	to tighten
(so-leh-y) **les lunettes de soleil**	sunglasses
remplacer	to replace
(tood-sweet) **tout de suite**	right away
(fahn-dew) **fendu**	cracked
(ruh-shahnzh) **une paire de rechange**	a spare pair

After studying the optometrist and shoemaker vocabulary, try to draw lines between the French words and their English equivalent:

1. réparer	A. the cobbler
2. des lunettes	B. the shoelaces
3. des chaussures	C. to tighten
4. fendu	D. the heel
5. la monture	E. shoes
6. le talon	F. glasses
7. serrer	G. lens
8. les lacets	H. frame
9. les verres	I. to repair
10. le cordonnier	J. cracked

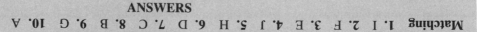

ANSWERS

Matching 1. I 2. F 3. E 4. J 5. H 6. D 7. C 8. B 9. G 10. A

ESSENTIAL SERVICES

(ser-vees) (eh-sahn-syel)
Services essentiels

25 La banque

(bahnk)
Bank

LES BILLETS ET LA MONNAIE

(bee-yeh) (mo-neh)
Bills and Coins

The basic unit of French currency is the **franc**, which is divided into 100 **centimes** *(sahn-teem)*. The following denominations of currency are presently in use:

5, 10, 20 copper-colored **centime** coins
50 **centime** coin (½ franc), 1, 2, 5, 50 (very rare) silver-colored **franc** coins
10 **franc** dark copper-colored coin which is replacing the 10 **franc** note still in circulation
10, 50, 100, 500 **franc** bills

If the exchange rate is 8 **francs** = $1.00, then the value of:

50 **francs** = \$ 6.25
100 **francs** = \$12.50
500 **francs** = \$62.50

The abbreviation for **francs** is **F**, and it is commonly used when referring to prices. Also bear in mind that when using numbers, the French use commas where we use periods, and periods where we use commas:

\$1.500,50 = fifteen hundred **francs**, fifty **centimes**.

To obtain the best exchange rate for your foreign currency, you will want to go to the nearest bank. Most French banks remain open from 9:30 A.M.–4:30 P.M. Some close for lunch, especially during the slower summer months. All banks close at noon on the day before a holiday.

Most large hotels will exchange your dollars if you are staying there. You can find **BUREAUX DE CHANGE** *(bew-roh)* in large banks, in airports and railroad stations, and at the border. **Attention!** If you are traveling during the weekend, don't forget to change your money at the border, as you may have difficulty finding a **bureau de change** open in small towns.

Courtesy of Ernst Klett Verlag, Stuttgart.

(sahn-teem)
Une pièce de dix centimes

Une pièce de vingt centimes

(pyehs)
Une pièce d'un demi-franc
(frahn)
½ franc
50 centimes

Une pièce d'un franc

une pièce de cinq francs
5 francs

Une pièce de dix francs
(frahn)
10 francs

(bee-yeh)
Un billet de dix francs

LES BANQUES, LE CHANGE, LES CHÈQUES DE VOYAGE

(shahnzh) *(shehk)* *(vwa-yahzh)*

Banks, Money Exchange, Traveler's Checks

Les gens et les choses

People and things

(ahn-plwah-yay)
l'employé de banque
bank employee

la banque
bank

(lee-keed)
l'argent liquide
cash

(ahn-pruhn)
l'emprunt (masc.)
loan (money you borrow)

(keh-syeh) *(keh-syehr)*
le caissier, la caissière
cashier (male and female)

l'argent
money

le billet de banque
banknote

(gee-sheh)
le guichet
teller's window

(bewl-tan) *(vehr-suh-mahn)*
le bulletin de versement
deposit slip

(kohnt)
le compte
account

(dee-rehk-tūhr)
le directeur
manager

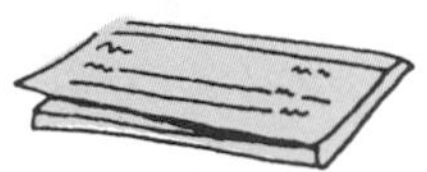

(kar-neh)
le carnet de chèques
checkbook

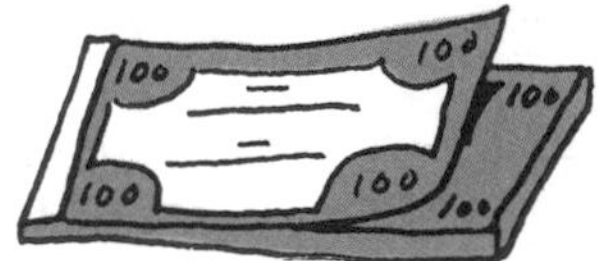

(vwa-yahzh)
le chèque de voyage
traveler's check

(mo-neh)
la monnaie
small change

Read the following dialogue out loud several times. It contains expressions you will need to conduct business in a bank.

Mr. Smith and his wife enter a bank in Paris in order to exchange some American dollars and traveler's checks.

M. SMITH	**Bonjour Monsieur. Je voudrais changer ce chèque de voyage de 100 dollars en francs français.** (chèque de voyage: traveler's checks)	Good day sir. I would like to exchange this $100 American traveler's check for French francs.
LE CAISSIER	**J'ai besoin de votre passeport.**	I need your passport.
M. SMITH	**Pourquoi?**	Why?
LE CAISSIER	**C'est comme ça. Il faut montrer une carte d'identité.** *(ee-dahn-tee-tay)*	That's the way it is. You have to show some identification.
M. SMITH	**Je l'ai oubliée à l'hôtel.**	I left it at the hotel.
MME SMITH	**J'ai mon passeport.**	I have my passport.
L'EMPLOYÉ	**Très bien, Madame.**	Very well, Madam.
MME SMITH	**Je voudrais aussi changer 500 dollars américains.**	I would also like to change 500 American dollars.
L'EMPLOYÉ	**Bon. Alors ça fait 600 dollars américains en tout?**	Okay. Then, it is 600 American dollars in all?
MME SMITH	**Oui.**	Yes.

L'EMPLOYÉ	That will be 4800 French francs. Take this slip to the cashier.
M. SMITH **Mais vous parlez anglais?**	But you speak English?
(stahzh) L'EMPLOYÉ **Bien sûr. J'ai fait un stage de deux ans à une banque à New York.**	Of course. I did a two-year internship at a bank in New York City.
(sa-pehr-lee-po-pet) (oh-ryay) M. SMITH **Saperlipopette! Vous auriez** *(pew)* **pu nous le dire plus tôt . . .**	For heavens sake! You could have told us earlier . . .
L'EMPLOYÉ (souriant) **Au revoir . . . et bon séjour en France!**	(smiling) Good-bye . . . and enjoy your stay in France!

(ko-mahn)

COMMENT . . .

How to . . .

(shahn-zhay)
changer
to exchange

(koor) (shahnzh)
le cours du change
exchange rate

(pay-yay)
payer
to pay

(day-poh-zay)
déposer
to deposit

(prayl-vay)
prélever
to withdraw

(oo-vreer) (kohnt)
ouvrir un compte
to open an account

(too-shay) (shek)
toucher un chèque
to cash a check

(see-nyay)
signer
to sign

Now see if you can remember these useful things. Match each expression or word to each picture by checking off the appropriate box:

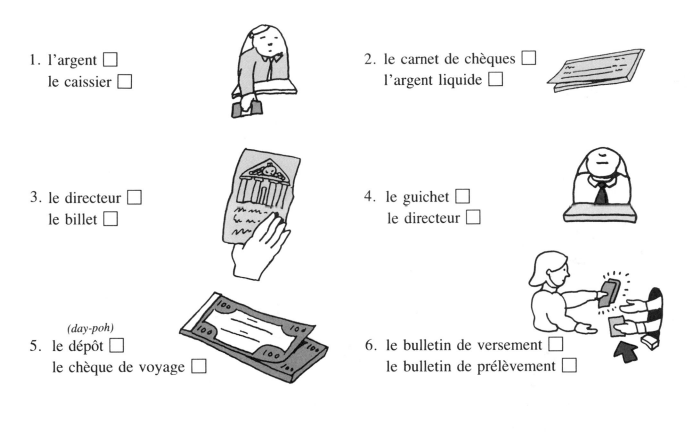

1. l'argent ☐
   le caissier ☐

2. le carnet de chèques ☐
   l'argent liquide ☐

3. le directeur ☐
   le billet ☐

4. le guichet ☐
   le directeur ☐

5. le dépôt ☐ *(day-poh)*
   le chèque de voyage ☐

6. le bulletin de versement ☐
   le bulletin de prélèvement ☐

Now, try to complete the following:

1. Je voudrais ____________ (exchange) dix dollars américains.

2. Je voudrais ____________ (withdraw) cinq cents francs.

3. Je voudrais ____________ (cash) un chèque.

4. Je voudrais ____________ (deposit) 500 francs.

ANSWERS

Match each expression **1.** le caissier **2.** le carnet de chèques **3.** le billet **4.** le guichet **5.** le chèque de voyage **6.** le bulletin de versement

Complete the following **1.** changer **2.** prélever **3.** toucher **4.** déposer

Match up the French expressions at the left with the English terms on the right:

1. L'emprunt
2. Les chèques de voyage
3. La monnaie
4. L'echange
5. Le caissier
6. Le guichet
7. Le compte
8. Le carnet de chèques

A. Exchange rate
B. Cashier
C. Loan
D. Small change
E. Teller's window
F. Traveler's checks
G. Checkbook
H. Account

(bahnk)

Comment aller à la banque?

Which way to the bank?

Suppose someone stops you on the street and asks for directions to get to the bank. You are now at the shoemaker's shop. Can you give him or her proper instructions? Use the map below.

ANSWERS

Banking 1. C 2. F 3. D 4. A 5. B 6. E 7. H 8. G

Which way to the bank Tournez à gauche. Allez tout droit. Tournez à gauche. Tournez à droite.

26 Le service de poste

(sehr-vees) *(post)*

Postal Service

(vyan)

Je viens de . . .

I just . . .

Remember the immediate future, simply formed with **aller** in the present tense followed by an infinitive? To express the immediate past, you simply use **venir** (to come) + **de** or **d'** before a vowel + infinitive. The English equivalent of this construction is: ''I just went to the post office.'' (*Je viens d'aller à la poste.*)

(ahn-vwa-yay) **Je viens d'envoyer une lettre à ma mère.**	I just sent a letter to my mother.
Tu viens d'arriver?	Did you (familiar) just arrive?
Il vient d'acheter une voiture.	He just bought a car.
Nous venons d'aller à Paris.	We just went to Paris.
Vous venez d'apprendre quelque chose de nouveau.	You just learned something new.
Marc et Marie viennent de partir.	Marc and Marie just left.

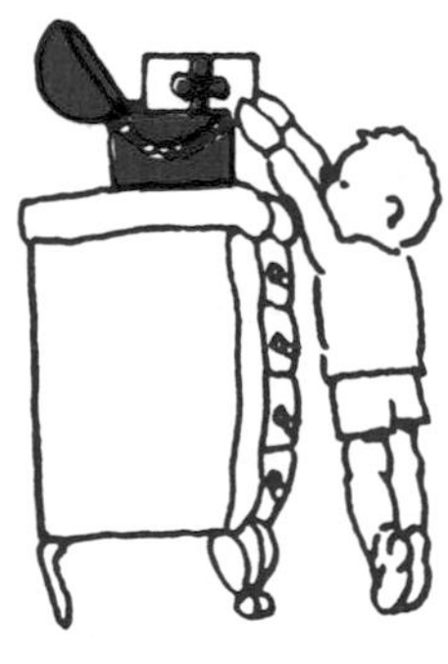

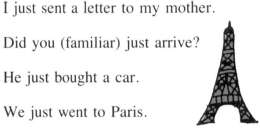

It's lunch time. Jeannot, 5 years old, comes home, out of breath and looking happy.

JEANNOT **Je viens de jouer au facteur,** *(fak-tūhr)* **maman!** *(ma-mahn)*	I just played mailman, mommy.
MAMAN **Au facteur? Comment peut-on jouer au facteur sans lettres?**	Mailman? How can one play mailman without letters?

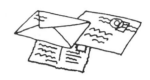

JEANNOT	**Mais j'ai des lettres.**	But I do have letters.
MAMAN	**Quelles lettres?**	What letters?
JEANNOT	**Dans la commode** *(ko-mod)* **de ta chambre, tu sais bien . . . le paquet de lettres avec un beau ruban** *(rew-bahn)* **rose autour** *(oh-toor)* **. . .**	In the bureau of your room, you know . . . the package of letters with a beautiful pink ribbon around . . .
MAMAN	**Oui . . . eh bien?**	Yes . . . so?
JEANNOT	**Eh bien! Je viens de mettre une lettre sous chacune** *(shah-kewn)* **des portes de notre rue.**	So! I just put one letter under each door of our street.

You may find it very useful, upon your arrival in France, to stop in a large post office and pick up their brochures for foreigners. Under the heading **"Les P.T. sont heureux de vous souhaiter** *(soo-eh-tay)* (to wish) **la bienvenue,"** *(byanv-new)* (welcome) (The French P.T. [Poste et Télécommunications] are glad to welcome you), these publications will give you all sorts of information **(en français, en anglais, en allemand, en italien et en espagnol)** about their services, which are generally efficient. They even give tourists some key phrases such as: **Y a-t-il un bureau de poste ouvert le dimanche matin?** The answer to that is yes, but only in large railroad stations. Mail **(le courrier)** is distributed twice a day (three times in businesses), and Paris has a unique service: **le pneumatique,** *(nūh-ma-teek)* which dispatches letters from one end of Paris to the other in two or three hours.

le facteur
mailman

la boîte aux lettres
mailbox

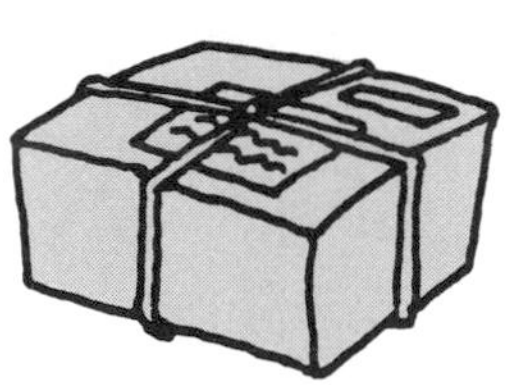

le paquet/le colis *(ko-lee)*
package

poste restante *(rehs-tahnt)*
general delivery

(gee-shay)
le guichet
window

la poste
post office

(koo-ryay)
le courrier
mail

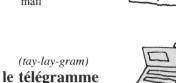

(a-frahn-sheer)
affranchir
to put stamps on a letter or package

(tay-lay-gram)
le télégramme
telegram

faire suivre
to forward

Jean et Françoise vont à la poste.

(John has quite a few chores to do. His Parisian friend Françoise helps him out.)

JEAN	**Combien de timbres faut-il que je mette sur cette lettre-avion pour Seattle?**	How many stamps should I put on this airmail letter to Seattle?
FRANÇOISE	**Je ne sais pas. Allons la faire peser à la poste.**	I don't know. Let's go and have it weighed at the post office.
JEAN	**Dans ce cas,** *(kah)* **je vais aussi envoyer ce colis à New York. D'où puis-je envoyer un télégramme à mon patron?** *(pa-trohn)*	In that case, I'll also mail this package to New York. From where can I send a telegram to my boss?
FRANÇOISE	**De la poste.**	From the post office.
JEAN	**C'est commode.** *(ko-mod)* **Je dois aussi faire un coup de téléphone interurbain. . .** *(an-teh-rewr-ban)*	That's handy. I must also make a long-distance telephone call. . . .
FRANÇOISE	**À la poste.**	At the post office.
JEAN	**Et il me faut payer la facture de mon dentiste . . .**	And I have to pay my dentist's bill. . . .
FRANÇOISE	**À la poste.**	At the post office.

JEAN *(ehks-tror-dee-nehr)* **Extraordinaire!** — Extraordinary!

Est-ce que je peux aussi faire nettoyer mon complet, louer une voiture, faire ma réservation *(ray-zehr-va-syohn)* **d'avion et manger de la glace au chocolat à la poste?** — Can I also have my suit cleaned, rent a car, make my plane reservation and eat a chocolate ice cream at the post office?

À LA POSTE

At the Post Office

FRANÇOISE **Voilà le guichet-colis.** — Here is the parcel post window.

LE POSTIER (postal employee): **Pourriez-vous remplir cette formule** *(for-mewl)* **s'il vous plaît?** — Could you please fill out this form?

JEAN **D'accord. Avez-vous des timbres?** — Okay. Do you have stamps?

LE POSTIER **Allez au guichet-timbres là-bas.** — Go to the stamp window over there.

JEAN **Il y a aussi des cartes postales?** — Are there also postal cards?

LE POSTIER **Bien sûr.** — Of course.

JEAN **Mademoiselle, pourriez-vous peser cette lettre?** — Miss, could you weigh this letter?

LA POSTIÈRE **Deux francs quatre-vingts.** — 2 francs 80.

JEAN **Et est-ce que vous avez de la glace au chocolat?** — And do you have any chocolate ice cream?

How about changing the immediate future into an immediate past as in the example below:

Je vais aller à la poste.	**Je viens d'aller à la poste.**
1. Jean va envoyer un colis.	Jean ______________ envoyer un colis.
2. Jean va aussi acheter des timbres-poste.	Jean ______________ acheter des timbres-poste.
3. Nous allons oublier notre passeport.	Nous ______________ oublier notre passeport.
4. Anne et Jean vont voyager en Europe.	Anne et Jean ______________ voyager en Europe.
5. Qu'est-ce que vous allez faire?	Qu'est-ce que vous ______________ faire?

Fill in blanks with French words:

Pour envoyer son ______________, Jean va au guichet-colis.

Jean achète aussi des ______________.

Les employés de la poste s'appellent les ______________.

ANSWERS

Immediate past **1.** vient d' **2.** vient d' **3.** venons d' **4.** viennent de **5.** venez de

Fill in blanks colis (paquet) timbres-poste facteurs

27 Le service téléphonique

(sehr-vees) (tay-lay-foh-neek)

Telephone Service

(a-loh) (a-loh)

ALLÔ? ALLÔ?

Hello? Hello?

(a-loh) **Allô? Allô?**	Hello . . . Hello?
(kee) (eh) (ta) (la-pa-reh-y) **Qui est à l'appareil?**	Who is it?
Je voudrais parler à . . .	I would like to speak to . . .
(me-sahzh) **Puis-je laisser un message?**	May I leave a message?
Dites à . . . que Marc Smith *(ra-play) (tar)* **va rappeler plus tard.**	Tell . . . that Mark Smith will call back later.
Mademoiselle/Monsieur!	Operator! (Address an operator as "mademoiselle" or "monsieur.")
(ko-mew-nee-ka-syohn) (moh-vehz) **La communication est mauvaise.**	This is a bad connection.
(ay-tay) (koo-pay) **Nous avons été coupés.**	We have been cut off.
C'est une erreur.	This is the wrong number.
(pay-say-vay) **Je voudrais faire un appel en P.C.V.**	I would like to make a collect call.
(pray-a-vee) **Je voudrais faire un appel avec préavis.**	I would like to make a person-to-person call.
(kee-tay) **Ne quittez pas!**	Don't hang up. (Wait a minute.)
(kohn-poh-say) **Composer un numéro**	To dial a number
(day-kro-shay) (ray-sehp-tūhr) **Décrocher (le récepteur)**	To pick up the receiver
(ra-kro-shay) **Raccrocher (le récepteur)**	To hang up
(a-new-ehr) **L'annuaire**	Telephone book
(zhuh-tohn) **Le jeton**	Token

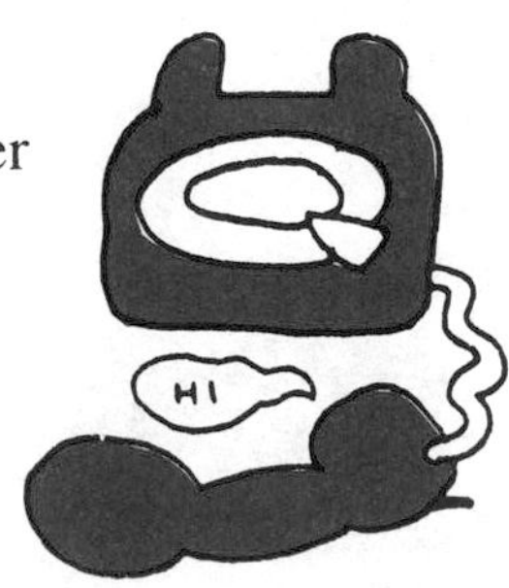

The easiest method for telephoning is to do it through the **réceptionniste** *(ray-sehp-syo-neest)* at the hotel. Another possibility is to go to the post office. Public pay phones often require a token **(un jeton)** *(zhuh-tohn)*, which can be purchased at cafés, the post office, etc. As you know, **les P. T. sont heureux de vous souhaiter la bienvenue**. But if you want to be challenged and to practice your **français**, you might follow the example of **Marc et Marie**, who wish to reach their friend **à Versailles** *(vehr-sa-y)*.

MARC (à un passant) **Pourriez-vous me dire où il y a une cabine téléphonique?**	(To a passerby) Could you tell me where there is a telephone booth?
LE PASSANT **Vous voyez l'écriteau avec un téléphone, devant ce café? Ça veut dire qu'il y a un téléphone public.**	You see the sign with a telephone on it, in front of that cafe? That means that there is a public telephone.
MARC **Merci, vous êtes très aimable. Viens, Marie.**	Thank you, you are very kind. Come on, Mary.

À LA CABINE TÉLÉPHONIQUE
(ka-been) (tay-lay-foh-neek)

At the Telephone Booth

MARIE **Tu as un jeton?**	Have you got a token?
MARC **Oui. (À lui-même): Je décroche, je mets le jeton dans la fente. J'attends la tonalité** *(to-na-lee-tay)* (dial tone)**. Bon, ça** (it's) **sonne** (ringing)**. Je compose le numéro: 44-53-42.**	Yes. (To himself): I pick up the receiver, I put the token into the slot, I wait for the dial tone. Good, it's ringing. I'm dialing the number: 44-53-42.
Allô? Allô?	Hello, hello?
Alice? C'est Marc à l'appareil.	Alice? This is Mark calling.
UNE VOIX *(vwah)* **Quel numéro appelez-vous?**	What number are you calling?

MARC **Le quatre quatre cinq trois . . . Zut! On a été coupé. Opérateur?**

Four four five three . . . Darn it! We've been cut off. Operator?

L'OPÉRATEUR **Allô, j'écoute.**

Hello, I'm listening.

MARC **Pouvez-vous me donner la communication avec Mme Alice Dupont à Versailles . . . .**

Can you connect me with Mrs. Alice Dupont in Versailles . . . .

L'OPÉRATEUR (très vite) *(day)* **D Daniel,** *(ew)* **U Ursule,** *(pay)* **P Pierre,** *(oh)* **O Oscar,** **N Nadine et** *(tay)* **T comme Théodore?**

(Very fast): D Daniel, U Ursula P Peter O Oscar N Nadine and T as in Theodore?

MARC (pris de panique) **Mademoiselle, je ne comprends pas un mot de ce que vous dites.**

(Suddenly panicky) Miss, I don't understand a word of what you're saying.

(He hangs up and leaves the booth.)

MARC **Viens, Marie. Nous allons retourner à l'hôtel et demander au** *(zhahn-tee)* **gentil réceptionniste de nous aider.**

Come on, Mary. We're going to return to the hotel and ask the nice receptionist to help us.

After studying the expressions at the beginning of this section and the dialogue, can you fill in the blanks in the sentences below?

1. Si je veux téléphoner, d'abord, je demande où il y a une ______________ (telephone booth).
2. Ensuite, je ______________ (pick up) le récepteur.
3. Puis j'attends la ______________ (dial tone).
4. Alors, je ______________ (dial the number).
5. Si la personne à qui je voudrais parler n'est pas là, je dis: "Puis-je laisser un ________ (message)?"

ANSWERS

Fill in blanks **1.** cabine téléphonique **2.** décroche **3.** tonalité **4.** compose le numéro **5.** message

28 Les docteurs/Les médecins

(dok-tūhr) *(mayd-san)*

Doctors

Les dentistes — Les hôpitaux

(dahn-teest) *(o-pee-toh)*

Dentists — Hospitals

UNE RÉPÉTITION GÉNÉRALE

(ray-pay-tee-syohn) *(zhay-nay-rahl)*

A Once Over . . .

(Paul and Anne are at it again. This time they test each other on the parts of the human body.)

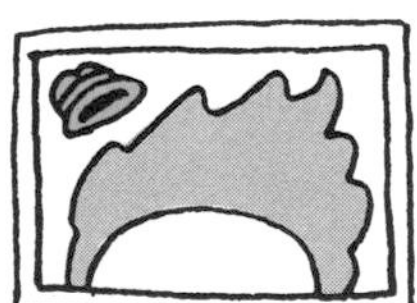

PAUL	**Alors, qui commence, toi ou moi?**	Well, who starts, you or me?
ANNE	**Tu me demandes en premier.**	You ask me first.
PAUL	**Bon. Qu'est-ce que tu as là?**	Good. What do you have there?
ANNE	*(shuh-vūh)* **Les cheveux.**	Hair.
PAUL	*(yūh)* **Entre les cheveux et les yeux?**	Between the hair and the eyes?
ANNE	*(frohn)* **Le front.**	The forehead.
PAUL	*(oh) (duh-sew)* **Au-dessus des yeux?**	Over the eyes?
ANNE	*(soor-see)* **Les sourcils.**	The eyebrows.

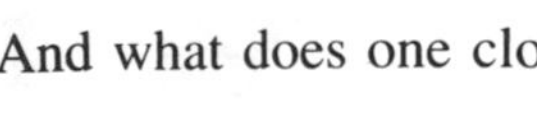

PAUL	**Et qu'est-ce qu'on ferme quand on dort?**	And what does one close when one sleeps?
	(poh-pyehr)	
ANNE	**Les paupières.**	The eyelids.
PAUL	**Et sur les paupières il y a . . .**	And on the eyelids there are . . .
	(seel)	
ANNE	**les cils.**	lashes.
PAUL	**Et entre les yeux il y a . . .**	And between the eyes there is
	(nay)	
ANNE	**le nez.**	the nose.
PAUL	**Et entre le nez et la bouche, beaucoup d'hommes ont** *(boosh)*	And between the nose and the mouth, many men have
	(moos-tash)	
ANNE	**une moustache.**	a moustache.
PAUL	**Tu as deux . . .**	You have two . . .
	(o-reh-y)	
ANNE	**oreilles**	ears
PAUL	**et deux . . .**	and two . . .
	(zhoo)	
ANNE	**joues**	cheeks
PAUL	**mais seulement un . . .**	but only one . . .
	(vee-zahzh)	
ANNE	**visage**	face
PAUL	**et seulement une . . .**	and only one . . .
	(tet)	
ANNE	**tête.**	head.
	(ree)	
PAUL	**Quand tu ris, on voit . . .**	When you laugh, one sees . . .
	(dahn)	
ANNE	**les dents**	the teeth
PAUL	**et quand tu vas chez le docteur, tu lui montres la**	and when you go to the doctor's, you show him the

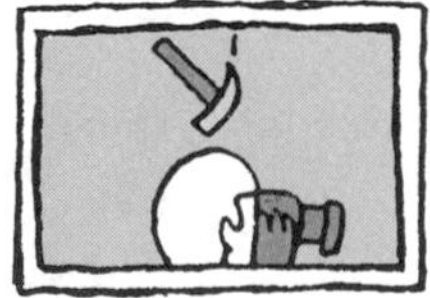

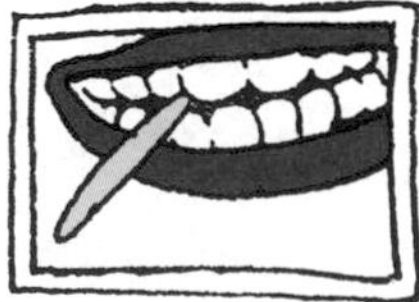

ANNE *(lahng)* **langue, aaaaaaah . . .** — tongue, aaa. . .

PAUL **Ça, c'est le...** — This is the. . .

ANNE *(mahn-tohn)* **menton** — chin

PAUL **et ça, le...** — and this, the. . .

ANNE *(koo)* **cou.** — neck.

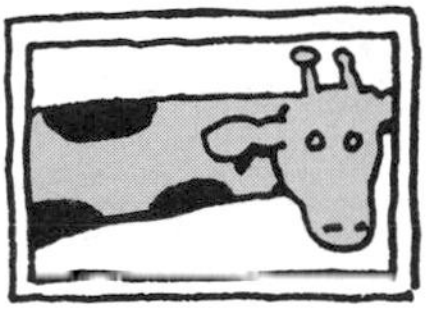

PAUL **Voilà deux...** — Here are two

ANNE *(ay-pohl)* **épaules** — shoulders,

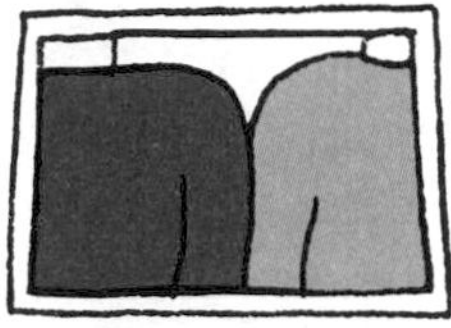

PAUL **deux...** — two . . .

ANNE *(brah)* **bras** — arms

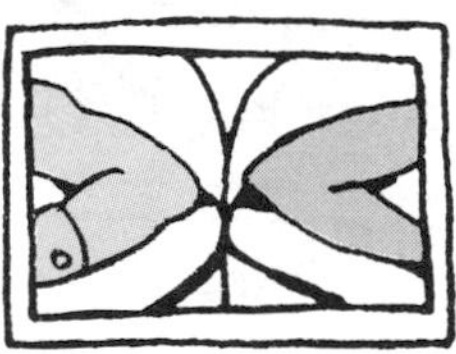

PAUL **et deux...** — and two. . .

ANNE *(kood)* **coudes** — elbows

PAUL **deux...** — two

ANNE *(man)* **mains** — hands

PAUL **et dix...** — and ten . . .

ANNE *(dwa)* **doigts.** — fingers.

PAUL **Mon tour maintenant.** — My turn now.

ANNE **Ça, c'est le** — This is the . . .

PAUL *(doh)* **dos** — back

ANNE **et là-devant, la . . .** — and here in front, the . . .

PAUL *(pwa-treen)* **poitrine.** — chest.

ANNE **Quelque chose te fait mal quand tu manges trop de gâteau:** — Something hurts you when you eat too much cake:

(es-to-ma)
PAUL **l'estomac.** — the stomach.

ANNE **Et un peu plus bas il y a le...** — And a little lower is the

(vahntr)
PAUL **ventre.** — belly.

ANNE **Et derrière il y a le . . .** — And behind there is the . . .

(de-ryer)
PAUL **derrière** — behind

ANNE **et d'ici jusque là tu as deux . . .** — and from here to there you have two . . .

(kwees)
PAUL **cuisses** — thighs

ANNE **et ensuite deux** — and then two . . .

(zhuh-noo)
PAUL **genoux** — knees

ANNE **et plus bas les deux . . .** — and farther down the two . . .

(mo-le)
PAUL **mollets** — calves

ANNE **jusqu'aux deux . . .** — down to the two . . .

(shuh-vee-y)
PAUL **chevilles.** — ankles.

ANNE **Et ce que tu te laves une fois par an, ce sont les . . .** — And what you wash once a year are the . . .

(pyay)
PAUL **pieds** — feet

ANNE **avec les dix . . .** — with the ten . . .

(or-te-y)
PAUL **orteils.** — toes.

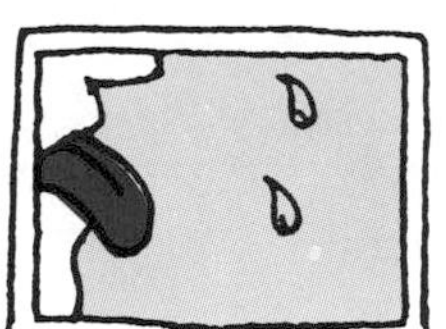

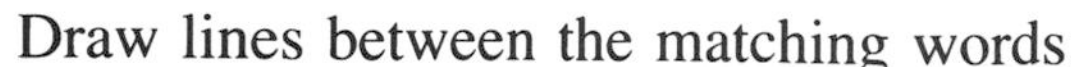

Draw lines between the matching words:

1. le front
2. les orteils
3. la bouche
4. les chevilles
5. la langue
6. les paupières
7. l'estomac
8. le visage
9. la moustache
10. les dents

A. tongue
B. face
C. eyelids
D. forehead
E. ankles
F. toes
G. stomach
H. mouth
I. teeth
J. moustache

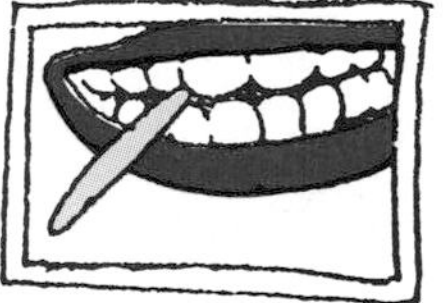

(sehn-teer)

Se sentir (bien, mal)

To feel

Do you remember the second group of **IR** verbs you studied in Chapter 5? When the verb **SENTIR** (to smell, to feel) is made reflexive, it is used to describe the state of one's health.

Toilettes (W.C.)

Dames **Messieurs**

Je me sens bien.	I feel well.
Je me sens mal.	I feel sick.
Je ne me sens pas très bien.	I don't feel very well.

Parts of the body are usually preceded with the definite article LE, LA, L', LES.

Je me lave les mains.	I wash my hands.
J'ai mal à la tête.	My head hurts, I have a headache.

Remembering that À + LE becomes AU and À + LES AUX, can you practice this construction with parts of the body?

Example: **J'ai mal à la tête.**
J'ai mal au dos.
J'ai mal aux oreilles.

ANSWERS

Match words **1.** (D) **2.** (F) **3.** (H) **4.** (E) **5.** (A) **6.** (C) **7.** (G) **8.** (B) **9.** (J) **10.** (I)

Draw lines between the expressions which match:

1. J'ai mal aux dents.
2. J'ai mal au dos.
3. J'ai mal à la tête.
4. J'ai mal au pied.
5. J'ai mal aux oreilles.
6. J'ai mal aux yeux.
7. J'ai mal à l'estomac.
8. J'ai mal au genou gauche.
9. Je me suis fait mal.
10. Je me suis fait mal au doigt.

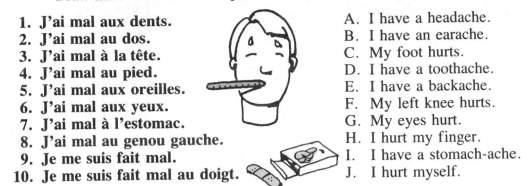

A. I have a headache.
B. I have an earache.
C. My foot hurts.
D. I have a toothache.
E. I have a backache.
F. My left knee hurts.
G. My eyes hurt.
H. I hurt my finger.
I. I have a stomach-ache.
J. I hurt myself.

In case of a minor medical complaint which cannot be solved with **des aspirines,** you can always walk into a **pharmacie** and say:

Excusez-moi Monsieur/Madame.	Excuse me.
(kohn-se-y) **Pouvez-cous me donner un conseil? J'ai très mal __________________.**	Can you give me some advice? My ________ hurts badly.

(far-ma-syan) *(far-ma-syehn)*
If the **pharmacien** or **pharmacienne** cannot help you, he/she will give you the address of a doctor. So will the hotel's receptionist. Doctors usually have consultation hours for patients who do not have an appointment. You may have to wait a long time, so it's better, if possible, to make an appointment ahead of time. In case of an emergency in Paris, you can call

(prohn) *(suh-koor)*
707.77.77, 336.03.86, the Police (17), or **Prompt Secours** (18), and even ask for an
prompt assistance

English-speaking doctor. In the provinces, all the emergency numbers are on page one of the telephone book. A few pharmacies remain open all night and during the weekend. The local paper carries a list. In case of a toothache, the procedure is the same.

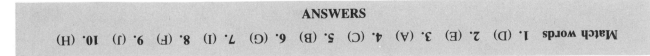

ANSWERS

Match words **1.** (D) **2.** (E) **3.** (A) **4.** (C) **5.** (B) **6.** (G) **7.** (I) **8.** (F) **9.** (J) **10.** (H)

DITES AAAAAAAAAH . . .

Say Aaaaaaaaah . . .

(gorzh)
Marie a mal à la gorge. (Mary has a sore throat.) She makes an appointment with Dr. Rebouteux, a general practitioner *(zhay-nay-rah-leest)* **(généraliste).**

LE DOCTEUR **Bonjour, Madame.** — Hello, madam.

(khes) (keen) (va) (pah)
Qu'est-ce qui ne va pas? — What's wrong?

(a) (pehn)
MARIE **Je peux à peine parler.** — I can hardly speak.

LE DOCTEUR **Ouvrez la bouche et dites "trente-trois."** — Open your mouth and say "trente-trois."

MARIE **Pourquoi trente-trois?** — Why 33?

LE DOCTEUR **C'est comme ça. Oui, la gorge est un peu rouge. Comment vous sentez-vous autrement?** *(oh-truh-mahn)* — That's the way it is. Yes, your throat is a little red. How do you feel otherwise?

(boo-shay)
MARIE **Mal. J'ai le nez bouché et j'ai mal à la tête.** — Poorly. I have a stuffed nose and a headache.

LE DOCTEUR **Prenons votre température.** — Let's take your temperature.

(Mary opens her mouth).

LE DOCTEUR **La température est normale. C'est un méchant rhume avec un peu d'angine . . . .** *(may-shahn) (rewm) (ahn-zheen)* — Your temperature is normal. It's a bad cold with a little angina . . . .

MARIE **Angine?** — Angina?

(an-fek-syohn)
LE DOCTEUR **Oui, une petite infection à la gorge. Je vais vous donner une ordonnance. Prenez un comprimé toutes les quatre heures.** *(kohn-pree-may)* — Yes, a mild throat infection. I'll give you a prescription. Take one pill every four hours.

(oo-vray) *(boosh)*

OUVREZ LA BOUCHE!

Open Wide!

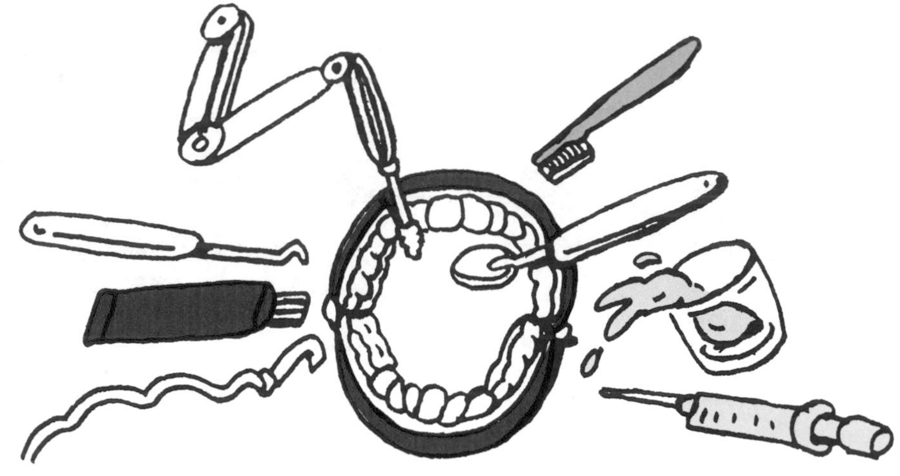

Mark has a toothache. A friend recommends a dentist with whom she is most satisfied. Mark's appointment is today at 2:00 P.M.

MARC (à la réceptionniste) **J'ai un rendez-vous.**	(To the receptionist) I have an appointment.
LA RÉCEPTIONNISTE **Avec le Docteur** *(bwee-sohn)* **Buisson?**	With Dr. Buisson?
MARC **Oui, pour deux heures.**	Yes, for 2 o'clock.
LA RÉCEPTIONNISTE **Votre nom, s'il vous plaît?**	Your name, please?
MARC **Marc Smith.**	Mark Smith.
LA RÉCEPTIONNISTE (Elle examine le livre de rendez-vous.) *(eh-feh)* **En effet.**	(She examines the appointment book.) That's correct.
LA RÉCEPTIONNISTE *(plas)* **Prenez place. Il y a du monde aujourd'hui. C'est votre première visite?**	Take a seat. There are a lot of people today. Is this your first visit?
MARC **Oui.**	Yes.

LA RÉCEPTIONNISTE **Pourriez-vous remplir cette carte s'il vous plaît?**

Could you fill out this card please?

(Une heure plus tard)

(One hour later)

(a-sees-tahnt) (dahn-ter)
L'ASSISTANTE DENTAIRE **Monsieur Smith?**

Mr. Smith?

MARC **Oui?**

Yes?

L'ASSISTANTE **Prenez place dans ce**
(foh-tuh-y)
fauteuil. Le docteur arrive.

Sit in this armchair. The doctor will be here soon.

(Quinze minutes plus tard.)

(15 minutes later)

LE DENTISTE **Monsieur Smith? Où avez-vous mal? Ici? Voyons . . . Ça**
(brahnl)
fait mal? Et ça? Oui—et ça branle un
(plohn-bahzh)
peu par ici. Le plombage est tombé.
(a-nehs-tay-zee)
Je vais vous faire une anesthésie
(lo-kahl) (boo-shay)
locale. Puis je vais boucher la dent
(tahn-po-rehr)
avec un amalgam temporaire. Ce bridge ici est mal placé et cette
(koo-ron) (mwa-tyay) (fee-shew)
couronne est à moitié fichue. Dans deux ou trois ans vous allez avoir
(dahn-tyay)
besoin d'un dentier.

Mr. Smith? Where does it hurt? Here? Let's see . . . It hurts? And that? Yes—and it wobbles a bit around here. The filling has fallen out. I'm going to give you a local anesthesia. Then I'll fill the tooth with a temporary amalgam. This bridge here doesn't sit well and this crown is half-finished. In two to three years you're going to need a denture.

(ray-zwee) (kūhr)
MARC **Cela me réjouit le coeur.**

That makes my heart rejoice.

LE DENTISTE **Au revoir Monsieur, et**
(bon) (va-kahns)
bonnes vacances!

Good-bye, and enjoy your vacation!

Can you match up the words in the left column with the definitions in the right column?

1. **généraliste**
2. **mal à la gorge**
3. **le nez bouché**
4. **rendez-vous**
5. **anesthésie locale**
6. **plombage**
7. **dentier**

A. stuffed nose
B. appointment
C. general practitioner
D. filling
E. sore throat
F. denture
G. local anesthesia

A L'HÔPITAL

At the Hospital

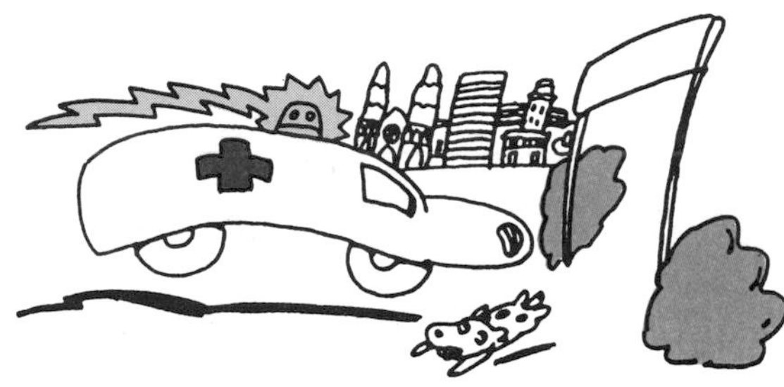

(André, Aunt Agnes's husband, has symptoms which look like a heart attack. The ambulance takes him to the hospital; Agnes and Suzanne stay in the waiting area.)

AGNÈS	**Tu es vraiment gentille** *(zhahn-te-y)* **d'être venue avec moi. Je suis un peu inquiète** *(an-kyet)***.**	You are really kind to have come with me. I am a little worried.
SUZANNE	**Où est-il maintenant?**	Where is he now?
AGNÈS	**Dans la salle des urgences** *(ewr-zhahns)***.**	In the emergency room.
SUZANNE	**Est-ce qu'il est souvent malade?**	Is he often sick?
AGNÈS	**Pas du tout. Il est costaud** *(kos-toh)* **comme un cheval.**	Not at all. He's as strong as a horse.
SUZANNE	**Voilà l'infirmière** *(an-feer-myehr)* nurse**.**	Here is the nurse.

ANSWERS

Match up 1. C 2. E 3. A 4. B 5. G 6. D 7. F

AGNÈS **Comment va mon mari?**

How is my husband?

L'INFIRMIÈRE **Tout va bien! Le docteur** *(muh-zewr)* **mesure** **sa** *(tahn-syohn)* **tension** *(ar-tay-ryehl)* **artérielle.** **Suivez-moi.** (In the room)

Everything is fine! The doctor is taking his blood pressure. Follow me.

AGNÈS **Alors, mon trésor, comment te sens-tu?**

So, my treasure, how are you feeling?

ANDRÉ **Un peu fatigué, mais bien autrement.**

A little tired, but fine otherwise.

AGNÈS (au docteur): **Docteur, qu'est-ce qu'il a?**

Doctor, what's the matter with him?

LE DOCTEUR **Un peu de** *(fa-teeg)* **fatigue, c'est tout.**

A little fatigue, that's all.

AGNÈS (à André) **Tu vois, mon chou? Je te répète tout le temps que tu travailles trop, tu ne fais pas assez d'exercise et tu fumes trop.**

You see, my darling? I'm always telling you that you work too much, don't take enough exercise and smoke too much.

Retenez

Remember

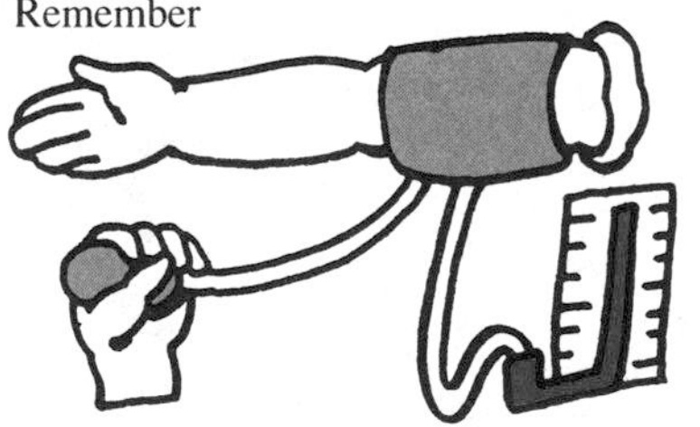

(fyehvr)
la fièvre
fever

(vee-zeet)
la visite
visit

la gorge
throat

(or-do-nahns)
l'ordonnance
prescription

(spay-see-men) (ew-reen)
le spécimen d'urine
urine specimen

(ma-lad)
le malade
patient

(tahn-syohn) (ar-tay-ryel)
la tension artérielle
blood pressure

(tahn-pay-ra-tewr)
la température
temperature

(an-feer-myehr)
l'infirmière
nurse

(zhay-nay-ra-leest)
le généraliste
general practitioner

(spay-sya-leest)
le spécialiste
specialist

(pwah)
le poids
weight

See if you can answer the following questions pertaining to the dialogues on the doctor, dentist, and hospital:

1. Pourquoi Marie va-t-elle chez le docteur? Parce qu'elle a
   A. mal à l'estomac
   (ma-la-dee)
   B. une maladie cardiaque
   illness
   C. mal à la gorge

2. Le docteur donne à Marie
   A. un conseil
   B. des comprimés
   C. une ordonnance

3. Marc va chez le dentiste
   A. parce qu'il a mal aux dents
   B. parce qu'il a besoin d'un dentier
   C. pour trouver une couronne

4. Qui est dans la salle d'attente du docteur Buisson?
   A. Jean
   B. beaucoup de monde
   C. un dentiste très patient

5. Qui a une petite crise?
   A. André
   B. Jean
   C. Agnès

ANSWERS

Dialogues 1. C 2. C 3. A 4. B 5. A

Have fun with the following puzzle:

ACROSS
3. prescription
5. hand
6. throat
7. nose
8. illness

DOWN
1. arm
2. hospital
3. ear
4. pill
9. tooth

ANSWERS

Puzzle ACROSS **3.** ordonnance **5.** main **6.** gorge **7.** nez **8.** maladie
DOWN **1.** bras **2.** hôpital **3.** oreille **4.** comprimé **9.** dent

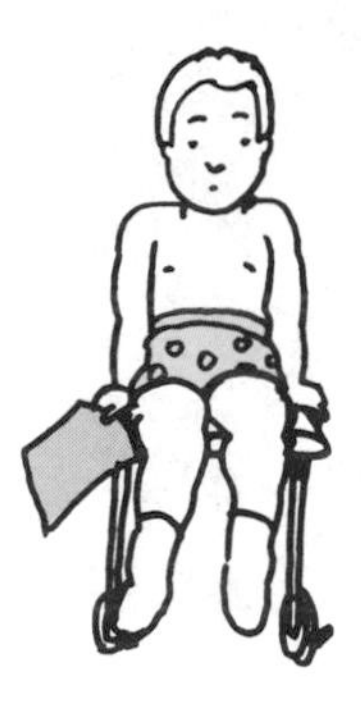

Un jeune homme entre dans la salle
(say-lehbr)
d'attente d'un célèbre spécialiste des
(o-sūhz)
maladies osseuses. Il dit à l'infirmière

qu'il voudrait parler au docteur en
(pree-vay)
privé. "Entrez ici," dit l'infirmière,
(day-za-bee-yay)
"déshabillez-vous et attendez."

A young man walks into the waiting room of a famous specialist of bone diseases. He tells the nurse that he would like to talk with the doctor in private. "Come in here," the nurse says, "get undressed and wait."

"Mais . . . ."

"But . . . ."

LE DOCTEUR **Qu'est-ce qui ne va pas?**

What's the matter with you?

"Je suis ici," répond le jeune homme,

"pour vous demander si vous voulez
(ruh-noov-lay) *(a-bon-mahn)*
renouveler votre abonnement

à "Paris-Match."

"I am here," replies the young man, "to ask you if you want to renew your subscription to "Paris-Match."

Can you remember? Just answer **vrai ou faux.**

1. ________ Le jeune homme voudrait parler au docteur et à l'infirmière.
2. ________ Le jeune homme est malade.
3. ________ Le docteur est un spécialiste du coeur.
4. ________ Le jeune homme demande au docteur s'il veut continuer son abonnement à "Paris-Match."

ANSWERS

Vrai ou faux **1.** F **2.** F **3.** F **4.** V

29 Comment obtenir de l'aide

(ob-tuh-neer) *(ehd)*

How to get help

Here is a little courtroom drama. As in English the speakers use the present tense to give a sense of immediacy to their remarks.

(zhewzh) LE JUGE judge	**Donc vous cassez votre parapluie sur le crâne** *(krahn)* **de votre mari.**	So you break your umbrella over your husband's skull.
(ay-pooz) L'ÉPOUSE the wife	**Un accident, Monsieur le Juge.**	An accident, your honor.
LE JUGE	**Comment est-ce possible?**	How is that possible?
L'ÉPOUSE	**Je n'ai pas l'intention** *(an-tahn-syohn)* **de casser le parapluie.**	I do not intend to break the umbrella.

COMMENT APPELER UNE AMBULANCE

(ahn-bew-lahns)

How to Call an Ambulance

If you need an ambulance in Paris, you can call **S.O.S.** (707.77.77 or 336.03.86), the **Police** (17) or **Prompt Secours** (18). In small towns, emergency telephone numbers are listed on page 1 of the telephone directory. If you are near a pharmacy you'll find help there.

(At a party, Jack meets Dr. Henri Lasanté, a health officer of the French government.)

JACQUES	**Qu'est-ce que je dois faire si ma femme a une crise cardiaque?**	What should I do if my wife has a heart attack?

LE DR. LASANTÉ **Pas de problème. Vous appelez ou demandez à quelqu'un d'appeler Prompt Secours et une ambulance va venir immédiatement. Ne dites pas: "Ma femme a mal au coeur" parce que "avoir mal au coeur" veut dire "avoir la nausée (noh-zay)." Dites:** ***"Ma femme vient d'avoir une crise cardiaque."***

No problem. You call or ask somebody to call the **Prompt Secours** and an ambulance will come immediately. Do not say: "My wife has mal au coeur" because this means to be nauseated. Say: "My wife just had a heart attack."

JACQUES **Les ambulances ont de l'oxygène (ok-see-zhehn) et tout l'équipement (ay-keep-mahn) nécessaire (nay-se-sehr)?**

The ambulances have oxygen and all the necessary equipment?

LE DR. LASANTÉ **Bien sûr.**

Of course.

Ne vous inquiétez pas.

Don't worry.

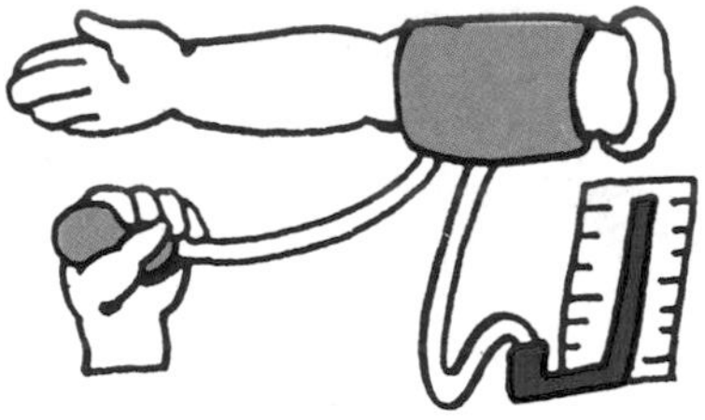

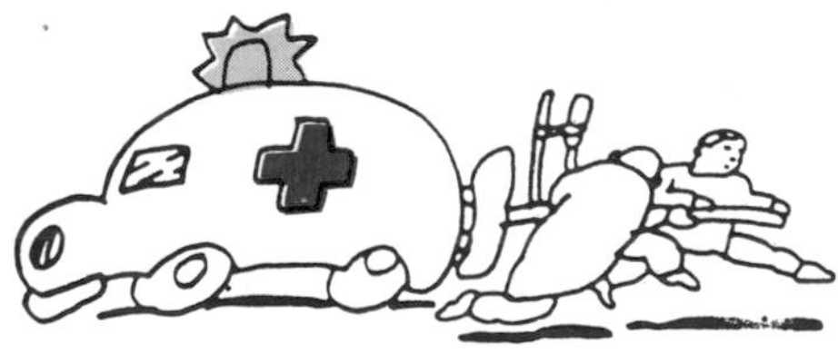

COMMENT APPELER LA POLICE (po-lees)

How to Call the Police

In case of emergency, ask the hotel's receptionist to call the police. If you are walking, ask a pedestrian or an **agent de police**:

Pouvez-vous me dire où est le commissariat?

Can you tell me where the police station is?

If you are traveling in the provinces, the number of the police is on the first page of the telephone book.

(At the same party, Jack meets a retired police official, Pierre Leflic.)

JACQUES **Quelle est la différence entre un**
(a-zhahn) *(zhahn-darm)*
agent de police, un gendarme et un
(say-ehr-es)
C.R.S.?

What's the difference between an "agent de police," a "gendarme" and a C.R.S.?

LEFLIC ***L'agent de police* dirige la circulation dans les villes. *Le gendarme* est sur les routes, en voiture**
(moh toh) *(mee lee tehr)*
ou à moto. Le *C.R.S.*, un militaire,
(mo-bee-lee-zay)
est mobilisé pour assurer l'ordre en
(ma-nee-fehs-ta-syohn)
cas de manifestation publique.

The *agent de police* regulates traffic in the cities. The *gendarme* is on the roads, in a car or on a motorcycle. The *C.R.S.*, a military man, is mobilized to keep order in the case of public demonstrations.

(pyay-tohn)
JACQUES **Est-ce que les piétons traversent la**
(an-tehr-dee)
rue quand c'est interdit, comme en Amérique?

Do pedestrians cross the street illegally as in America?

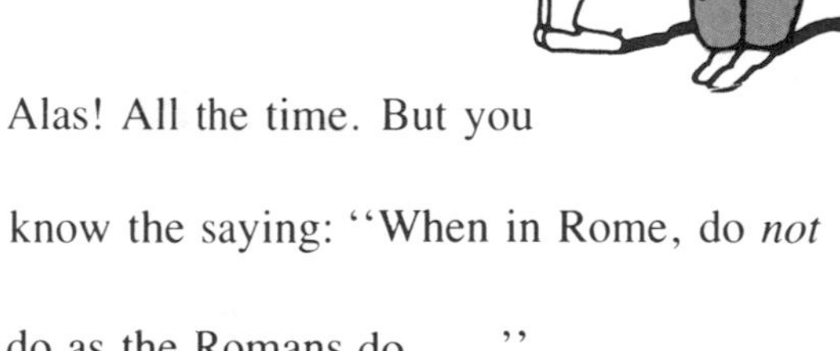

(ay-lahs) (tool) (tahn)
LEFLIC **Hélas! Tout le temps. Mais vous**
(deek-tohn)
connaissez le dicton: À Rome, *ne* faites *pas* comme les Romains . . ."

Alas! All the time. But you know the saying: "When in Rome, do *not* do as the Romans do . . ."

BEFORE YOU LEAVE

Avant de partir

Now we have come to the final step in the learning process, and the most important one. What will you do in the following situations? It may be worthwhile to look over each unit to help you.

Situation 1: Faisons connaissance

1. It is day and you meet someone. What do you say in order to start a conversation?
   A. À bientôt
   B. Bonjour
   C. Au revoir

2. You have just run into a friend. What do you say?
   A. Merci
   B. Salut
   C. Au revoir

3. You introduce the friend to your wife. You say:
   A. Je te présente . . .
   B. Je vous en prie . . .
   C. Je vais bien merci . . .

4. Someone asks you how you are. Which of the following is *not* possible as an answer?
   A. Pas mal, merci
   B. Très bien, merci
   C. Bonjour, merci

Situation 2: L'arrivée

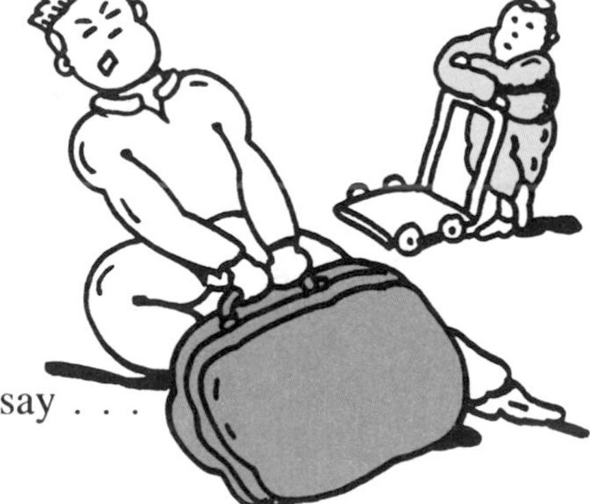

1. You do not have a reservation at the hotel. What do you say?
   A. Comment allez-vous, Monsieur?
   B. Excusez-moi, Monsieur, je n'ai pas de réservation.
   C. Bonjour, Monsieur, comment vous appelez-vous?

2. You want to say that you would like a room. You say:
   A. S'il vous plaît, je voudrais une chambre.
   B. S'il vous plaît, je ne veux pas de salle de bain.
   C. S'il vous plaît, je veux une fenêtre dans ma chambre.

3. You want to inquire about price and what is included. So you say . . .
   A. Pouvez-vous me dire où sont les toilettes?
   B. Pouvez-vous me dire combien coûte la chambre et si le service est compris?
   C. Pouvez-vous me dire comment vous vous appelez?

ANSWERS

Situation 1 1. B 2. B 3. A 4. C **Situation 2** 1. B 2. A 3. B

Situation 3: Allons voir les curiosités

1. You are on foot and you want to find a certain street. You ask a passerby the following:
   A. Pardon, où allez-vous?
   B. Pardon, où est la rue du Cherche-Midi?
   C. Pardon, où habitez-vous?

2. The passerby might give you various directions such as . . .
   A. À gauche, à droite, tout droit . . .
   B. Demain, hier, aujourd'hui . . .
   C. Le bureau de poste, la banque, le bureau de tabac . . .

3. Now you have just gotten onto a bus. You want to ask where to get off. You say . . .
   A. Excusez-moi, combien coûte le billet?
   B. Excusez-moi, où dois-je descendre pour la rue . . .
   C. Excusez-moi, comment vous appelez-vous?

4. You have flagged down a taxi, but before getting on you want to know how much it would cost to get to **la rue Molière.**
   A. Excusez-moi, est-ce que la rue Molière est loin?
   B. Excusez-moi, savez-vous où est la rue Molière?
   C. Excusez-moi, c'est combien pour aller à la rue Molière?

5. You have forgotten your watch. You stop a passerby to ask what time it is. You say . . .
   A. Pardon, quelle heure est-il?
   B. Pardon, j'ai une montre.
   C. Pardon, quel temps fait-il?

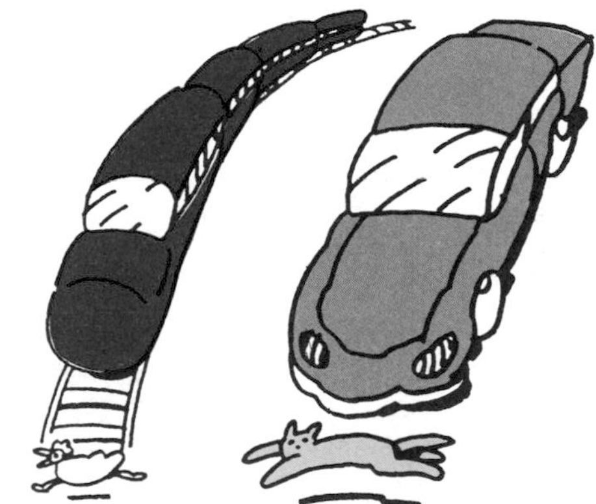

6. The passerby would *not* answer . . .
   A. Il est deux heures vingt-cinq.
   B. C'est demain.
   C. Il est une heure et demie.

7. You are at the train station and want to buy a ticket.
   A. Excusez-moi, combien coûte un billet pour Lyon?
   B. Excusez-moi, où est Lyon?
   C. Excusez-moi, quelle heure est-il?

8. The clerk answers that there is no room left on the train. He might say something like . . .
   A. Je suis désolé, mais vous êtes porteur.
   B. Je suis désolé, mais vous ne parlez pas français.
   C. Je suis désolé, mais il n'y a pas de place.

9. You want to say to someone that you are American and speak only a little French. You might say . . .
   A. Je suis américain, je parle un tout petit peu le français.
   B. Je parle américain, je ne suis pas français.
   C. Je ne suis pas français, je suis américain.

Situation 3 1. B 2. A 3. B 4. C 5. A 6. B 7. A 8. C 9. A

10. You want to rent a car cheaply. You might ask the clerk . . .
   A. Je voudrais une voiture pas trop chère.
   B. Je voudrais une voiture pas trop sale.
   C. Je voudrais une voiture pas trop bon marché.

11. You want to fill up your car. You might say . . .
   A. S'il vous plaît, une voiture jaune.
   B. S'il vous plaît, faites le plein.
   C. S'il vous plaît, c'est trop cher.

12. A service station attendant might tell you that your car needs repairs. He would *not* say...
   A. Votre voiture est belle.
   B. Votre voiture a besoin de nouveaux freins.
   C. Votre voiture a besoin d'un nouveau moteur.

13. You ask a "camping employee" if there are essential services. You would *not* say . . .
   A. Est-ce qu'il y a de l'eau?
   B. Est-ce qu'il y a des toilettes?
   C. Est-ce qu'il y a un cinéma?

14. As an answer to "Quelle est la date d'aujourd'hui?" (What's today's date?), you would not hear . . .
   A. C'est le trente mars.
   B. C'est le deuxième jour.
   C. C'est le trois mai.

15. To ask an airline employee at what time your flight leaves, you would say . . .
   A. Pardon, à quelle heure part mon vol?
   B. Pardon, quand arrive mon vol?
   C. Pardon, vous volez souvent?

16. With which statement does the picture go?
   A. Je voudrais louer une voiture pour une semaine.
   B. Je voudrais deux billets aller-retour pour Paris en deuxième classe.
   C. À quelle heure part le vol pour Zurich?

Situation 4: Les distractions

1. You are at a ticket agency. The clerk would *not* ask you . . .
   A. Vous voulez un billet d'opéra?
   B. Vous voulez un billet de cinéma?
   C. Vous voulez un billet d'avion?

2. If someone were to ask you what your favorite sport was **(Quel est votre sport préféré?)**, you would *not* say . . .
   A. J'aime le tennis.
   B. J'aime la natation.
   C. J'aime le français.

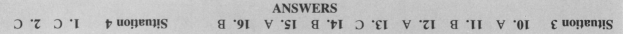

ANSWERS

Situation 3 10. A 11. B 12. A 13. C 14. B 15. A 16. B **Situation 4** 1. C 2. C

Situation 5: Choisissant des repas

1. You want to ask what the restaurants in France are like. You would ask . . .
   A. On mange bien en France?
   B. Comment sont les restaurants?
   C. Où sont les restaurants?

2. As a possible answer, you would *not* hear . . .
   A. Ils sont à Paris.
   B. Il y a beaucoup de restaurants.
   C. Ils sont bons.

3. When a waiter asks you to order, he might say . . .
   A. Vous désirez?
   B. Vous payez?
   C. Vous finissez?

4. To see the menu, you would say . . .
   A. Puis-je voir la cuisine?
   B. Puis-je voir la carte?
   C. Puis-je voir le directeur?

5. One of the following is not connected with eating . . .
   A. droguerie
   B. restaurant
   C. assiette

6. If you wanted to order some vegetables you would say . . .
   A. Une assiette de soupe chaude, s'il vous plaît.
   B. Un plat de légumes, s'il vous plaît.
   C. Des pamplemousses, s'il vous plaît.

7. After which course would you expect to be served your salad?
   A. l'entrée
   B. le fromage
   C. le dessert

8. An example of a dessert you might order is . . .
   A. du poisson
   B. de la glace
   C. de la confiture

9. At the end of a meal you say to the waiter/waitress . . .
   A. Le couteau, s'il vous plaît.
   B. Le pourboire, s'il vous plaît.
   C. L'addition, s'il vous plaît.

10. How would you ask if the tip is included on your bill?
    A. Le petit déjeuner est servi?
    B. La taxe est correcte?
    C. Le service est compris?

ANSWERS

Situation 5 1. B 2. A 3. A 4. B 5. A 6. B 7. A 8. B 9. C 10. C

Situation 6: Au magasin

1. Which of the following would you *not* say in a clothing store?
   A. Pardon, combien coûte cette chemise?
   B. Pardon, combien coûte ce pain?
   C. Je voudrais des chaussures, des chaussettes et des cravates.

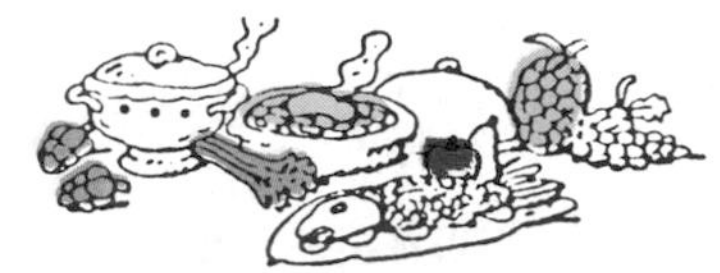

2. One of the following lists has nothing to do with clothing . . .
   A. complet bleu, robe de laine, chemise blanche
   B. gants de cuir, chaussures du soir, chemise de soie
   C. légumes, viandes, fruits

3. You would *not* hear which of the following in a butcher's shop?
   A. Combien coûtent les fruits?
   B. La viande coûte 18 francs le kilo.
   C. Le veau est frais.

4. You want to order a drug at the pharmacy. You might say . . .
   A. Je voudrais ces légumes, s'il vous plaît.
   B. Je voudrais ce médicament, s'il vous plaît.
   C. Je voudrais ces fruits, s'il vous plaît.

5. A pharmacist would *not* ask you one of the following . . .
   A. Voulez-vous une bouteille de vin?
   B. Voulez-vous des aspirines?
   C. Avez-vous une ordonnance?

6. You are at the laundry. You would *not* ask one of the following . . .
   A. Pouvez-vous laver et repasser ces chemises pour demain?
   B. Faites-vous aussi le nettoyage à sec?
   C. Combien coûtent les chaussures?

7. You are at the barber's and want a haircut. You might say . . .
   A. S'il vous plaît, donnez-moi un paquet de cigarettes.
   B. S'il vous plaît, coupez-moi les cheveux très courts.
   C. S'il vous plaît, donnez-moi un billet.

8. The hairdresser might ask you . . .
   A. Voulez-vous une mise en plis?
   B. Voulez-vous un biscuit?
   C. Voulez-vous un journal?

ANSWERS

Situation 6 **1.** B **2.** C **3.** A **4.** B **5.** A **6.** C **7.** B **8.** A

9. Choose the store for each question (match them up):

A. Combien coûte la réparation de mes chaussures?	1. cordonnerie
B. Est-ce qu'il me faut une nouvelle montre?	2. papeterie
C. Combien coûtent un journal et une revue?	3. magasin de photographie
D. Pouvez-vous développer les photos?	4. magasin de disques
E. Combien coûtent ces disques?	5. horlogerie
F. Est-ce que vous vendez du papier à lettres?	6. bureau de tabac
G. Combien coûte cette robe?	7. bijouterie
H. Cette bague est magnifique.	8. magasin de confection-dames

10. Each of these stores is selling an item which should be carried by another store. Can you correct the situation?

A. **PRÊT-À-PORTER**
1. **robes**
2. **collants**
3. **saucisson**
4. **jupes**

B. **SOUVENIRS**
1. **viande froide**
2. **reproductions**
3. **cartes postales**
4. **foulards**

C. **BOULANGERIE**
1. **croissants**
2. **pain**
3. **linge**
4. **petits fours**

D. **CHARCUTERIE**
1. **bagues**
2. **jambon**
3. **pâté**
4. **salami**

Situation 7: Services essentiels

1. You are at a bank and wish to exchange a traveler's check . . .
   A. Excusez-moi, pourriez-vous me dire l'heure?
   B. Excusez-moi, pourriez-vous me changer ce chèque de voyage?
   C. Excusez-moi, pourriez-vous me donner un cadeau?
2. A bank employee would *not* ask you . . .
   A. S'il vous plaît, remplissez cette formule.
   B. S'il vous plaît, signez ici.
   C. S'il vous plaît, mangez du pain.
3. You want to buy stamps at a post office. You would say . . .
   A. S'il vous plaît, je voudrais acheter du fromage.
   B. S'il vous plaît, je voudrais acheter des journaux.
   C. S'il vous plaît, je voudrais acheter des timbres.

4. Which of the following would you *not* say in a post office?
   A. Je voudrais envoyer cette lettre par avion.
   B. Je voudrais envoyer ce colis.
   C. Je voudrais écrire une lettre maintenant.

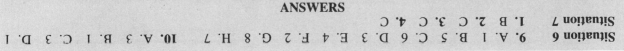

ANSWERS

Situation 6 **9.** A 1 B 5 C 6 D 3 E 4 F 2 G 8 H 7 **10.** A 3 B 1 C 3 D 1

Situation 7 **1.** B **2.** C **3.** C **4.** C

5. You answer a phone call with . . .
   A. Allô
   B. Au revoir
   C. À bientôt

6. You want to make a long distance phone call. You would say . . .
   A. Excusez-moi, je voudrais payer la facture téléphonique.
   B. Excusez-moi, je voudrais faire un appel interurbain.
   C. Excusez-moi, je voudrais votre numéro de téléphone.

7. You want to ask someone how to dial a number. You would say . . .
   A. S'il vous plaît, comment faut-il composer le numéro?
   B. S'il vous plaît, où est le téléphone?
   C. S'il vous plaît, combien coûte la communication?

8. Which of the following would *not* be used to seek help in an emergency?
   A. S'il vous plaît, appelez une ambulance.
   B. S'il vous plaît, appelez la police.
   C. S'il vous plaît, dites-moi où vous habitez.

9. You would *not* say one of the following to a doctor.
   A. Docteur, j'ai mal à la tête.
   B. Docteur, j'ai besoin d'un parapluie.
   C. Docteur, j'ai de la fièvre.

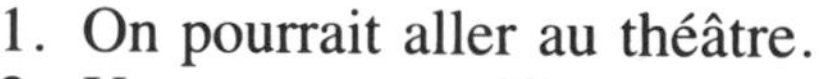

10. Can you match the questions in the left column with statements in the right column?

   A. Comment vous appelez-vous?
   B. Où descendons-nous pour aller au cinéma Broadway?
   C. Quelle heure est-il?
   D. Où puis-je acheter du lait?
   E. Pourriez-vous me couper les cheveux?
   F. Avez-vous des journaux en anglais?
   G. Il y a un trou dans ma chaussure. Pouvez-vous la réparer?
   H. Avez-vous des timbres?
   I. Combien coûte un billet aller-retour à Cannes pour quatre personnes?
   J. Est-ce qu'il y a un garage près d'ici?
   K. Quel temps fait-il?
   L. Qu-est-ce que tu veux faire ce soir?

   1. On pourrait aller au théâtre.
   2. Un temps magnifique!
   3. À la laiterie.
   4. Allez au guichet-timbres.
   5. Aimez-vous les cheveux courts?
   6. Je ne peux pas la réparer.
   7. Oui, nous avons un bon choix de journaux anglais et americains.
   8. À l'arrêt après la Concorde.
   9. Il est midi.
   10. Oui, au coin de la prochaine route.
   11. 800 francs par personne.
   12. Je m'appelle Marc Smith.

ANSWERS

Situation 7 **5.** A **6.** B **7.** A **8.** C **9.** B **10.** A. 12 B. 8 C. 9 D. 3 E. 5 F. 7 G. 6 H. 4 I. 11 J. 10 K. 2 L. 1

Use the target word on top to answer the question. Then, check the answer on the back.

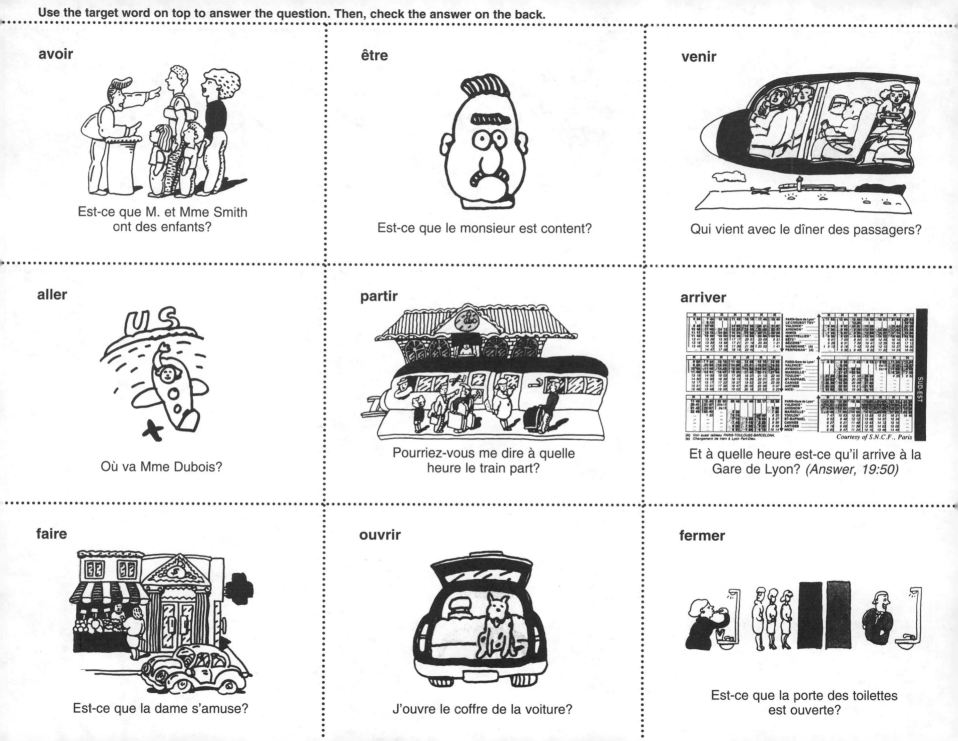

avoir

Est-ce que M. et Mme Smith ont des enfants?

être

Est-ce que le monsieur est content?

venir

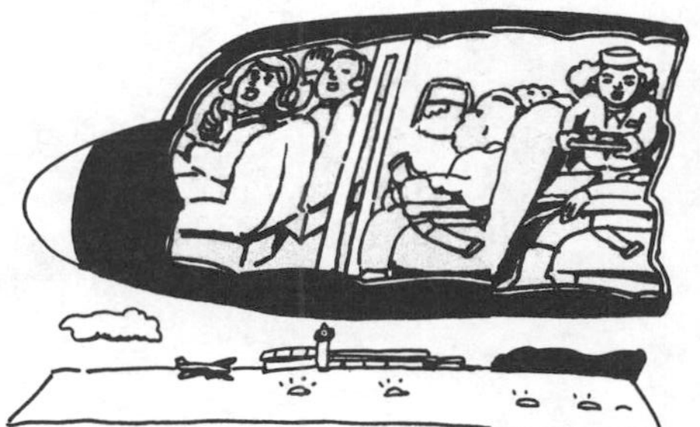

Qui vient avec le dîner des passagers?

aller

Où va Mme Dubois?

partir

Pourriez-vous me dire à quelle heure le train part?

arriver

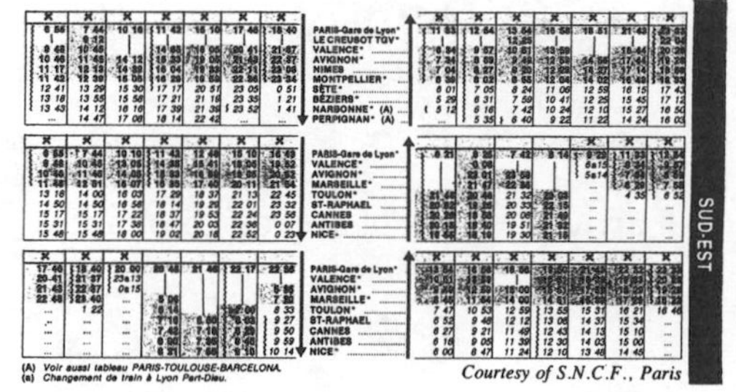

Courtesy of S.N.C.F., Paris

Et à quelle heure est-ce qu'il arrive à la Gare de Lyon? *(Answer, 19:50)*

faire

Est-ce que la dame s'amuse?

ouvrir

J'ouvre le coffre de la voiture?

fermer

Est-ce que la porte des toilettes est ouverte?

L'hôtesse de l'air **vient**.

Non, il **est** fâché.

Oui, ils **ont** un fils et une fille.

Il **arrive** à dix-neuf heures cinquante.

Il **part** à quinze heures.

Elle **va** aux Etats-Unis.

Non, elle est **fermée**.

Oui, **ouvre**-le pour le chien.

Non, elle **fait** ses courses.

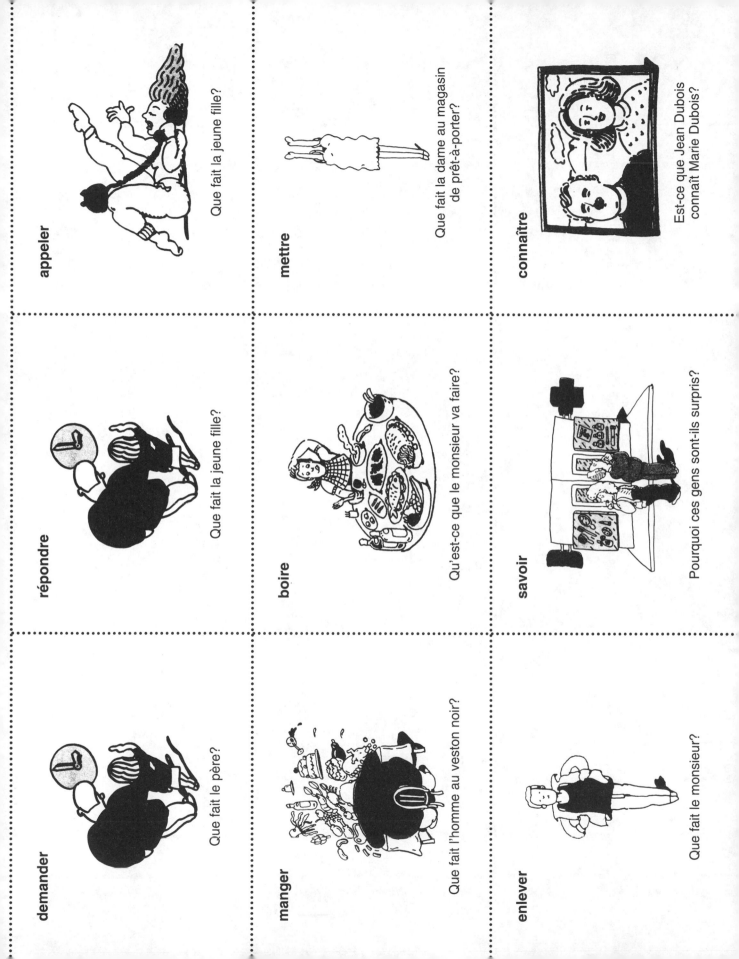

demander

Que fait le père?

répondre

Que fait la jeune fille?

appeler

Que fait la jeune fille?

manger

Que fait l'homme au veston noir?

boire

Qu'est-ce que le monsieur va faire?

mettre

Que fait la dame au magasin de prêt-à-porter?

enlever

Que fait le monsieur?

savoir

Pourquoi ces gens sont-ils surpris?

connaître

Est-ce que Jean Dubois connaît Marie Dubois?

Elle **appelle** son petit ami au téléphone.

Elle **répond**: “Il est trois heures, papa”.

Il **demande** à sa fille quelle heure il est.

Elle **met** une robe.

Il va **boire** du vin.

Il **mange** de bon appétit.

Il la **connaît** bien sûr, c’est sa femme!

Parce qu’ils ne **savent** pas que
les pharmacies américaines ne sont
pas comme les “drugstores” américains.

Il **enlève** son veston.

bon, bonne

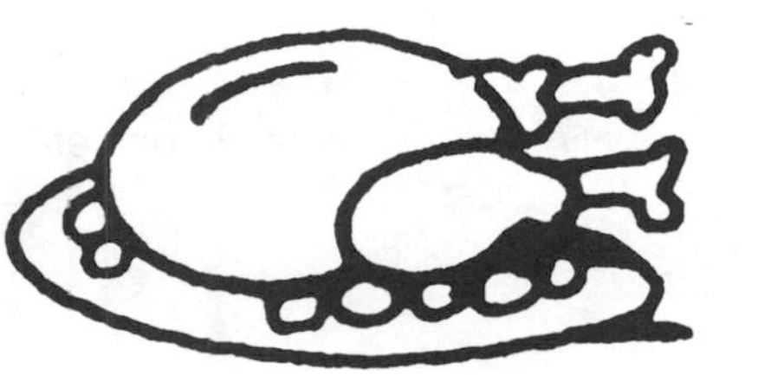

Le garçon: "Tout va bien, Monsieur"?

assez

Le banquier a l'air content, pourquoi?

beaucoup

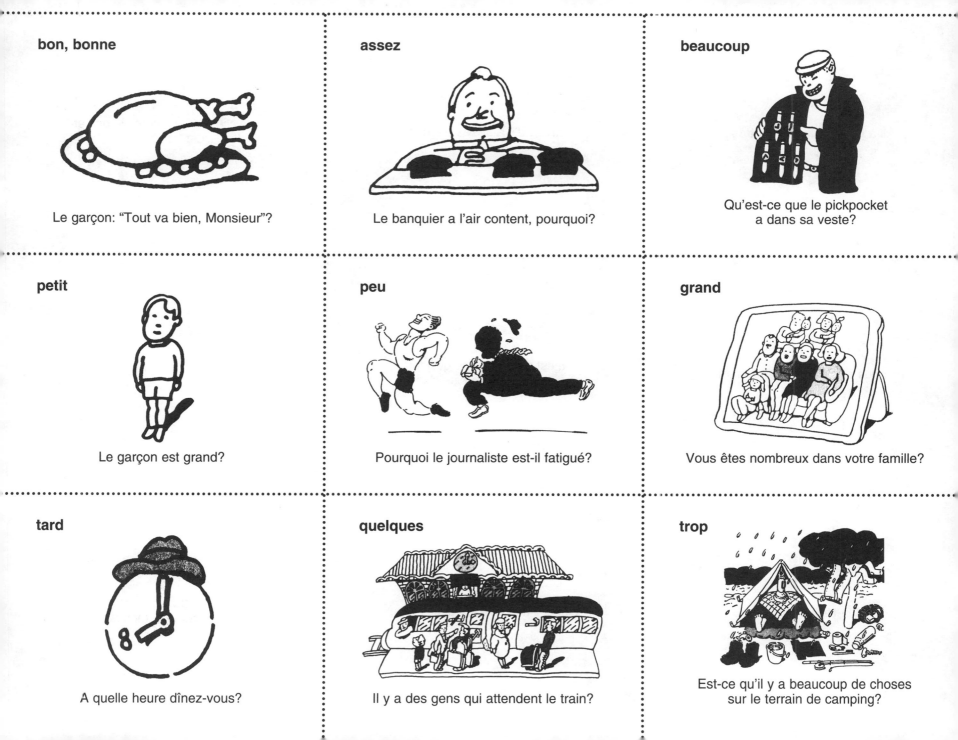

Qu'est-ce que le pickpocket
a dans sa veste?

petit

Le garçon est grand?

peu

Pourquoi le journaliste est-il fatigué?

grand

Vous êtes nombreux dans votre famille?

tard

A quelle heure dînez-vous?

quelques

Il y a des gens qui attendent le train?

trop

Est-ce qu'il y a beaucoup de choses
sur le terrain de camping?

Il a **beaucoup** de montres.

Parce qu'il a **assez** d'argent.

Le client: "Oui, merci, le poulet est très **bon**".

Oui, nous avons une **grande** famille.

Il est fatigué parce qu'il fait **peu** d'exercise.

Non, il est **petit**.

Il y a **trop** de choses.

Oui, il y a **quelques** passagers.

En général vers huit heures, **tard** pour les américains.

la chaise

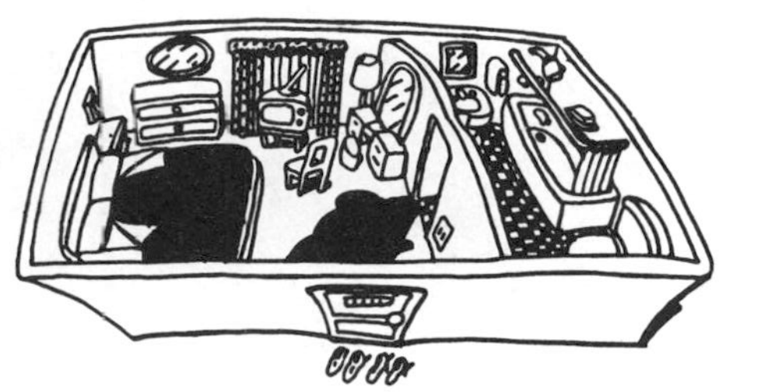

Il y a un fauteuil dans la chambre d'hôtel?

l'agent de police

Qui est l'homme à droite?

la boulangerie

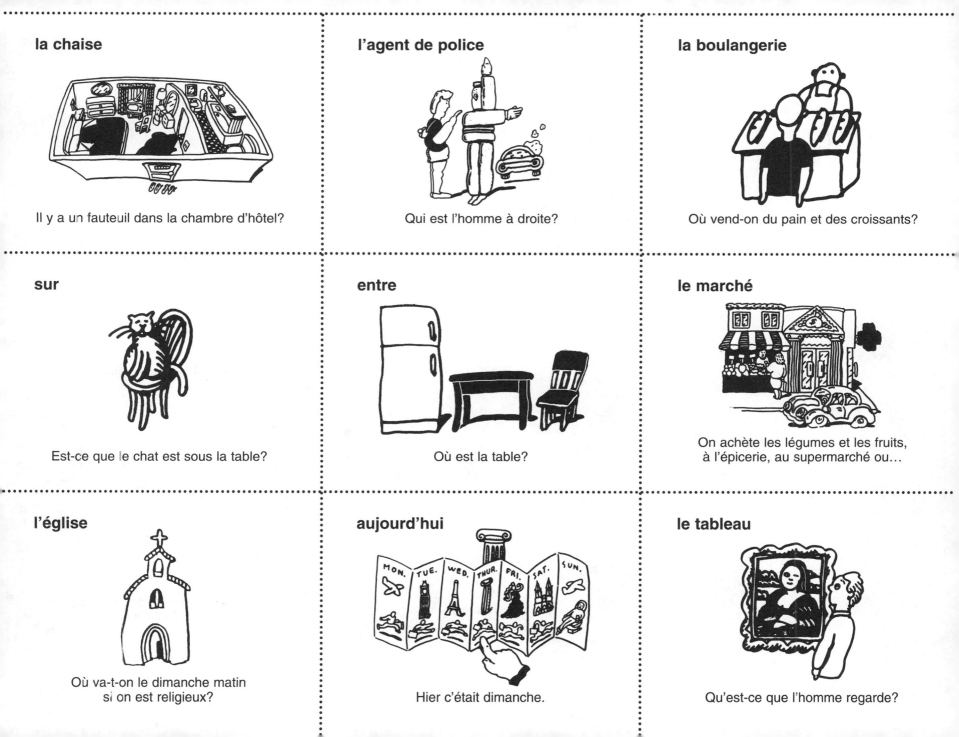

Où vend-on du pain et des croissants?

sur

Est-ce que le chat est sous la table?

entre

Où est la table?

le marché

On achète les légumes et les fruits, à l'épicerie, au supermarché ou…

l'église

Où va-t-on le dimanche matin si on est religieux?

aujourd'hui

Hier c'était dimanche.

le tableau

Qu'est-ce que l'homme regarde?

A la **boulangerie**.	C'est un **agent de police**.	Non, mais il y a une chaise.
...au **marché**.	**Entre** le réfrigérateur et la chaise.	Non, il est **sur** la chaise.
Il regarde un **tableau**.	**Aujourd'hui** c'est lundi.	On va à la synagogue, à la mosquée ou à l'**église**.

aimer

Mme Dubois semble fâchée, pourquoi?

détester

Est-ce que cet homme est content?

dire

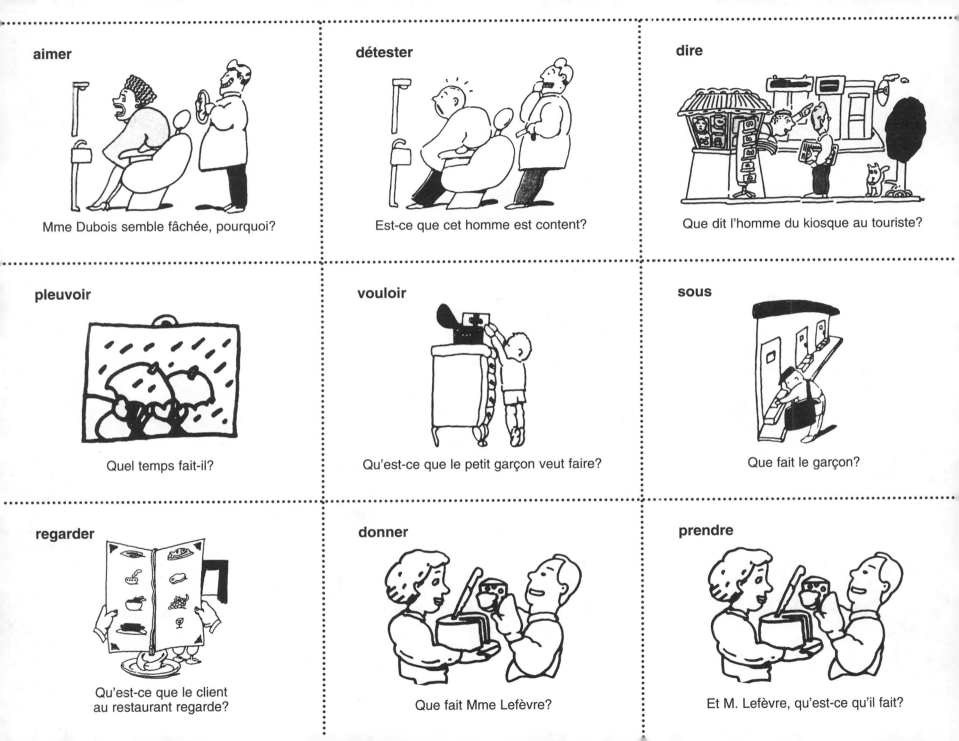

Que dit l'homme du kiosque au touriste?

pleuvoir

Quel temps fait-il?

vouloir

Qu'est-ce que le petit garçon veut faire?

sous

Que fait le garçon?

regarder

Qu'est-ce que le client
au restaurant regarde?

donner

Que fait Mme Lefèvre?

prendre

Et M. Lefèvre, qu'est-ce qu'il fait?

Il lui **dit** où il peut acheter des cigarettes.

Non! Il **déteste** être chauve!

Parce qu'elle n'**aime** pas avoir les cheveux blonds!

Il met une lettre **sous** la porte.

Il **veut** prendre quelque chose dans la boîte.

Il **pleut**.

Il **prend** du fromage.

Elle **donne** du fromage à son mari.

Il **regarde** le menu.

le poisson

La sole est une viande?

le fromage

Aimez-vous le Brie?

la jupe

Qu'est-ce que tu vas mettre ce soir pour aller chez Jeanne?

la chaussure

Elles sont beaucoup trop grandes pour moi, ces...

la pâtisserie

Où trouve-t-on les meilleurs éclairs au chocolat?

le kilo

Deux livres américaines de sucre font...

le litre

Combien de "quarts" y a-t-il dans un litre?

la demi-douzaine

Donnez-moi six citrons, s'il vous plaît.

le panier

Qu'est-ce qu'il y a devant la fermière?

Je vais mettre ma **jupe** rouge et un chemisier beige.

Oui, c'est un excellent **fromage**.

Non, c'est un **poisson**.

...900 grammes de sucre en France, presque un **kilo**.

A la **pâtisserie** Duroflet, là-bas.

...chaussures!

Il y a trois grands **paniers**.

Alors, une **demi-douzaine**?

Un **litre** et un "quart", c'est presque la même chose.

dans

Est-ce que les passagers sont dans un avion?

voir

Que voyez-vous sur le dessin?

désirer

Qu'est-ce que le jeune homme désire?

sans

L'école a une porte, mais a-t-elle des fenêtres.

avec

Avec qui est-ce que la passante parle?

en

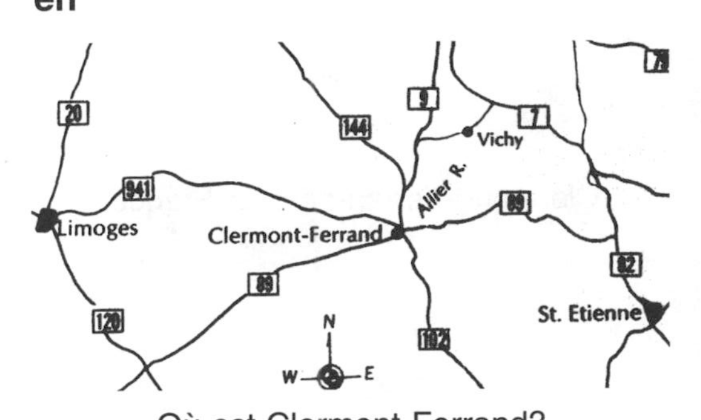

Où est Clermont-Ferrand?

et

Qu'est-ce que le dessin représente?

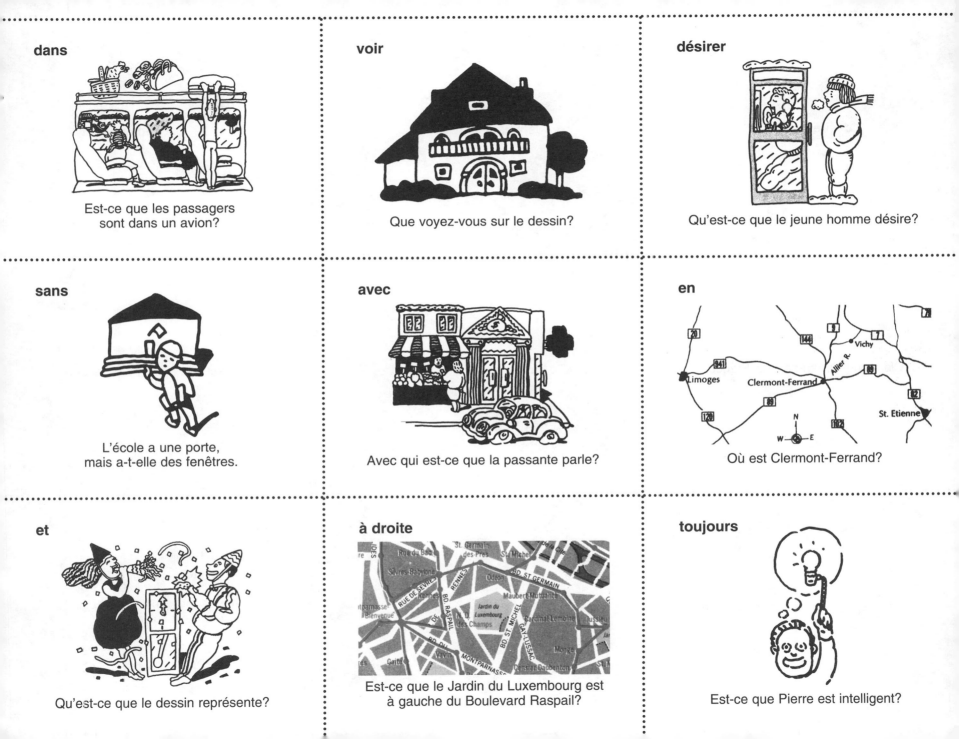

à droite

Est-ce que le Jardin du Luxembourg est à gauche du Boulevard Raspail?

toujours

Est-ce que Pierre est intelligent?

Il **désire** téléphoner.

Je **vois** une maison.

Non. Ils sont **dans** un train.

Clermond-Ferrand est **en** France.

Elle parle **avec** la marchande.

Non, c'est une école **sans** fenêtres.

Oui, il a **toujours** des idées intéressantes.

Non, il est **à droite**.

Il représente un homme **et** sa femme qui s'amusent.

le guichet

Où est le caissier?

la monnaie

Excusez-moi, je n'ai qu'un billet de cent francs.

la bicyclette

Est-ce que le facteur apporte les lettres en voiture?

la bouche

Chez le dentiste, on doit ...

les yeux

Ma soeur a les yeux bruns, mais moi, ...

la main

Tu écris avec la main droite?

le cou

Les girafes ont une petite tête, mais . . .

la langue

Jean-Pierre, comme tu es impoli!
Tu sais bien qu'on ne doit jamais ...

le nez

Ce monsieur a un grand nez.

Non, il livre les lettres à **bicyclette**.

Ça ne fait rien, voilà de la **monnaie**.

Il estau **guichet** de la banque.

Non, j'écris avec la **main** gauche.

...J'ai les **yeux** bleus.

...ouvrir la **bouche**.

Moi, j'ai un petit **nez** en trompette.

...tirer la **langue**!

...un **cou** très long.

le chien

Est-ce que les Smith aiment les animaux?

le portefeuille

Où est l'argent?

montrer

Que fait le touriste?

jouer

Qu'est-ce que les garçons font?

courir

Est-ce que l'homme marche?

entrer

Qu'est-ce que les touristes vont faire?

attendre

Que fait le piéton?

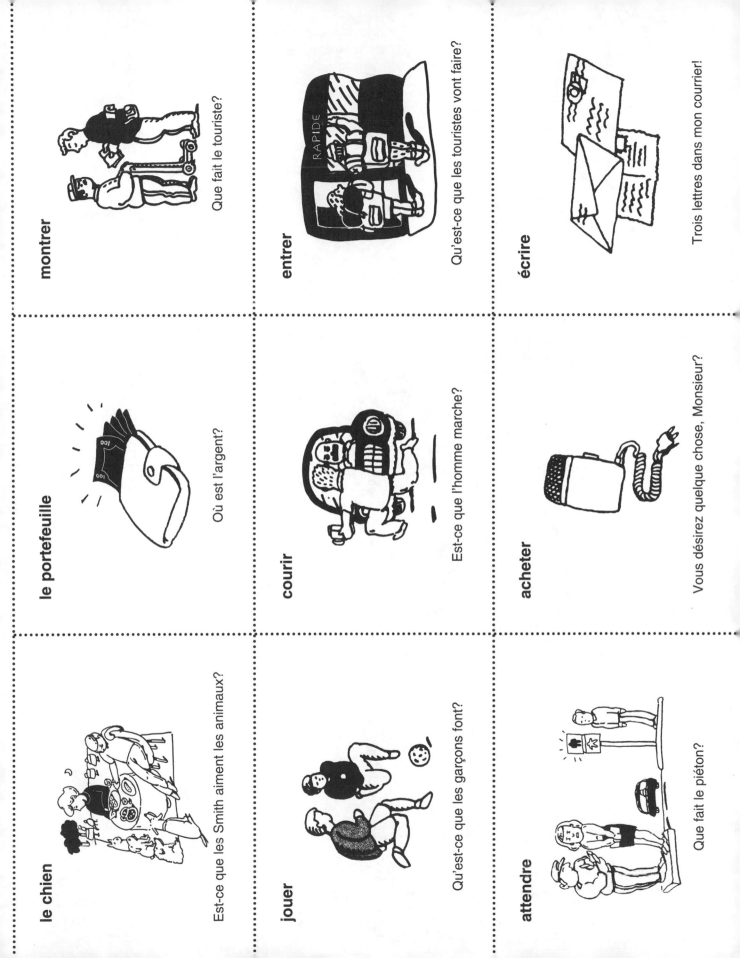

acheter

Vous désirez quelque chose, Monsieur?

écrire

Trois lettres dans mon courrier!

Il **montre** son passeport à l'inspecteur.

Dans le **portefeuille**.

Oui, ils adorent les **chiens**.

Ils vont **entrer** dans le train.

Non, il **court**.

Ils **jouent** au foot.

Maintenant, je dois **écrire** à mes amis!

Oui, je voudrais **acheter**
un rasoir électrique.

Il **attend** le feu vert pour traverser.

la brosse

A la droguerie, on vend des produits de beauté, des peignes,...

la machine à laver

Quelle erreur est-ce que Susan fait?

se raser

Que fait l'homme?

le journal, les journaux

Au kiosque, on ne vend pas de cigarettes mais on vend...

la papeterie

Où achète-t-on du papier à lettres ou des enveloppes?

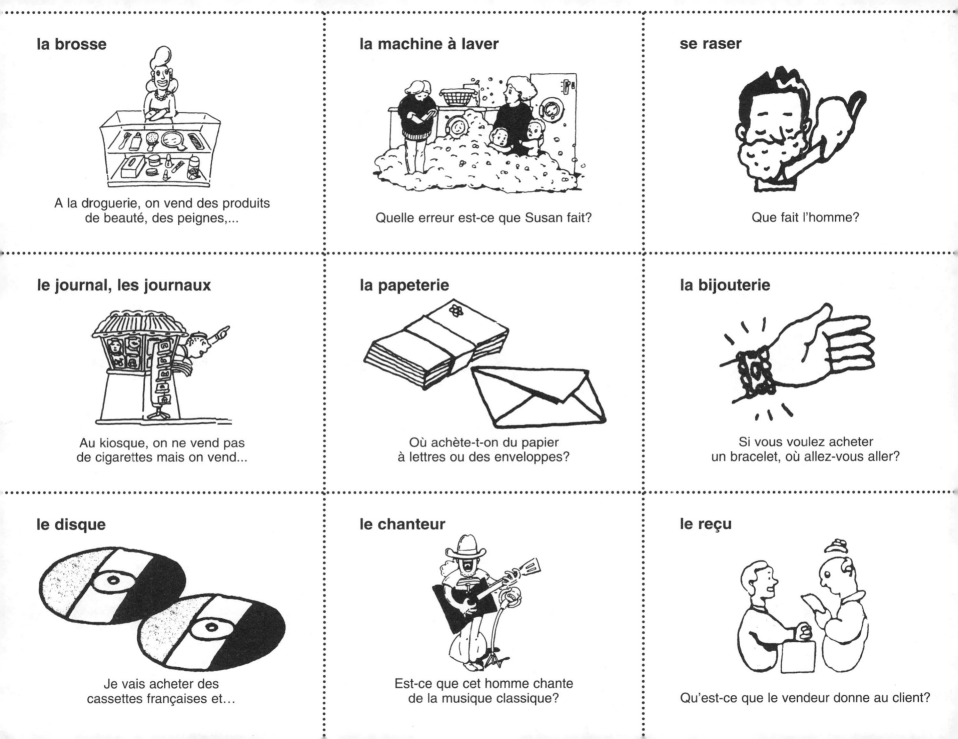

la bijouterie

Si vous voulez acheter un bracelet, où allez-vous aller?

le disque

Je vais acheter des cassettes françaises et…

le chanteur

Est-ce que cet homme chante de la musique classique?

le reçu

Qu'est-ce que le vendeur donne au client?

Il **se rase**.

Elle met trop de lessive dans la **machine à laver**.

…des **brosses à cheveux** et beaucoup d’autres choses.

A la **bijouterie**.

A la **papeterie**.

…des **journaux**, des cartes postales, des magazines.

Il lui done un **reçu**.

Non, c’est un **chanteur** folklorique.

...deux **disques** compacts pour David.